Apuleius' Cupid and Psyche

An Intermediate Latin Reader

Latin Text with Running Vocabulary and Commentary

Karen Krumpak
Evan Hayes
Stephen Nimis

Apuleius' *Cupid and Psyche*: An Intermediate Latin Reader: Latin Text with Running Vocabulary and Commentary

First Edition

ISBN-10: 1940997097

ISBN-13: 9781940997094

Published by Faenum Publishing, Ltd.

Cover Design: Evan Hayes

Fonts: Garamond

editor@faenumpublishing.com

Table of Contents

Acknowledgments

The idea for this project grew out of work that we, the authors, did with support from Miami University's Undergraduate Summer Scholars Program, for which we thank Martha Weber and the Office of Advanced Research and Scholarship. Work on the series, of which this volume is a part, was generously funded by the Joanna Jackson Goldman Memorial Prize through the Honors Program at Miami University. We owe a great deal to Carolyn Haynes and the 2010 Honors & Scholars Program Advisory Committee for their interest and confidence in the project.

The technical aspects of the project were made possible through the invaluable advice and support of Bill Hayes, Christopher Kuo, and Daniel Meyers. The equipment and staff of Miami University's Interactive Language Resource Center were a great help along the way. We are also indebted to the Perseus Project, especially Gregory Crane and Bridget Almas, for their technical help and resources. We also profited greatly from advice and help on the POD process from Geoffrey Steadman. All responsibility for errors, however, rests with the authors themselves.

To John:

Amo enim et efflictim te…diligo aeque ut meum spiritum,
nec ipsi Cupidini comparo. (*The Golden Ass* 5.6)

Introduction

The aim of this book is to make the story of "Cupid and Psyche" from Apuleius' *The Golden Ass* accessible to intermediate students of Ancient Latin. The running vocabulary and grammatical commentary are meant to provide everything necessary to read each page so that readers can progress through the text, improving their knowledge of Latin while enjoying one of the most delightful stories from antiquity.

Apuleius' "Cupid and Psyche" is a great text for intermediate readers. Its plot resembles familiar fairy tales such as "Beauty and the Beast" and "Cinderella," but its literary texture is typical of the rest of the Golden Ass. The sentence structure and grammatical constructions are relatively simple, but the unusual word order and vocabulary necessitate extra attention. Readers will learn to resist the temptation to make assumptions based on word order in favor of paying attention to the endings of the Latin words, particularly nouns and adjectives. For this reason, we have been more generous than usual in providing vocabulary in the page by page glossaries.

Apuleius of Madaura

Lucius Apuleius Madaurensis (c. 125-180 CE) was born in the Roman province of Africa. He studied philosophy and rhetoric in Athens and Rome, traveled to Egypt, and was awarded a prestigious priesthood in his home province. In his Apology, he defends himself against a charge of magic made by the family of his wife, a wealthy widow who was thought to have been bewitched by Apuleius. His most famous work is the Golden Ass, from which the story of Cupid and Psyche is taken.

Apuleius' *The Golden Ass*

Apuleius' *The Golden Ass*, also known as *Metamorphoses*, the larger narrative in which the story of Cuptid and Psyche is embedded, is an adaptation of a lost Greek text with the title *Metamorphoses*. An adaptation or epitome of this lost text survives in Greek among the works of Lucian with the name *Lucius, or The Ass*. There are some specific and general similarities between these two surviving works that make a relationship of some kind beyond a doubt (Mason 1994). Both extant works display a ribald sense of humor through an interest in magic and sex. But whereas Lucian's hero ends his tale with a comic conclusion befitting the rest of the story, Apuleius' hero ends his journey with a religious transformation that mirrors his physical metamorphosis back into a man. His transformation is due to the kindness of the goddess Isis, to whom Lucius then pledges himself. After the bawdy stories throughout the entirety of the novel, this conversion comes as a surprise, especially considering the novel is narrated by Lucius recalling these events after his transformation. There is significant scholarly debate about the sincerity and the meaning of the religious ending of Apuleius' novel, but this too large an issue to be addressed here.

The Story of Cupid and Psyche

Another difference between Lucian's *Onos* and the *Golden Ass* is that the latter includes a number of embedded tales, told by various narrators and reported to us by Lucius as part of his adventures. The Cupid and Psyche story is by far the longest of these embedded tales. Its narrator is a drunken old hag who is the servant of a band of robbers; she tells the story to a young captive girl in order to soothe her anxieties. Our hero Lucius, at this point in the novel already changed into an ass by magic, overhears the story and is moved to tears. While ignoring this narrative context deprives the story of some of its meaning, this is the most autonomous episode in the entire novel. Even as the literary popularity of Apuleius in general has waxed and waned over the centuries, admiration for the story of Cupid and Psyche has been nearly universal. With its narrative of betrayal and redemption and a harrowing descent into the underworld, the tale of Cupid and Psyche has been viewed as a parallel to the novel as a whole, as well as an allegory for the redemption of the soul. But it has also been admired as a light-hearted fairy tale ending in marital bliss – a simple tale told to the frightened captive that fittingly includes a beautiful maiden, romance, an adventure with difficulties that must be overcome, and final redemption and acceptance into the realm of the gods.

There has been considerable discussion of the sources for the Cupid and Psyche story, with some emphasizing its folklore affinities, while others emphasize its literary qualities and allusions. There is also disagreement about whether the tale should be seen as an allegory for Lucius' redemption at the end of the novel, or as a contrast to the novel's conclusion. The many symbolic and mysterious elements have prompted various psychological interpretations as well as interpretations grounded in contemporary mystery religions (of which Isis worship is a prime example). These same elements have also been adduced to a support a more philosophical interpretation along the lines of contemporary Platonic ideas. Excellent summaries of characteristic work along these different lines can be found in the bibliographical survey by Schlam and Finkelpearl (2000).

The Latin Style of Apuleius

The Latin style of Apuleius can perhaps be best characterized with the term *amplificatio*. He is fond of describing ordinary things with elaborate pleonasm. Note the examples in the following selection:

> 4.28: *Iamque proximas civitates et attiguas regiones fama pervaserat deam quam caerulum profundum pelagi peperit et ros spumantium fluctuum educavit....*
>
> Soon the news spread through neighbouring cities and the lands beyond its borders, that the goddess herself, born from the blue depths of the sea, emerging in spray from the foaming waves....

Although Apuleius tends to avoid elaborate periodic sentences in the manner of Cicero, at times it can be easy to lose the thread of the narrative in the midst of descriptions and specifications. Rhetorical effects, such as alliteration and assonance, parallelism and rhythm, anaphora, antithesis and hyperbole abound in the story.

Here is a good example of assonance and alliteration produced by a series of elaborations (5.10):

> *... fomentis olidis et pannis sordidis et foetidis cataplasmatibus manus tam delicatas istas adurens nec uxoris officiosam faciem sed medicae laboriosam personam sustinens ....*
>
> with his odious fomentations, sordid bandages, and fetid poultices, soiling these delicate hands of mine; nor ever am I playing the role of a normal wife, but the burdensome role of doctor ....

In addition, Apuleius is fond of using unusual words, archaisms and colloquialisms, and in using ordinary words in unusual ways, even changing the gender of nouns in a number of instances. These aspects of Apuleius' language have been studied thoroughly by L. Callebat, who argues that Apuleius' mannered use of vocabulary, word order and syntax is part of an effort to create a new poetic prose:

> The language of the Metamorphoses affirms the primacy of the aesthetic and asserts the noble status of prose. In a world undergoing profound changes, in a cultural context marked by the deterioration of traditional genres, especially poetic genres, the promotion of literary

> fantasy narrative in prose becomes sanctioned.... Beyond the formal game, a universe is suggested where being intermixes with seeming, the natural with the strange, where objects are not properly integrated into a familiar reality, where there are metaphorical projections through which language transcribes the fantastic or, in the "Tale of Psyche," the marvelous (Callebat 1993: 1662-63).

And again,

> The Tale of Cupid and Psyche reveals in its many correspondences, in its mixing of multiple registers, in the proliferation of its images, and in its insistent search for artifice, a specific status of Art: Art living its own life, a happy rival of the real universe. The Tale of Cupid and Psyche, a story of love, life and art. (Callebat 2000: 54).

Texts, Translations and Commentaries

Finkelpearl, Ellen D. *An Apuleius Reader: Selections from the Metamorphoses. Text and Commentary*. Mundelein, IL: Bolchazy-Carducci Publishers, Inc., 2012.

Gaselee, S., ed. and tr. *The Metamorphoses.* London: William Heinemann, 1915.

Gollnick, James. *Love and the Soul: Psychological Interpretations of the Eros and Psyche Myth*. Waterloo, Ont.: Wilfrid Laurier University Press, 1992.

Hanson, J. A., ed. and tr. *The Metamorphoses.* Cambridge: Harvard University Press. 1996.

Kenney, E. J. *Apuleius: Cupid and Psyche. Text, Translation and Commentary.* Cambridge: Cambridge University Press, 1990.

Relihan, Joel C., tr. *Apuleius. The Golden Ass. Or, A Book of Changes.* Indianapolis/Cambridge: Hackett, 2007.

Ruden, S., tr. *The Golden Ass*. New Haven: Yale University Press, 2011.

Ruebel, James S. *Apuleius: Metamorphoses, Book I: Text and Commentary. Wauconda*: Bolchazy-Carducci, 2000.

Zimmerman, M. et al., *Apuleius Madaurensis. Metamorphoses, Book IV 28-35, V and VI 1-24. The Tale of Cupid and Psyche. Text, Introduction and Commentary.* Groningen: Egbert Forsten, 2004.

Critical Studies

Callebat, Louis. "Le conte d'Amour et Psyché : un style « décadent »." *Fontes* 3 N° 5-6 (2000), 45-54.

Callebat, L. "Formes et modes d'expression dans les oeuvres d'Apulée." *ANRW* II 34.2 (1993), 1600-1664.

Callebat, L. "La prose des Metamorphoses: genèse et spécifité," in *Aspects of Apuleius' Golden Ass.* Vol. II (Groningen: Forsten, 1998) 167-83.

Mason, H. J. "Greek and Latin Versions of the Ass Story." *ANRW* II 34.2 (1993), 1665-1707.

Schlam, Carl C. "Cupid and Psyche: Folktale and Literary Narrative," in *Groningen Colloquia on the Novel* V, ed. Heinz Hofmann (Groningen: Forsten, 1993), 63-73.

Schlam, C. and Ellen D. Finkelpearl. *A Review of Scholarship on Apulerius' Metamorphoses 1970-1998.* Lustrum 42 (2000).

Maaskant-Kleibrink M. "Psyche's Birth," in *Groningen Colloquia on the Novel* Vol. III, ed. Heinz Hofmann (Groningen: Forsten, 1990), 13-33.

How to use this book

The page-by-page vocabularies gloss all but the most common words. We have endeavored to make these glossaries as useful as possible without becoming fulsome, so there is a lot of repetition. Since in this story vocabulary is likely to present the biggest problem to intermediate readers, we have been more generous than is usual in such texts. Apuleius uses many words and many unfamiliar words, and often just knowing the declension of a substantive or the conjugation of a verb can be crucial. It is our assumption that having too much vocabulary is not as serious a problem as too little, so we have consistently sought to err in that direction. Words occurring frequently in the text can be found in an appendix in the back, but it is our hope that most readers will not need to use this appendix often. For details on the format of glossing various parts of speech, see "Glossing Conventions" below.

The commentary is almost exclusively grammatical, explaining subordinate clauses, uses of cases, and idioms. A brief grammatical summary details the meaning of the technical terms used in the commentary, although most of these will be familiar to intermediate readers of Latin. A good strategy is to read a passage in Latin, check the glossary for unusual words and consult the commentary as a last resort. We have kept cultural and rhetorical information to a minimum, and it is our expectation that readers will only consult the commentary when something is troubling grammatically. There is considerable repetition in the commentary, and it is meant as a safety net rather than something to be read completely. Our work thus has a more modest aim than a traditional literary commentary: to facilitate reading, rather than studying, this Latin text.

Two excellent literary commentaries have been published on the story of Cupid and Psyche, that of E. J. Kenney (1960) and that of Zimmerman et al. (2004). Kenney publishes the text with a translation on facing pages with a separate commentary. Zimmerman et al. (like the other Groningen commentators) print each Latin sentence individually, followed by a translation and commentary on that sentence. Both commentaries contain extensive information about all aspects of the text, with copious bibliography. Our contribution has a more limited focus aimed at helping intermediate readers navigate through the text, but we have made full use of these and other resources, including the Perseus Project. An idiomatic translation by A. S. Kline can be found online at http://www.poetryintranslation.com/klineasapuleius.htm. The older Loeb edition of Gasselee, with Latin and English on facing pages, is also available online in pdf format.

The Latin text is based on L. C. Purser, *Cupido et Psyche* (London, 1913), which is in the public domain. It was digitized by Konrad Schroder and is posted on the Latin Library. Here and there we have corrected some errors and made minor changes in the name of readability. This is not a scholarly edition; for that one should turn to the edition of Zimmerman et al.

An Important Disclaimer:

This volume is a self-published "Print on Demand" (POD) book, and it has not been vetted or edited in the usual way by publishing professionals. There are sure to be some factual and typographical errors in the text, for which we apologize in advance. The volume is also available only through online distributors, since each book is printed when ordered online. However, this publishing channel and format also account for the low price of the book; and it is a simple matter to make changes when they come to our attention. For this reason, any corrections or suggestions for improvement are welcome and will be addressed as quickly as possible in future versions of the text.

Please e-mail corrections or suggestions to editor@faenumpublishing.com.

About the Authors:

Karen Krumpak is a 2014 graduate in Classics, English Literature, and History at Miami University.

Evan Hayes is a graduate in Classics and Philosophy at Miami University and the 2011 Joanna Jackson Goldman Scholar.

Stephen Nimis is an Emeritus Professor of Classics at Miami University and Professor of English and Comparative Literature at the American University in Cairo.

Glossing Conventions

Adjectives of two and three terminations will be formatted thus:

bonus, -**a**, -**um**

facilis, -**e**.

Single termination adjectives will have the genitive indicated thus:

fallax, **falacis** (*gen.*)

Participles will generally be glossed as a verb, but some present participles (particularly where their verbal force has been weakened) are glossed as nouns or adjectives: e.g.

parens, -**entis**, *m*: "a parent"

or as a single termination adjective: e.g.,

patiens, **entis** (*gen.*): "patient"

Many perfect participles and gerundives are also glossed as adjectives,

erectus, -**a**, -**um**: "upright"

periclitabundus, -**a**, -**um**: "testing"

Adverbs will be identified as such (*adv.*) when there is some ambiguity.

Regular infinitives are indicated by conjugation number: e.g.,

laudo (1)

moneo (2)

Where principal parts are predictable, as in the case of most first conjugation verbs, only the conjugation number will be given in the glossary. This format is used even in the case of unpredictable perfect forms, if the word occurring in the text is based on the present stem (present, future, imperfect tenses). Elsewhere the principal parts will be provided in their standard form.

Simple syntactical information such as "+ gen." or "+ inf." will often be cited in the glossary with verbs and adjectives. However, the lexical information given for most words is minimal and sometimes specific to the context. To get a broader sense of Apuleius' peculiarities of language, it will be necessary to consult the commentaries or critical literature cited above.

Abbreviations used in the commentary

abl. – ablative
abs. – absolute
acc. – accusative
act. – active
adj. – adjective
adv. – adverb
apoc. – apocopated
appos. – apposition
attend. – attendant
circum. – circumstantial
com. – command
comp. – comparative
concess. – concessive
dat. – dative
delib. – deliberative
desc. – description
dir. – direct
f. – feminine
fut. – future
gen. – genitive
imper. – imperative
impf. – imperfect
ind. – indirect
inf. – infinitive
intrans. – intransitive
loc. – locative
m. – masculine
neut. – neuter
neg. – negative
nom. – nominative
obj. – object
part. – participle
pass. – passive
perf. – perfect
pl. – plural
plupf. – pluperfect
pr. – present
pred. – predicative
pron. – pronoun
purp. – purpose
quest. – question
resp. – respect
s. – singular
sc. – scilicet
sep. – separation
st. – statement
subj. – subjunctive
sync. – syncopated

Grammatical terms used in the commentary

The grammatical terms used in the commentary are organized below according to syntactical category with brief explanations and examples. For more detailed information, see Allen and Greenough, *New Latin Grammar* (available on Perseus) or Charles Bennett *New Latin Grammar* (available on the Latin Library).

1. Uses of Cases

NOMINATIVE

The nominative case is the used for the subject of finite verbs and the predicate of verbs of being, seeming, etc.

GENITIVE

The genitive is commonly used to express a relationship between one noun and another, especially a limiting relationship. Some verbs also take the genitive as their object instead of the accusative.

Material: The genitive denotes what a thing consists of:

flumina lactis: "rivers *of milk*"

Objective: the genitive can indicate the object of an action implied by a substantive:

metus hostium, "the fear felt toward the enemy:

Partitive (genitive of the whole): The genitive indicates the whole to which a part belongs:

quibuscumque auri vel monilium: "whatever *of gold or jewels*"

Possession: The genitive denotes possession, including the belonging of an object, quality, feeling, or action to a person or thing:

viscera sororis, the heart *of the sister*.

Predicative: A genitive can be used with verbs of being, seeming, etc.

sciscitari ... unde natalium: "to question whence was *his parentage*"

Quality (characteristic, description): The genitive is used to describe a person or thing:

maritum incerti status: "a husband *of uncertain status*"

Separation: The genitive can express separation:

requiem malorum: "a respite *from her evils*"

Specification (respect): the genitive expresses the respect in which something is the case:

furens *animi*: "raging *with respect to the mind*"

Subjective: The genitive can indicate the subject of an action implied by a substantive:

metus *hostium*, "fear *of the enemy*" i.e. the enemy's fear

Value: The genitive of is used with verbs of rating and buying:

parvi existimare, "to consider it *of small value*"

After verbs and adjectives: The genitive is used to complete the meaning of certain adjectives, such as *plenus* (full of) or *egenus* (in need of). It is also used after certain verbs, such as *memini* (to remember), *misereror* (to pity), *paeniteo* (to regret), *metuo* (to fear), etc. These will be indicated in the commentary simply as "gen. after *memini*"

DATIVE

The Dative case is chiefly used to indicate the person for whom an action happens or a quality exists.

Adjectives: many adjectives, such as *similis* (similar to) and *complacitus* (pleasing to), take the dative. These will be noted in the commentary simply as "dat. after similis"

Agent: the dative expresses the agent of an action with impersonal verbs.

opus expeditum approbato mihi: "let the completed work be approved *by me*"

Indirect Object: The recipient of the action of the verb is put in the dative case.

suae conjugi praecepta sortis enodat: "he makes clear the order of the oracular response *to his own wife*"

Purpose: the dative denotes the object for which something is done.

nuptiis destimatam esse: "that you had been destined *for marriage*"

Reference (advantage, interest): the dative identifies the person interested, concerned, benefited by an action.

nobis...geris: "you bear *for us*"

Verbs and Compound Verbs: Verbs such as *credere* (to believe in), *suadere* (persuade), etc., take the dative case, as do many intransitive verbs with a prefix, such as *accedo* (to come near to), *obstare* (to stand in the way of), etc. These will be indicated in the commentary simply as "dat. after *credere*"

ACCUSATIVE

The accusative case is used for the direct object of transitive verbs, for the subject of an infinitive in indirect statement and other complements of a verb, to indicate place to which, and duration of time.

Adverbial: the accusative of adjectives can be used adverbially:

simile ... fluctuat: she fluctuates *similarly*

Direct Object: the direct object of verbs is in the accusative case:

commeantem populi...adprecantur: "the people beseech *her passing*"

Duration: The accusative shows the extent of space or duration of time:

diem totum lacrimis...consumit: "she wastes in tears *all day long*"

Exclamation: The accusative is used in short exclamatory phrases.

beatos illos qui super gemmas et monilia calcant!: "*happy* are those who tread upon gems and necklaces!"

Place to Which: Used to convey the location travelled to, often with a preposition:

domus suas contendunt: "they hasten *to their own homes*"

Predicative: Causative verbs like *facere* can take a second predicative accusative.

maritum proceritas spatii fecerat alienum: "the great length of intervening space had made her husband *a stranger*"

Respect: The accusative may be used with an adjective or verb to denote the part concerned.

fragrans balsama Venus: "Venus, fragrant *with balsam*"

Subject of Infinitives: In indirect discourse and other expressions that are complemented by an infinitive, the subject of the infinitive is in the accusative case.

non maria sed terras Venerem aliam...pullulasse: "(the rumor spread) that not *the sea* but *the lands* have sprouted another Venus"

me necesse est ... frequentare: "it is necessary *that I* frequent"

Supine: Accusative supines occur after verbs of motion in order to express purpose.

completum festinat: "he hastens *in order to fill*"

ABLATIVE

Nouns in the ablative case are used often adverbially, generally expressing motion away from something, instrument, location, and many other relations.

Ablative Absolute: Combined with a participle, adjective, or noun, the ablative conveys the circumstance (time, cause, or condition) of a particular action.

perlata fabula: "the tale having been anounced"

Accordance: Usually with *de* or *ex*, the ablative expresses that in accordance with which a thing is done or judged.

meis precibus, oro, largire: "bestow, I beg, *in accordance with my prayers*"

Agent: The agent of a passive verb is expressed by the ablative usually with the preposition *ab*.

laudatur ab omnibus: she is praised *by all*"

Cause: Cause may be expressed by an ablative with or without a presposition.

sive perfidia pessima sive invidia noxia: "whether *because of most disloyal treachery* or *because of noxious envy*"

Circumstance: a circumstance or situation attendant to a verb can be expressed with the ablative:

ut solet aestu: "as is the habit *in the summer heat*"

Psyche cum sua perspicua pulchritudine: "Psyche *with her own clear beauty*"

Comparison: Comparative adjectives followed by the ablative express comparison.

> patre meo seniorem maritum: "a husband older *than my father*"

Degree of Difference (measure of difference) is indicated by the ablative:

> paulo facilior: "easier *by a little*"

Manner: Often with *cum,* manner is also denoted by the simple ablative.

> animo tanto iratum: "furious *with so much spirit*"
>
> perfectis ... cum summo maerore: "completed *with the greatest sadness*"

Means (Instrument): The ablative expresses the means by which an action is accomplished:

> sufficienti recreata somno: "restored *by sufficient sleep*"
>
> flammis et sagittis armatus: equipped *with the fires and arrows*"

Place Where: Often denoted by the preposition *in* along with the ablative; the preposition is commonly ommitted in poetry or poetic prose.

> sudo resedit vertice: "sit down *on the clear and bright peak*"

Place From Which: The ablative denotes the place a noun has moved from usually with a preposition.

> caelo commeantem: "travelling *from heaven*"

Quality (description) : Quality is regularly denoted by the ablative.

> maiores...quamvis gratissima specie: "the elders, although *with a very pleasing appearance*"
>
> rara canitie: "*with a rare gray hair*"

Separation: Separation is expressed with or without a preposition especially with verbs and adjectives of deprivation, freedom, and want.

> spiritus corpore tuo fuerit sejugatus: "the spirit will have been separated *from your body*"

Source: Also called origin or descent, ablative of source is denoted by the ablative with or without a prepostion.

> utroque parente prognatae: "descended *from each parent*"

Specification: The ablative of specification provides details with respect to which anything is or is done.

> vesania turgidae: "swollen *with madness*"

Time: Both time when and time within which are denoted by the ablative.

nocte: abl. time, "at night"

diutino tempore: "in the course of a long time"

LOCATIVE

The locative case is used for the location of towns and small islands of first and second declension, *humus*, *domus*, *rus*, and sometimes countries and large islands as an alternative to ablative of place where.

Psyche domi residens: "Psyche remaining seated *at home*"

2. Uses of the Subjunctive

Independent Uses of the Subjunctive

Deliberative questions occur when the speaker wonders what he or she should do.

quid agam? quo me conferam?: "What am I to do? Where am I to take myself?"

Hortatory, Jussive, Prohibition Clauses

Jussive and hortatory subjunctives "urges" some action in a more polite manner than an imperative. "Hortatory" applies to first person "let us..."); "jussive" applies to second and third person (may you..., let her..."); "prohibition" refers to the negative (don't...).

virgo ista teneatur: pr. pass., "let that maiden be held"

consilium validum requiramus: let us seek strong counsel"

neque respondeas, immo nec prospicias: "neither answer nor look towards"

The volitive subjunctive expresses a wish for the future:

moriar: "may I die"

Dependent Uses of the Subjunctive

Tenses of the subjunctive in subordiante clauses follow the *sequence of tenses*: present or perfect subjunctive for primary sequence, imperfect or pluperfect for secondary sequence.

tense of main clause	*same time or time after main verb*	*time before main verb*
present or future tense	present subjunctive	perfect subjunctive
past tense	imperfect subjunctive	pluperfect subjunctive

Anticipatory Clauses: The subjunctive is used with priusquam when the action is anticipated or contingent:

> prius…quam caream: pr. subj. anticipatory, "before I would be without"

Concessive clauses with *cum* or *quamvis* take the subjunctive:

> quamvis…nemo pareret: "although no one appeared"
>
> cum te scilicet amator aliquis primus invenerit: "*although* surely some lover first *discovered*"

Conditions: The subjunctive is used in future less vivid and contrafactural conditions (see below)

Cum Causal Clauses: When *cum* introduces a causal clause, the subjunctive is used:

> cum…possitis: "since you are able"

Cum Circumstantial Clauses: When *cum* introduces a general circumstance rather than a specific time, the subjunctive is used

> cum…celebrarent…cum…nuncuparent: "When they were celebrating…when they were calling…"
>
> cum…coerceas et…praecludas: "when you limit and…you block"

Cum Temporal clauses refering to past actions in secondary sequence regularly take the subjunctive.

> cum ... pererrasset: "when she had wandered"

Indefinite Temporal Clauses take the subjunctive:

> quoad…mitigetur: "until it may be lightened (whenever that may be)"

Indirect commands are an example of a jussive noun clause used as the object of a verb. For more on jussive noun clauses, see below.

> Zephyro praecipe ... sistat: "order Zephyrus *to establish*"
>
> petit de te Venus ... mittas: "Venus asks you *to send*"

Indirect questions are formed with the subjunctive following the sequence of tenses and introduced by an interrogative word.

> periclitabor an oppido forti animo singularique prudentia sis praedita: " I will test *whether you are* gifted with an exceedingly strong mind and a remarkable good sense"

Indirect statement: The subjunctive is used with *quod* to introduce an alleged statement, as opposed to a statement of fact.

> quod manibus meis alumnatus sim, profecto scitis omnes: "*that I have nurtured him* with my own hands, you all know perfectly well."

Noun Clauses clauses following certain verbs are introduced with our without *ut* or *ne* with the subjunctive, as in indirect commmands:

> patere vel pauculos dies delitescam, "Allow *that I may hide* a few days"
>
> faxo ... *paeniteat*: "I will cause it *to be a source of regret*"

Proviso clauses: *dummodo*, *dum*, and *modo* with the subjunctive express a proviso:.

> dum tamen scias aeumulos tos cavere: subj. in proviso cls., "*so long as you know* to beware your rivals"

Purpose Clauses explain the purpose behind the action of the main clause and is usually introducted by *ut* or *ne*.

> Interim Cupido...coercebatur acriter ne vulnus gravaret: "Meanwhile Cupid was steadfastly confined, *lest he aggravate the wound*"

Quod, *quia* and *quoniam* can take the subjunctive when the cause is alleged, rather than stated as a fact:

> Veneris familiam male audire, quod tu vero marino natatu secesseritis: "... that the family of Venus was being reproached, *because (so they claimed) you have withdrawn* to your marine swimming"

Relative Clauses of Characteristic: Relative clauses in the subjunctive suggest that that the clause does not simply state a fact but rather indicates another type of subjunctive clause such as purpose, result, cause, concession, etc. They are called relative clauses of characteristic for introducing a defining quality or characteristic.

> corpus quale peperisse Venerem non paeniteret: "a body *such as would not displease* Venus to have birthed"

Result clauses explain the outcome of the action in the main clause, often with an adverb in the main clause signalling the result clause. Result clauses are usually introduced by *ut* or *ut non*.

> pupugit altius, ut roraverint parvulae guttae: "she pricked more deeply, *so that small drops moistened*"

3. Indirect Statements, Questions, and Commands

Indirect statements are formed with the accusative plus infinitive after verbs of saying, thinking, etc.

> fama pervaserat <u>deam…conversari</u>: "the rumor had spread *that the goddess lives*." The direct statement would be *dea conversatur*, "the goddess lives"

When a statement is attributed to someone other than the author or main speaker, *quod* + subj. may be used instead.

> <u>quod manibus meis alumnatus sim</u> scitis omnes: "you all know *that I have raised him with my own hands*"

Indirect questions are formed with the subjunctive following the sequence of tenses and introduced by an interrogative word:

> Deinde nuntiatio <u>quid adveneris</u>: "Afterwards with you having announced *why you have arrived*"

Indirect Commands are formed with the subjunctive, with or without *ut* or *ne*, and are a type of jussive noun clauses (see section on the subjunctive above):

> Zephyro praecipit…<u>efflaret</u>: "he ordered Zephyr *to blow*."

> monuit ac saepe terruit <u>ne…quaerat</u>: "he warned her and often scared her *not to seek*"

The accusative + infinitive construction can also be used:

> quae <u>te ... addici</u> jusserat, "who had ordered *you to be doomed*"

4. Conditional sentences

Future more vivid conditions express a future *probability*. The protasis (the clause expressing the condition, i.e. the "if" clause) can be the future or future perfect, the apodosis (the clause expressing consequence, i.e. the "then" clause) is the future tense or some equivalent. In English this is expressed with the present tense in the protasis, future tense in the apodosis: "If she comes…then I will go."

> nisi…<u>praecaves</u>, <u>congredietur</u>: "unless *you are cautious, she will approach*"

Future less vivid conditions express a future *possibility* and thus use the potential subjunctive in the apodosis and present or perfect subjunctive in the protasis; In English, "If it should…then it would…" or "If it were to…then it would."

> Tunc injuriae meae litatum crediderim, cum eius comas…deraserit: "*I would believe* him to have made recompense for my injury, when (i.e. if) *she should have clipped* his hairs"

Contrafactual conditions indicate an untrue premise and conclusion and use the subjunctive mood: imperfect subjunctive for the present (i.e. "if he were now doing this, he would be doing badly"); pluperfect subjunctive for the past (i.e. "if he had done this, he would have done badly").

> nisi ferrum manibus evolasset, fecisset: "if the steel *had not flown* from her hand, *she would have done* it"

Rhetorical terms used in the commentary

Alliteration – the repetition of the same consonant.

> 5.22: purpureas…pererrantes

Anaphora – the repetition of the same word or phrase at the beginning of successive clauses.

> 4.31: Per...per...per: 5.1, 5.2 5.13

Apostrophe - a sudden break in the narrative to address some person or object who is not present:

> 5.23: Hem, audax et temeraria lucerna! "Alas bold lantern!"

Assonance – the close repetition of a vowel sound

> 4.33: affatu…accepto: the a-sounds create a dignified tone

Asyndeton – the ommission of a conjunction between parts of a sentence

> 5.6: cupitis adnuat…videat…mulceant…conferat

Chiasmus – the reversed repetition of words or concepts in the same or in modified form

> 5.5: Psyche dulcissima et cara uxor: noun/adj./adj./noun, "Psyche sweetest and beloved wife

Epithet – an adjective or descriptive phrase expressing a quality characteristic of the person mentioned, especially when frequently applied to that person

> 5.18: Psyche misella, also misera, miserrima

Hendiadys - ("one through two) the use of two nouns linked by a conjunction instead of a noun and adjective:

6:1: spem et votum, "the hope of a prayer"

Litotes - (undestatement) is the use of two negatives to produce a positive:

5.5: nihil non sentiebatur, "nothing of him was not perceived

Personification – the attribution of a personal nature or human characteristic to something nonhuman

5.26: conscio luminei, "the lamp was her confidant"

Polysyndeton – excessive use of conjunctions in succession

5.4: et inscenderat et…fecerat et...discesserat

Transferred epithet - when an epithet is transferred from its proper noun to one with which it is associated,

5.12: sarcinae nesciae rudimento miratur, "she wondered at the experience of her ignorant burden" but Psyche is ignorant, not the burden

Other terminology

Apocopation – when a word is formed by the removal of the end of a longer word

4.28: habuere: apoc. perf. (=habuerunt), "these had daughters"

Syncopation – the contraction of a word by omission of part of the middle

6.21: perieras: sync. plupf. (=periveras), "you would have been destroyed

Hapax Legomenon – a word or form having a single recorded use

6.19: polentacium: as an adjective

Periphrastic: the use of a participle and a form of the verb esse to create a tense:

5.16: exterminanda est: (gerundive) "she must be banished" literally, "she is (one who) ought to be banished"

Lucius Apuleius

Cupid and Psyche

Cupid and Psyche

The youngest of three beautiful princesses is so beautiful that she inspires men to worship her as a "new Venus."

[4.28] Erant in quadam civitate rex et regina. Hi tres numero filias forma conspicuas habuere, sed maiores quidem natu, quamvis gratissima specie, idonee tamen celebrari posse laudibus humanis credebantur, at vero puellae junioris tam praecipua tam praeclara pulchritudo nec exprimi ac ne sufficienter quidem laudari sermonis humani penuria poterat. Multi denique civium et advenae copiosi, quos eximii spectaculi rumor studiosa celebritate congregabat,

---

advena, **-ae** *m*: a foreigner
celebritas, **-atis** *f*: a multitude
celebro, (1): to celebrate, honor
civis, **-is** *m*: a fellow citizen
civitas, **-atis** *f*: a city
congrego, (1): to assemble
conspicuus, **-a**, **-um**: notable, conspicuous
copiosus, **-a**, **-um**: abundant
credo, (3), **credidi**: to think
denique: indeed
eximius, **-a**, **-um**: extraordinary
exprimo, (3), **expressi**: express
forma, **-ae** *f*: beauty
gratus, **-a**, **-um**: pleasing
idonee: (*adv.*) adequately
junior, **-ius**: younger
laudo, (1): to praise
laus, **laudis** *f*: praise
natus, **-us** *m*: birth, age
ne...quidem: not even
penuria, **-ae** *f*: want
praecipuus, **-a**, **-um**: especial
praeclarus, **-a**, **-um**: famous, noble
pulchritudo, **-inis** *f*: beauty
regina, **-ae** *f*: a queen
rex, regis, *m*: a king
rumor, **-oris** *m*: a rumor
sermo, **-onis**, *m*: speech
species, **-ei** *f*: appearance
spectaculum, **-i** *n*: a spectacle
studiosus, **-a**, **-um**: eager, zealous
sufficienter: (*adv.*) sufficiently
tres, **-ia**: three

---

numero...forma...natu: abl. specification, "three *in number*...conspicuous *in beauty*...greater *by birth*," i.e. "older"
habuere: apocopated perf. (=*habuerunt*), "these have had"
gratissima specie: abl. quality, "with a very pleasing appearance"
celebrari: pr. pass. inf. complementing *posse*, "to be able *to be celebrated*"
posse: pr. inf. in ind. st. after *credebantur*, "were believed *to be able*..."
exprimi...laudari: pr. pass. inf. complementing *poterat*, "able *to be expressed*...*to be praised*"
penuria: abl. means, "praised *by the poverty* of human speech"
studiosa celebritate: abl. circumstance, "in an eager multitude"

inaccessae formonsitatis admiratione stupidi et admoventes oribus suis dexteram primore digito in erectum pollicem residente ut ipsam prorsus deam Venerem religiosis venerabantur adorationibus. Jamque proximas civitates et attiguas regiones fama pervaserat deam quam caerulum profundum pelagi peperit et ros spumantium fluctuum educavit jam numinis sui passim tributa venia in mediis conversari populi coetibus, vel certe rursum novo caelestium

---

admiratio, **-onis** *f.* admiration
admoveo, (2), **admovi**: move up, bring X (*acc.*) to Y (*dat.*)
adoratio, **-onis** *f.* act of worship or prayer
attiguus, **-a**, **-um**: neighboring
caelestis, **-e**: heavenly
caerulus, **-a**, **-um**: blue, cerulean
coetus, **-us** *m*: society
converso, (1): to turn around, abide, live
dextera, **-ae** *f.* right hand
digitus, **-i** *m*: a finger
educo, (1): to rear
erectus, **-a**, **-um**: upright
fama, **-ae** *f.* fame
fluctus, **-us** *m*: a wave
formonsitas, -tatis, *f.* beauty
inaccessus, **-a**, **-um**: inaccessible, unapproachable
medius, **-a**, **-um**: midst of
numen, -inis, *n*: divine power
pario, (3), **peperi**: give birth to, beget
passim: everywhere
pelagus, **-i** *n*: a sea
pervado, (3), **pervasi**: spread through
pollex, **-icis** *m*: a thumb
primoris, **-e**: first
profundum, **-i** *n*: depths
prorsus: (*adv.*) in short
proximus, -a, -um: nearest
regio, **-onis** *f.* a region
religiosus, **-a**, **-um**: reverent
resido, (3), **residi**: settle
ros, roris *m*: spray
spumo, (1): to froth
stupidus, **-a**, **-um**: stunned
tribuo, (3), **tribui**: grant
veneror, (1): adore, worship
venia, **-ae** *f.* favor

---

oribus suis: dat. with compound verb, "moving their right hand *to their ears*"
primore...residente: abl. abs., "*with the tip of the finger settling* onto the upright thumb," a gesture of pious adoration
ut ipsam...deam Venerem: "as though the goddess Venus herself"
pervaserat: plupf., "the rumor *had spread throughout*"
deam...conversari: pr. pass. inf. in ind. st. after *pervaserat*, "that the goddess lives"
quam...peperit: relative clause, "the goddess *whom the sea begot,*" i.e. Venus
tributa venia: abl. abs., "favor having been granted"
novo...germine: abl. means, "by means of a new bud"

stillarum germine non maria sed terras Venerem aliam virginali flore praeditam pullulasse.

Men travel to honor her as the rumor of her beauty spreads, leaving the shrines to Venus neglected.

[29] Sic immensum procedit in dies opinio, sic insulas jam proxumas et terrae plusculum provinciasque plurimas fama porrecta pervagatur. Jam multi mortalium longis itineribus atque altissimis maris meatibus ad saeculi specimen gloriosum confluebant. Paphon nemo Cnidon nemo ac ne ipsa quidem Cythera ad

---

altus, **-a**, **-um**: deep
Cnidos, **-i** *f.* Cnidus, a city in Caria with a famous statue of Venus
confluo, (3), **confluxi**, **confluxus**: to flock
Cythera, **-orum** *n*: Cythera, an island with Venus' most famous shrine
flos, **-oris** *m*: a flower
germen, **-inis** *n*: a sprout, bud
gloriosus, **-a**, **-um**: glorious
immensum: to an enormous extent
insula, **-ae** *f.* island
iter, **itinineris** *n*: a journey
mare, **-is** *n*: a sea
meatus, **-us** *m*: a channel
nemo, **-inis** *m*: no one, nobody
opinio, **-onis** *f.* rumor
Paphos, **-i** *f.* Paphos, a city on the island of Cyprus
pervagor, (1): spread widely through (+ *acc.*)
plurimus, **-a**, **-um**: most
plusculum, **-i** *n*: a larger amount of (+ *gen.*)
porrigo, (3), **porrexi**, **porrectus**: to extend
praeditus, **-a**, **-um**: gifted
procedo, (3): to proceed
provincia, **-ae** *f.* a province
proxumus, **-a**, **-um**: nearest
pullulo, (1): to sprout
saeculum, **-i** *n*: age
specimen, **-iminis** *n*: a specimen
stilla, **-ae** *f.* a drop of liquid
virginalis, **-e**: maidenly, virginal

---

non maria sed terras: acc. subject of *pullulasse* in ind. st., "that *not the sea but the lands* have sprouted"
virginali flore: abl. means after *praeditam*, "gifted *with a maidenly flower*," i.e. a virgin
pullulasse: syncopated perf. inf. (=*pullulavisse*) in ind. st., "that they have sprouted"
Sic...sic: climactic anaphora. See also 5.1, 5.9.
in dies: "day by day"
porrecta: perf. part. agreeing with *fama*, "the fame *having been extended*"
mortalium: partitive gen., "many *of mortals*"
itineribus atque meatibus: abl. means, "were flocking *by journeys and channels*
Paphon...Cnidon...Cythera: acc. place to which without preposition because they are names of islands or cities, "to Paphos, to Cnidos, and...to Cythera"
ne...quidem: "*not even* Cythera itself" Cythera had Venus' most famous shrine

conspectum deae Veneris navigabant; sacra differuntur, templa deformantur, pulvinaria proteruntur, caerimoniae negleguntur; incoronata simulacra et arae viduae frigido cinere foedatae. Puellae supplicatur et in humanis vultibus deae tantae numina placantur, et in matutino progressu virginis, victimis et epulis Veneris absentis nomen propitiatur, jamque per plateas commeantem populi frequentes floribus sertis et solutis adprecantur. Haec honorum caelestium ad puellae mortalis cultum inmodica translatio verae Veneris

---

absens, **-entis** (*gen.*): absent
adprecor, (1), **adprecatus sum**: to beseech
ara, **-ae** *f.* altar
caerimonia, **-ae** *f.* a ceremony
cinus, **-eris** *n*: ashes
commeo, (1): to pass, come and go
conspectus, **-us** *m*: a sight
cultus, **-us** *m*: worship, cult
deformo, (1): to disgrace
differo, (3): to postpone
epulum, **-i** *n*: a feast
foedo, (1): to soil, darken
frequens, **-entis** (*gen.*): crowded
frigidus, **-a**, **-um**: cold, lifeless
honor, **-oris** *m*: honor
incorono, (1): to wreathe
inmodicus, **-a**, **-um**: immoderate, excessive
matutinus, **-a**, **-um**: early
navigo, (1): to sail
neglego, (3): to neglect
nomen, **-inis** *n*: a name
placo, (1): to placate, appease
platea, **-ae** *f.* a street
progressus, **-us** *m*: advance
propitio, (1): to sooth
protero, (3), **protrivi**: tread under foot
pulvinar, **-aris** *n*: a cushioned couch
sacrum, **-i** *n*: a sacrifice
sertus, **-a**, **-um**: wreathed together
simulacrum, **-i** *n*: a statue
solutus, **-a**, **-um**: unbound
supplico, (1): to pray, supplicate
templum, **-i** *n*: a temple
translatio, **-onis** *f.* transfer to another
verus, **-a**, **-um**: true
victima, **-ae** *f.* a victim, animal for sacrifice
viduus, **-a**, **-um**: bereft
vultus, **-us** *m*: a face, expression

---

incoronata: perf. part. agreeing with *simulacra*, pred., "statues were left *unwreathed*"
viduae: "bereft," having the connotation of widowed or unmarried
foedetae: perf. part. pred., "bare altars were *darkened*"
frigido cinere: abl. means, "darkened *with cold ash*"
supplicatur: impersonal, "it was supplicated to" + dat.
in matutino progressu: abl. time, "in her early morning advance"
victimis et epulis: abl. means, "is soothed *with victims and feasts*"
commeantem: pr. part. acc. agreeing with implied dir. obj. of *adprecantur*, "the people beseech *her passing*..."

vehementer incendit animos, et impatiens indignationis capite quassanti fremens altius sic secum disserit:

Venus is enraged at the insult and informs her son Cupid of the impudence of Psyche, the princess.

[30] "En rerum naturae prisca parens, en elementorum origo initialis, en orbis totius alma Venus, quae cum mortali puella partiario majestatis honore tractor et nomen meum caelo conditum terrenis sordibus profanatur! Nimirum communi nominis piamento vicariae venerationis incertum sustinebo et imaginem meam circumferet puella moritura. Frustra me pastor ille cuius justitiam

---

almus, **-a**, **-um**: nourishing
altius, **-a**, **-um**: more shrilly
animus, **-i** *m*: feelings, pride
caelum, **-i** *n*: heaven
caput, -itis *n*: a head
circumfero, **-ferre**, **-tuli**, **-latus**: to carry around
communis, **-e**: public
condo, (3), **condidi, conditus**: to found
dissero, (3): to discuss
elementum, **-i** *n*: element
en: behold! lo!
fremo, (3): to rage
frustra: in vain
imago, **-inis** *f*: a likeness, image
impatiens, **-entis** (*gen.*): unable to hold back (+ *gen.*)
incendo, (3): to provoke, aggravate
incertum, **-i** *n*: uncertainty
indignatio, **-onis** *f*: indignation
initialis, **-e**: initial, original
justitia, **-ae** *f*: justice
majestas, **-atis** *f*: dignity (of a god)
morior, (4), **moritus sum**: to die
natura, **-ae** *f*: nature
nimirum: (*adv.*) evidently
orbis, **-is** *m*: a sphere, world
origo, **-inis** *f*: a source
partiarius, **-a**, **-um**: shared
pastor, **-oris** *m*: a shepherd
piamentum, **-i** *n*: atoning sacrifice
priscus, **-a**, **-um**: ancient, early, former
profano, (1): to desecrate
quasso, (1): to shake repeatedly
sordes, **-is** *f*: filth
sustineo, (2): to put up with
terrenus, **-a**, **-um**: earthly
tracto, (1): to treat
vehementer: (*adv.*) very much
veneratio, **-onis** *f*: veneration
vicarius, **-a**, **-um**: vicarious, substituted

---

capite quassanti: abl. abs., "with her head shaking"
fremens: pr. part., "*raging* more shrilly"
quae...tractor: relative clause, "I who am (mis)treated"
partiario honore: abl. manner, "treated *with shared honor*"
caelo: abl. place., "established *in heaven*"
terrenis sordibus: abl. means, "desecrated *by earthly filth*"
circumferet: fut., "will carry around"
mortitura: fut. act. part., "a girl *destined to die*"
pastor ille: "that famous shepherd" refers to Paris, who chose Venus as the most beautiful goddess

fidemque magnus comprobavit Iuppiter ob eximiam speciem tantis praetulit deabus. Sed non adeo gaudens ista, quaecumque est, meos honores usurpaverit: jam faxo eam huius etiam ipsius inlicitae formonsitatis paeniteat." Et vocat confestim puerum suum pinnatum illum et satis temerarium, qui malis suis moribus contempta disciplina publica flammis et sagittis armatus per alienas domos nocte discurrens et omnium matrimonia corrumpens impune committit tanta flagitia et nihil prorsus boni facit. Hunc, quamquam genuina

---

adeo: (*adv.*) certainly
alienus, **-a**, **-um**: another's
armo, (1): to equip
committo, (3): to commit
comprobo, (1): to sanction, approve
confestim: immediately
contemno, (3): to despise, condemn
corrumpo, (3): to infect
disciplina, **-ae** *f.* discipline
discurro, (3): to roam
domus, -i *f.* a home
eximius, **-a**, **-um**: extraordinary, remarkable
fides, **-ei** *f.* faith
flagitium, **-i** *n*: a disgrace, scandal
flamma, **-ae** *f.* a flame, fire of love
formonsitas, **-atis** *f.* beauty
gaudeo, (2): to be glad, rejoice
impune: (*adv.*) with impunity
inlicitus, **-a**, **-um**: illegal
matrimonium, **-i** *n*: a marriage
mos, moris *m*: manner, behavior (*pl.*)
nihil: nothing
nox, noctis *f.* a night
paeniteo, (2): to regret
pinnatus, **-a**, **-um**: winged
praefero, **-ferre**, **-tuli**, **-latus**: to prefer
prorsus: (*adv.*) absolutely
publicus, **-a**, **-um**: public
quaecumque: whoever
quamquam: although
sagitta, **-ae** *f.* an arrow
satis: (*adv.*) sufficiently, fairly
species, **-ei** *f.* a sight, beauty
temerarius, **-a**, **-um**: reckless
usurpo, (1): to usurp
voco, (1): to summon

---

tantis...deabus: dat. after *paretulit*, "preferred (me) *to such great goddesses*," namely, Juno and Minerva
gaudens: pr. part., "but certainly not *rejoicing*"
usurpaverit: fut. perf., "will have usurped"
faxo: archaic fut. of *facio* (=*faciam*), "I will make it so that" + subj.
huius...ipsius inlicitae formonsitatis: gen. after *paeniteat*, "regret for *this illegal beauty itself*"
paeniteat: impersonal pr. subj. volitive after *faxo*, "I will see to it *that there is regret* to X (acc.) for Y (gen.)"
malis suis moribus: abl. manner, "with his own wicked behavior"
contempta disciplina publica: abl. abs., "public discipline having been condemned"
flammis et sagittis: abl. instrument, "equipped *with the fires and arrows*"
nocte: abl. time, " in the night"
nihil boni: "nothing of good"
Hunc...stimulat: "this one (Cupid) she (Venus) goads on"

licentia procacem, verbis quoque insuper stimulat et perducit ad illam civitatem et Psychen — hoc enim nomine puella nuncupabatur— coram ostendit,

Venus entrusts Cupid with the task of punishing Psyche.

[31] et tota illa perlata de formonsitatis aemulatione fabula gemens ac fremens indignatione: "per ego te," inquit, "maternae caritatis foedera deprecor, per tuae sagittae dulcia vulnera, per flammae istius mellitas uredines, vindictam tuae parenti sed plenam tribue et in pulchritudinem contumacem severiter vindica idque unum et pro omnibus unicum volens effice: virgo ista amore

---

aemulatio, **-onis** *f.* a rivalry
amor, **-oris** *m*: love
caritas, **-atis** *f.* love, affection
contumax, **-acis**: insolent
coram: (*adv.*) in person, face to face
deprecor, (1), **deprecatus sum**: to entreat
dulcis, -e: sweet
efficio, (3): to bring about, execute
fabula, **-ae** *f.* a story, tale
flamma, **-ae** *f.* a flame, ardor
foedus, **-eris** *n*: a bond
fremo, (3): to murmur
gemo, (3): to moan
genuinus, **-a**, **-um**: inborn
indignatio, **-onis** *f.* indignation, anger
insuper: in addition
licentia, **-ae** *f.* outspokenness
maternus, **-a**, **-um**: maternal
mellitus, **-a**, **-um**: honey-sweet
nuncupo, (1): to call
ostendo, (2): to point out
perduco, (3): to lead
perfero, **-ferre**, **-tuli**, **-latus**: to announce
plenus, **-a**, **-um**: full
procax, **-acis**: impudent, undisciplined
pulchritudo, **-inis** *f.* beauty
sagitta, **-ae** *f.* an arrow
severiter: (*adv.*) severely
stimulo, (1): to incite, rouse to frenzy
tribuo, (3): to bestow
uredo, **-inis** *f.* a burning sensation
verbum, -i *n*: a word
vindico, (1): to punish
vindicta, **-ae** *f.* vengeance
volens, **-entis** (*gen.*): willing
vulnus, **-eris** *n*: a wound, wound of love

---

genuina licentia: abl. specification with *procax*, "impudent *with inborn outspokenness*"
hoc...nomine: abl. means, "called *with this name*"
Psychen: the Greek word for "soul"
tota illa perlata...fabula: abl. abs., "with that whole tale having been announced"
indignatione: abl. manner, "murmuring *with indignation*"
Per ego te: the word order is formulaic, "I entreat you by" + acc.
Per...per...per: note the anaphora
tribue...vindica...effice: imper., "bestow!...punish!...execute!"
tuae parenti: dat. advantage, "punished *on behalf of your parent*"
sed: emphasizes *plenam*, "bestow the vengeance *and what's more* bestow the full vengeance"

fraglantissimo teneatur hominis extremi, quem et dignitatis et patrimonii simul et incolumitatis ipsius Fortuna damnavit, tamque infimi ut per totum orbem non inveniat miseriae suae comparem." Sic effata et osculis hiantibus filium diu ac pressule saviata proximas oras reflui litoris petit, plantisque roseis vibrantium fluctuum summo rore calcato, ecce jam profundi maris sudo resedit vertice, et ipsum quod incipit velle, set statim, quasi pridem praeceperit, non moratur marinum obsequium: adsunt Nerei filiae chorum

---

adsum, **-esse**: be present (+ *dat.*)
calco, (1): to tread
chorus, **-i** *m*: a chorus
compar, **-aris** *m:* an equal
damno, (1): to condemn X (acc) to lose Y (gen.
dignitas, **-atis** *f.* status
ecce: behold!
effor, (1), **effatus sum**: to declare, speak
extremus, **-a**, **-um**: lowest
fluctus, **-us** *m*: a wave
fortuna, **-ae** *f.* fortune, fate
fraglantissimus, **-a**, **-um**: most ardent, passionate
hio, (1): to be open-mouthed
homo, **-inis** *m*: a man
incipio, (3): to begin
incolumitas, **-atis** *f.* safety
infimus, **-a**, **-um**: lowest, vilest
invenio, (4): to find
litus, **-oris** *n*: a coast
mare, **-is** *n*: a sea
marinus, **-a**, **-um**: marine
miseria, **-ae** *f.* suffering
moror, (1), **moratus sum**: to delay
Nereius, **-i** *m*: Nereus, old Greek god of the sea
obsequium, **-i** *n*: a retinue
ora, **-ae** *f.* a shore, coast
orbis, **-is** *m*: sphere (world)
osculum, **-i** *n*: lips
patrimonium, **-i** *n*: inheritance
peto, (3): to make for
planta, **-ae** *f.* a sole (of foot)
praecipio, (3), **praecepi**: anticipate
pressule: (*adv.*) while pressing against
pridem: some time ago, previously
profundus, **-a**, **-um**: boundless
refluus, **-a**, **-um**: flowing back
resideo, (2), **resedi**: sit down
ros, **roris** *m*: spray of water
roseus, **-a**, **-um**: rose-colored
savior, (1), **saviatus sum**: to kiss
sudus, **-a**, **-um**: clear and bright
teneo, (2): to hold
vertex, **-icis** *m*: a peak
vibro, (1): to glitter

---

teneatur: pr. pass. subj. jussive, "*let* that maiden *be held*"
dignitatis...ipsius: the genitives indicate what he is condemned to lose
ut non inveniat: pr. act. subj. in result clause, "so vile *that she might not find*"
miseriae suae: dat. after *comparem*, "an equal *to her own misery*"
effata...saviata: pf. part. deponent nom., "having spoken...having kissed"
plantisque roseis: abl. means, "treaded on *with rose-colored soles*"
summo rore calcato: abl. abs., "the top of the water having been treaded on"
sudo...vertice: abl. place where, "on the clear and bright peak"
ipsum quod incipit velle: "that which he begins to wish"
quasi pridem praeceperit: perf. subj. indicating an alleged motive, "as if he had already ordered it"
Nerei filiae: "the daughters of Nereus;" nymphs

canentes et Portunus caerulis barbis hispidus et gravis piscoso sinu Salacia et auriga parvulus delphini Palaemon; jam passim maria persultantes Tritonum catervae hic concha sonaci leniter bucinat, ille serico tegmine flagrantiae solis obsistit inimici, alius sub oculis dominae speculum progerit, curru bijuges alii subnatant. Talis ad Oceanum pergentem Venerem comitatur exercitus.

---

auriga, **-ae** *m*: a charioteer
barba, **-ae** *f.* a beard
bijugis, **-e**: yoked two abreast
bucino, (1): to give signal with
caerulus, **-a**, **-um**: blue
cano, (3): to sing
caterva, **-ae** *f.* a troop, band
comitor, (1), **comitatus sum**: to escort
concha, **-ae** *f.* a conch-shell, horn
currus, **-us** *m*: a chariot
delphinus, **-i** *m*: a dolphin
exercitus, **-us** *m*: a navy
flagrantia, **-ae** *f.* a blaze
gravis, **-e**: heavy
hispidus, **-a**, **-um**: rough
inimicus, **-a**, **-um**: harmful
leniter: (*adv.*) lightly
obsisto, (3): to resist, withstand
Oceanus, **-i** *m*: Ocean
oculus, -i *m*: an eye
Palaemon *m*: Palaemon, Roman sea god
parvulus, **-a**, **-um**: very small
passim: everywhere
pergo (3): to mae one's way
persulto, (1): to leap
piscosus, **-a**, **-um**: teeming with fish
Portunus, **-i** *m*: Portunus, Roman sea god
progero, (3): to carry before
sericus, **-a**, **-um**: silken
sinus, **-us** *m*: a lap
sol, **solis** *m*: sun
sonax, **-acis**: making a sound, sounding
speculum, **-i** *n*: a mirror
subnato, (1): to swim under
tegmen, **-inis** *n*: a covering
Tritonum *m*: Triton

Portunus: old Roman sea god connected to harbors (*portus*)
Salacia: old Roman sea goddess connected to the rocking of the sea (*salum*)
auriga: nom. in apposition to *Palaemon*, "Palaemon *the charioteer*"
Palaemon: Roman sea god, often depicted riding dolphins
Tritonum catervae: group of divine beings who blow conch-shells and attend Neptune, "bands of Tritons"
hic...ille...alius...alii: "one...another...yet another...still others"
concha sonaci: abl. of means, "giving the signal *with the sounding conch-shell*"
flagrantiae: dat. with compound verb *obsisto*, "resists...*the blaze*"
solis...inimici: gen., "blaze *of the harmful sun*"
curru (=currui): dat. with compound *subnatant*, "swim under *the charriot*"
pergentem: pr. part. agreeing with *Venerem*, "Venus *proceeding*"

Psyche's sisters are married but Psyche's beauty isolates her. The king consults the oracle of Apollo at Miletus.

[32] Interea Psyche cum sua sibi perspicua pulchritudine nullum decoris sui fructum percipit. Spectatur ab omnibus, laudatur ab omnibus, nec quisquam, non rex, non regius, nec de plebe saltem cupiens eius nuptiarum petitor accedit. Mirantur quidem divinam speciem, sed ut simulacrum fabre politum mirantur omnes. Olim duae majores sorores, quarum temperatam formositatem nulli diffamarant populi, procis regibus desponsae jam beatas nuptias adeptae, sed Psyche virgo vidua domi residens deflet

---

accedo, (3): to approach
adipiscor, (3), **adeptus sum**: to secure
cupio, (3): to be eager for, desire
decor, **-oris** *m*: beauty, grace
defleo, (2): to lament
despondeo, (2), **despopondi**, **desponsus**: to betroth
diffamo, (1): to publish widely
fabre: (*adv.*) skillfully
formositas, **-atis** *f*: beauty
fructus, **-us** *m*: enjoyment, reward
laudo, (1): to praise
major, -oris; older
miror, (1), **miratus sum**: to admire
nuptiae, -arum *f*: a marraige
olim: formerly
percipio, (3): to gain
perspicuus, **-a**, **-um**: clear
petitor, **-oris** *m*: a candidate, suitor
plebs, **-ebis** *f*: common people
politus, **-a**, **-um**: refined, polished
procus, **-i** *m*: a suitor
pulchritudo, **-inis** *f*: beauty, excellence
regius, **-a**, **-um**: royal
resideo, (2): to remain seated
saltem: even, so much as
simulacrum, **-i** *n*: an image, statue
soror, -oris *f*: a sister
species, **-ei**, *f*: beauty
specto, (1): to look at, consider
temperatus, **-a**, **-um**: mild, moderate
viduus, **-a**, **-um**: unmarried

---

cum...pulchritudine: abl. circumstance, a colloquial use, "with her beauty"
ab omnibus...ab omnibus: abl. agent, "she is considered *by all*, she is praised *by all*"
eius: objective gen. with *cupiens*, "desirous *of her*"
nuptiarum: objective gen. with *petitor*, "suitor *of marriage*"
petitor: pred. nom., "no one approached *as a suitor*"
ut...mirantur: parenthetical clause of comparison, "just as all admire"
diffamarant: syncopated plupf., "none *had published widely*"
regibus: dat. pred. with *procis*, "to suitors (who were) *kings*"
desponsae: perf. part., "having already been betrothed"
adeptae (sc. erant): "they had already secured"
domi: locative, "at home"

desertam suam solitudinem, aegra corporis, animi saucia, et quamvis gentibus totis complacitam odit in se suam formositatem. Sic infortunatissimae filiae miserrimus pater suspectatis caelestibus odiis et irae superum metuens dei Milesii vetustissimum percontatur oraculum, et a tanto numine precibus et victimis ingratae virgini petit nuptias et maritum. Sed Apollo, quamquam Graecus et Ionicus, propter Milesiae conditorem, sic Latina sorte respondit:

---

aeger, **-gra**, **-grum**: ill
animus, **-i** *m*: spirit
caelestis, **-e**: heavenly
complacitus, **-a**, **-um**: favorable (+ *dat.*)
conditor, **-oris** *m*: an author
desertus, **-a**, **-um**: lonely
gens, **gentis** *f*: people
Graecus, **-a**, **-um**: Greek
infortunatus, **-a**, **-um**: unfortunate, unhappy
ingratus, **-a**, **-um**: thankless
Ionicus, **-a**, **-um**: Ionic, Ionian
ira, **-ae** *f*: ire, wrath
Latinus, **-a**, **-um**: Latin
maritus, -i m: a husband
metuo, (3), **metui**: fear
odeo, (4): to hate
odium, **-i** *n*: hatred
oraculum, **-i** *n*: an oracle
percontor, (1), **percontatus sum**: to inquire
peto, (3): to beg, entreat, ask (for)
prex, precis, *f*: a prayer
quamquam: although
respondeo, (2), **respondi**: answer
saucius, **-a**, **-um**: wounded
solitudo, **-inis** *f*: solitude
sors, sortis *f*: an oracular response
superus, **-i** *m*: a god
suspecto, (1): to be suspicious of
vetustissiumus, **-a**, **-um**,: most ancient
victima, **-ae** *f*: an animal for sacrifice

---

aegra corporis, animi saucia: gen. specification; note the chiastic order, "ill *of body*, *in spirit* wounded"
quamvis...complacitam: pr. part. concessive, "*although favorable* to all people"
gentibus totis: dat. with *complacitam*, "favorable *to all people*"
suspectatis caelestibus odiis: abl. abs., "heavenly hatred having been suspected"
irae: gen. after *metuens*, "fearing *the wrath*"
superum: syncopated (=*supererum*) gen. pl., "of the gods"
dei Milesii: "of the Milesian god," Apollo, who has a famous oracle near Miletus, but also alluding to the "Milesian tale" see below
precibus et victimis: abl. means, "he begs *with prayers and animals for sacrifice*"
ingratae virgini: dat. ind. obj., "for the thankless maiden"
propter Milesiae conditorem: "for the sake of the author of the Milesian [tale];" Milesian tales were baudy stories, like many of the stories in this novel. The adjective also occurs in the preface to the whole work.

Apollo replies: Psyche must be offered in marriage to an unknown evil and left alone on a cliff.

[33] "montis in excelsi scopulo, rex, siste puellam
Ornatam mundo funerei thalami.
Nec speres generum mortali stirpe creatum,
Sed saevum atque ferum vipereumque malum,
Quod pinnis volitans super aethera cuncta fatigat
Flammaque et ferro singula debilitat,
Quod tremit ipse Jovis, quo numina terrificantur,
fluminaque horrescunt et Stygiae tenebrae."

---

aether, **-eris** *n*: heaven, sky
creo, (1): to create, sire
cunctus, **-a**, **-um**: entire
debilito, (1): to weaken, cripple
excelsus, **-a**, **-um**,: lofty
fatigo, (1): to harass
ferrum, **-i** *n*: a sword
ferus, **-a**, **-um**: wild
flamma, **-ae** *f*: a flame
flumen, **-inis** *n*: a river, flood
funereus, **-a**, **-um**: funereal
gener, **-eri** *m*: a son-in-law
horresco, (3): to dread
Jovis, **-is** *m*: Jupiter
mons, **montis** *m*: a mountain
mundus, **-i** *m*: a dress, fashion
orno, (1): to dress, adorn
pinna, -ae *f*: a feather
saevus, **-a**, **-um**: cruel
scopulum, -i n: a rock
singulus, **-a**, **-um**: every
sisto, (3): to set up
spero, (1): to hope for
stirps, **-irpis** *f*: race
Stygius, **-a**, **-um**: Stygian
tenebra, **-ae** *f*: darkness (*pl.*), gloom
terrifico, (1): to terrify
thalamus, **-i** *m*: a marriage
tremo, (3): to tremble
vipereus, **-a**, **-um**: of a viper, viper-like
volito, (1): to fly about

---

montis...: the meter is elegaic couplets rather than dactylic hexameters, the usual form of oracles
siste: s. imper., "set up!"
mundo: abl. specification, "adorned *in the fashion*"
Nec speres: pr. subj. in prohibition, "Do not hope…"
mortali stirpe: abl. source, "created *from the human race*"
pinnis: abl. means, "flying *on wings*"
flammaque et ferro: abl. means, "weakens *with flame and sword*"
singula: acc. neut. pl., "everything"
quo: abl. s. referring to *malum*, "an evil *of whom*"
numina terrificantur: "the gods are terrified"

Rex olim beatus affatu sanctae vaticinationis accepto pigens tristisque retro domum pergit suaeque conjugi praecepta sortis enodat infaustae. Maeretur, fletur, lamentatur diebus plusculis. Sed dirae sortis jam urget taeter effectus. Jam feralium nuptiarum miserrimae virgini choragium struitur, jam taedae lumen atrae fuliginis cinere marcescit, et sonus tibiae zygiae mutatur in querulum Lydii modum cantusque laetus hymenaei lugubri finitur ululatu et puella nuptura deterget lacrimas ipso suo flammeo. Sic adfectae domus

---

adfectus, **-a**, **-um**: impaired
affatus, **-us** *n*: speech
ater, **-tra**, **-trum**: black
beatus, **-a**, **-um**: blessed
cantus, **-us** *m*: a song
choragium, **-i** *n*: gear, trappings
ciner, **-eris** *n*: ashes
conjunx, **-ugis** *f*: a spouse
detergeo, (2): to wipe away
dirus, **-a**, **-um**: dire
effectus, **-us** *m*: execution
enodo, (1): to make clear
feralis, **-e**: fatal
finio, (4): to end
flammeum, **-i** *n*: a veil
fleo, (2): to cry for
fuligo, **-inis** *f*: a soot
hymenaeus, **-i** *m*: a Greek wedding chant
infaustus, **-a**, **-um**: unlucky, inauspicious
lacrima, -ae f: a tear
laetus, **-a**, **-um**: happy
lamento, (1): to lament
lugubris, **-e**: mournful
lumen, -inis n: light
maereo, (2): to bewail
marcesco, (3): to wither, become weak
modus, **-i** *m*: a manner
muto, (1): to change
nubo, (3), **nupsi**, **nuptus**: to marry
olim: (*adv.*) formerly
pigo, (3): to be weakened
plusculus, **-a**, **-um**: rather more
praeceptum, **-i** *n*: an order
querulus, **-a**, **-um**: querulous
retro: (*adv.*) backwards, back
sonus, **-i** *m*: a noise, sound
sors, sortis *f*: an oracular response
struo, (3): to build
taeda, -ae *f*: a torch
taeter, **-tra**, **-trum**: foul
tibia, **-ae** *f*: pipes
tristis, **-e**: sorrowful
ululatus, **-us** *m*: howling
urgeo, (2): to press
vaticinatio, **-onis** *f*: prophecy
zygius, **-a**, **-um**: belonging to the yoke of marriage

---

affatu...accepto: abl. abs., "with the speech having been accepted"
domum: accusative of place to which, "proceeds back *to home*"
conjugi: dat. ind. obj., "makes clear *to his wife*"
miserrimae virgini: dat. advantage, "is set out for *the most miserable maiden*"
tibiae zygiae: gen., "of the yoking pipes," referring to part of the traditional marriage feast
Lydii modum: "the manner of the Lydians," i.e. a mournful and melancholic tone
lugubri ululatu: abl. manner, "ends *with a mournful howling*"
ipso suo flammeo: abl. means, "wipe away *with her own veil itself*"

triste fatum cuncta etiam civitas congemebat luctuque publico confestim congruens edicitur justitium.

Psyche urges her parents to accept fate and end their grief.

[34] Sed monitis caelestibus parendi necessitas misellam Psychen ad destinatam poenam efflagitabat. Perfectis igitur feralis thalami cum summo maerore sollemnibus toto prosequente populo vivum producitur funus, et lacrimosa Psyche comitatur non nuptias sed exsequias suas. Ac dum maesti parentes et tanto malo perciti nefarium facinus perficere cunctantur, ipsa illa filia talibus eos

---

caeleste, **-is** *n*: heavens
civitas, **-atis** *f.* a city
comitor, (1), **comitatus sum**: to accompany, attend funeral
confestim: (*adv.*) at once
congemo, (3): to lament
congruo, (3): to be appropriate for
cunctor (1): delay, hesitate (+ *inf.*)
cunctus, **-a**, **-um**: every
destinatus, **-a**, **-um**: destined, fixed
dum: while
edico, (3): to proclaim
efflagito, (1): to request, demand, insist
exsequia, **-ae** *f.* funeral procession (*pl.*)
facinus, **-oris** *n*: a deed
fatum, **-i** *n*: fate
feralis, **-e**: funereal
funus, **-eris** *n*: a corpse
igitur: therefore
justitium, **-i** *n*: cessation of judicial and all public business, due to national calamity
lacrimosus, **-a**, **-um**: weeping
luctus, **-us** *m*: grief
maeror, **-oris** *m*: mourning
maestus, **-a**, **-um**: mournful
misellus, **-a**, **-um**: poor
moneo, (2): to warn
necessitas, **-atis** *f.* necessity, obligation
nefarius, **-a**, **-um**: wicked
parens, -entis, m; parent
pareo, (2): to obey
percitus, **-a**, **-um**: stirred up
perficio, (3): to complete, execute
poena, **-ae** *f.* punishment
produco, (3): to lead forward
prosequor, (3), **prosecutus sum**: to escort
publicus, **-a**, **-um**: public
solleme, **-is** *n*: a solemn observance
thalamus, **-i** *m*: a marriage
tristis, **-e**: sad
vivus, **-a**, **-um**: living

---

luctuque publico: abl. desc., "laments *in public grief*"
parendi: gerund gen., "the necessity *of obeying*"
Perfectis...sollemnibus: abl. abs., "With the solemn observance having been completed..."
cum summo maerore: abl. manner, "with the greatest mourning"
toto prosequente populo: abl. abs., "with all people escorting"
tanto malo: abl. means, "stirred *by such great misfortune*"
talibus...vocibus: abl. means, "encourages *with such a voice*"

adhortatur vocibus: "Quid infelicem senectam fletu diutino cruciatis? Quid spiritum vestrum, qui magis meus est, crebris ejulatibus fatigatis? Quid lacrimis inefficacibus ora mihi veneranda foedatis? Quid laceratis in vestris oculis mea lumina? Quid canities scinditis? Quid pectora, quid ubera sancta tunditis? Haec erunt vobis egregiae formonsitatis meae praeclara praemia. Invidiae nefariae letali plaga percussi sero sentitis. Cum gentes et populi celebrarent nos divinis honoribus, cum novam me Venerem ore consono nuncuparent, tunc dolere, tunc flere, tunc me jam quasi peremptam

---

adhortor, (1), **adhortatus sum**: to encourage
canities, **-ei** *f.* white/gray hair
celebro, (1): to celebrate
consonus, **-a**, **-um**: harmonious
creber, **-era**, **-erum**: constant
crucio, (1): to torment, torture
diutinus, **-a**, **-um**: long lasting, long
doleo, (2): to grieve
egregius, **-a**, **-um**: extraordinary
ejulatus, **-us** *m*: wailing, lamentation
fatigo, (1): to weary, tire
fleo, (2): to weep
fletus, **-us** *m*: weeping
foedo, (1): to defile, stain
formonsitas, **-atis** *f.* beauty
gens, **gentis** *f.* a nation, people
honor, **-oris,** *m:* honor
inefficax, **-acis**: useless, ineffectual
infelix, **-icis** *(gen.)*: unfortunate
invidia, **-ae** *f.* envy
lacero, (1): to harm, ruin
letalis, **-e**: deadly, mortal
magis: (*adv.*) more nearly
nefarius, **-a**, **-um**: wicked
nuncupo, (1): to call
pectus, **-oris** *n*: a heart
percutio, (3), **percussi**, **percussus**: to strike
perimo, (3), **peremi**, **peremptus**: to destroy
plaga, **-ae** *f.* a blow
praeclarus, **-a**, **-um**: splendid
praemium, **-i** *n*: a reward
sanctus, **-a**, **-um**: sacred
scindo, (3): to tear
senecta, **-ae** *f.* old age
sentio, (4): to perceive, realize
sero: (*adv.*) too late
spiritus, **-us** *m*: a breath
tundo, (3): to beat, bruise
uber, **-eris** *n*: a breast
venero, (1): to adore, honor
vox, vocis f: a voice

---

fletu diutino: abl. means, "torment *with long lasting weeping*"
crebris ejulatibus: abl. means, "weary *with constant wailing*"
lacrimis inefficacibus: abl. means, "stain *with ineffectual tears*"
veneranda: fut. pass. part., "faces *that ought to be honored*"
mea lumina: n. acc. pl., "why ruin *my eyes* in your eyes"
egregiae formonsitatis meae: objective gen., "rewards *of my extraordinary beauty*"
letali plaga: abl. means, "struck *by the deadly blow*"
Cum...celebrarent...cum...nuncuparent: impf. subj. in cum circumstantial clause, "When they were celebrating...when they were calling"
divinis honoribus: abl. means, "celebrate *with divine honors*"
ore consono: abl. manner, "call *with harmonious speech*"
dolere...flere...lugere: inf. with *debuistis*, "ought *to grieve...to cry...to mourn*"

lugere debuistis. Jam sentio jam video solo me nomine Veneris perisse. Ducite me et cui sors addixit scopulo sistite. Festino felices istas nuptias obire, festino generosum illum maritum meum videre. Quid differo, quid detrecto venientem, qui totius orbis exitio natus est?"

The king and queen leave Psyche at the appointed mountain, from which she is softly taken from the cliff by Zephyr to a safe landing.

[35] Sic profata virgo conticuit ingressuque jam valido pompae populi prosequentis sese miscuit. Itur ad constitutum scopulum montis ardui, cuius in summo cacumine statutam puellam cuncti

---

addico, (3), **addixi**: doom, assign
arduus, **-a**, **-um**: steep, towering
cacumen, **-inis** *n*: a peak
constitutus, **-a**, **-um**: appointed
conticesco, (2), **conticui**: to fall silent
cunctus, **-a**, **-um**: all
debeo, (2): to be obliged to (+ *inf.*)
detrecto, (1): to reject
differo, **differre**, **-diuli**, **dilatus**: to put off
duco, (3): to lead
exitium, **-i** *n*: ruin
felix, **-icis** (*gen.*): happy, blessed
festino (1): to hasten
generosus, **-a**, **-um**: noble
ingressus, **-us** *m*: a step, approach
lugeo, (2): to mourn
misceo, (2), **miscui**: mix, join X (*acc.*) to Y (*dat.*)
mons, **montis** *m*: a mountain
nascor, (3), **natus sum**: to be born
obeo, (4): to go to meet, die
orbis, **-is** *m*: a sphere (world)
pereo, (4), **perivi**: to pass away, be ruined
pompa, **-ae** *f*: a procession
profor, (1), **profatus sum**: to speak out
prosequor, (3), **prosecutus sum**: to escort
sentio, (4): to feel, think
sisto, (3): to set up
sors, **sortis** *f*: fate
statuo, (3) **statutus**: to establish, place
validus, **-a**, **-um**: strong, firm

---

perisse: syncopated (=*perivisse*) perf. act. inf. in ind. st., "see *that I have been ruined*"
solo...nomine: abl. means, "ruined *by the name only*"
Ducite...sistite: imper., "Lead and set me up!"
scopulo: abl. place where, "on the rock"
obire: inf. of purpose, "hasten *to meet*," with the connotation "to die"
venientem: pr. part., "reject *the one who is coming*"
ingressu...valido: abl. manner, "with a firm approach" i.e. with determination
pompae: dat. after *miscuit*, "she joined herself to *the procession*"
Itur: archaic impersonal verb, "it is gone," i.e. "she goes"
cuius: gen., "on the peak *of which*"
in summo cacumine: abl. of place where, "on the highest peak"

deserunt, taedasque nuptiales, quibus praeluxerant, ibidem lacrimis suis extinctas relinquentes dejectis capitibus domuitionem parant. Et miseri quidem parentes eius tanta clade defessi, clausae domus abstrusi tenebris, perpetuae nocti sese dedidere. Psychen autem paventem ac trepidam et in ipso scopuli vertice deflentem mitis aura molliter spirantis Zephyri vibratis hinc inde laciniis et reflato sinu sensim levatam suo tranquillo spiritu vehens paulatim

---

abstrudo, (3), **abstrusi, -trusus**: to hide
aura, **-ae** *f.* a breeze, breath
clades, **-is** *f.* a disaster
clausus, **-a**, **-um**: locked
dedo, (3), **dedidi**: devote (to)
defessus, **-a**, **-um**: weary
defleo, (2): to lament, cry bitterly
dejectus, **-a**, **-um**: downcast, dejected
desero, (3): to desert
domuituo, **-onis** *f.* a returning home
extinguo, (3) **extinctus**: to destroy, extinguish
hinc: from here
ibidem: in that very place
inde: from there
lacinia, **-ae** *f.* hem of garment, dress (*pl.*)
levo, (1): to lift off
miser, **-era**, **-erum**: wretched, unhappy
mitis, **-e**: mild
molliter: (*adv.*) softly
nuptialis, **-e**: of marriage, nuptial
paro, (1): to prepare
paulatim: (*adv.*) little by little
paveo, (2): to be frightened
perpetuus, **-a**, **-um**: perpetual, everlasting
praeluceo, (2), **praeluxi**: light the way (for)
reflo, (1): to blow back again
relinquo, (3): to abandon
sensim: (*adv.*) gradually
sinus, **-us** *m*: a fold
spiro, (1): to blow
taeda, **-ae** *f.* a pine torch
tenebra, **-ae** *f.* darkness
tranquillus, **-a**, **-um**: calm
trepidus, **-a**, **-um**: jumpy, agitated
veho, (3): to bear, carry
vertex, **-icis** *m*: a peak
vibro, (1): to cause to wave
Zephyrus, **-i** *m*: Zephyr, the west wind

---

lacrimis suis: abl. means, "extinguished *by their own tears*"
deiectis capitibus: abl. manner, "*with downcast heads*... they prepare"
quibus: abl. means, "*by which* they had lit"
extinctas: perf. part. agreeing with *taedas*, "torches *having been extinguished*"
relinquentes: pr. part. with nom., "they *abandoning*"
tanta clade: abl. means, "weary *with so great a disaster*"
abstrusi: perf. part. with reflexive meaning, "the parents...having hidden themselves"
tenebris: abl. place where, "in the darkness"
dedidere: apocopated perf. (=*dediderunt*), "they have devoted themselves to" + dat.
spirantis: pr. part. agreeing with *Zephyri*, "of Zephyr *blowing*"
vibratis...laciniis: abl. abs., "with the dress having been waved"
reflato sinu: abl. abs., "with the fold having been blown back again"
suo tranquillo spiritu: abl. means, "carrying her *with his own calm breath*"

per devexa rupis excelsae vallis subditae florentis cespitis gremio leniter delapsam reclinat.

Psyche finds herself in a pleasant grove surrounding a magnificent palace.

[5.1] Psyche teneris et herbosis locis in ipso toro roscidi graminis suave recubans, tanta mentis perturbatione sedata, dulce conquievit. Jamque sufficienti recreata somno placido resurgit animo. Videt lucum proceris et vastis arboribus consitum, videt fontem vitreo latice perlucidum; medio luci meditullio prope fontis

---

animus, **-i** *m*: heart, spirit
arbor, **-oris** *f.* a tree
cespes, **-itis** *m*: grassy ground, earth
conquiesco, (3), **conquievi**: rest, to sleep
consero, (3), **consevi**, **consitus**: to sow, plant
delabor, (3), **delapsus sum**: to glide down
devexum, **-i** *n*: a slope
excelsus, **-a**, **-um**: lofty
florens, **-entis** *(gen.)*: flowering
fons, fontis, f: a fountain
gramen, **-inis** *n*: turf
gremium, **-i** *n*: a lap, bosom
herbosus, **-a**, **-um**: grassy
latex, **-icis** *m*: water
leniter: (*adv.*) gently
lucus, **-i** *m*: a sacred grove
meditullium, **-i** *n*: interior
medius, **-a**, **-um**: middle of
mens, **mentis** *f.* mind
perlucidus, **-a**, **-um**: transparent
perturbatio, **-onis** *f.* a disturbance
placidus, **-a**, **-um**: calm
procerus, **-a**, **-um**: lofty
prope: near (+ *acc.*)
reclino, (1): to bend back, recline
recreo, (1): to restore
recubo, (1): to recline
resurgo, (3): to rise
roscidus, **-a**, **-um**: dewy
rupes, **-is** *f.* a cliff
sedatus, **-a**, **-um**: untroubled
sedo, (1): to calm
somnus, -i m: sleep
suavis, **-e**: pleasant, sweet
subdo, (3): to place under
sufficiens, **-entis** *(gen.)*: sufficient
tener, **-era**, **-erum**: tender, soft
torus, **-i** *m*: a bed
valles, **-is**: valley
vastus, **-a**, **-um**: vast
vitreus, **-a**, **-um**: of glass, glassy

---

gremio: abl. place where, "in the bosom…"
delapsam: perf. part. deponent, "the girl *having flown down*"
teneris et herbosis locis: abl. place where, "in soft and grassy places"
ipso: emphatic, "on a *veritable* bed"
tanta…perturbatione sedata: abl. abs., "with so great a disturbance having been calmed"
sufficienti…somno: abl. means, "restored *by sufficient sleep*"
placido animo: abl. manner, "with a calm heart"
lucum…consitum: acc., "sees *a grove having been planted with*" (+ abl.)
proceris et vastis arboribus: abl. specification after *consitum*, "planted *with lofty and vast trees*"
vitreo latice: abl. specification, "transparent *with glassy water*"
medio…meditullio: abl. place where, "in the very middle of the interior"

adlapsum domus regia est, aedificata non humanis manibus, sed divinis artibus. Jam scies ab introitu primo dei cuiuspiam luculentum et amoenum videre te diversorium. Nam summa laquearia citro et ebore curiose cavata subeunt aureae columnae, parietes omnes argenteo caelamine conteguntur bestiis et id genus pecudibus occurrentibus ob os introeuntium. Mirus prorsum homo – immo semideus vel certe deus – qui magnae artis suptilitate

---

adlapsus, **-us** *m*: a gliding up
aedifico, (1): to construct
amoenus, **-a**, **-um**: beautiful
argenteus, **-a**, **-um**: silver
ars, **artis** *f*: a skill
aureus, **-a**, **-um**: golden
bestia, **-ae** *f*: a wild beast
caelamen, **-inis** *n*: a raised ornamentation
cavo, (1): to carve in relief
citrum, **-i** *n*: wood of the citron tree
columna, **-ae** *f*: a column
contego, (3): to cover up
curiose: (*adv.*) elaborately
deus, **-i** *m*: a god
diversorium, **-i** *n*: accommodation
domus, **-i** *f*: a house
ebur, **-oris** *n*: ivory
genus, **-eris** *n*: a kind
homo, **-inis** *m*: a man
immo: more correctly
introeo, **-ire**, **-ivi**, **-itus**: to enter
introitus, **-us** *m*: an entrance
laquear, **-aris** *n*: a rafter
luculentus, **-a**, **-um**: bright
manus, -us f: a hand
mirus, **-a**, **-um**: wonderful, amazing
occurro, (3): to run to meet
os, oris *n*: a face, mouth
paries, **-etis** *m*: a wall
pecus, **-udis** *f*: a herd
prorsum: (*adv.*) in short
quispiam: some
regius, **-a**, **-um**: regal
semideus, **-i** *m*: a demigod
subeo, **-ire**, **-ivi**, **-itum**: to extend underneath
summus, **-a**, **-um**: highest
suptilitas, **-atis** *f*: acuteness

---

non humanibus sed divinis: abl. means, "constructed *not by human hands but by divine skills*"
videre te: ind. st. after *scies,* "you will know *that you are seeing*"
citro et ebore: abl. specification, "carved *from citron wood and ivory*"
columnae: nom. subject of *subeunt,* "*columns* support the rafters"
argenteo caelamine: abl. means, "covered *by raised silver ornamentation*"
bestiis...pecudibus occurrentibus: abl. abs., "with wild beasts and herds running"
id genus: adverbial acc., "of that kind"
ob os introeuntium: "running *towards the face of those entering*"
Mirus: nom. pred., "*amazing* was the man"
efferavit: perf., "who *has animated*"
suptilitate: abl. manner, "with acuteness"

tantum efferavit argentum. Enimvero, pavimenta ipsa lapide pretioso caesim deminuto in varia picturae genera discriminantur: vehementer iterum ac saepius beatos illos qui super gemmas et monilia calcant! Jam ceterae partes longe lateque dispositae domus sine pretio pretiosae totique parietes solidati massis aureis splendore proprio coruscant, ut diem suum sibi domus faciat licet sole nolente: sic cubicula, sic porticus, sic ipsae balneae fulgurant. Nec setius opes ceterae majestati domus respondent, ut equidem illud

---

argentum, **-i** *n*: silver
balnea, **-ae** *f.* a bath
beatus, **-a**, **-um**: blessed
caesim: (*adv.*) by cutting
calco, (1): to tread upon
corusco, (1): to glitter
cubiculum, **-i** *n*: a bedroom
deminuo, (3), **deminui**, **deminutus**: to make smaller
dies, diei m: a day
discrimino, (1): to divide up
dispono, (3), **disposui**, **dispositus**: to arrange
domus, **-us** *f.* a house
effero, (1): to brutalize, animate
enimvero: to be sure
equidem: (*adv.*) truly
fulguro, (1): to glitter
gemma, **-ae** *f.* a gem
genus, **-eris** *n*: a style
iterum: again
lapis, **-idis** *m*: a jewel
late: (*adv.*) widely
licet: even though
longe: (*adv.*) far
majestas, **-atis** *f.* majesty, grandeur
massa, **-ae** *f.* a mass, weight
monile, **-is** *n*: a necklace
nolo, nolle, nolui: refuse to
ops, opis *f.* wealth (*pl.*)
paries, **-etis** *m*: a wall
pars, partis *f.* a part
pavimentum, **-i** *n*: pavement
pictura, **-ae** *f.* a picture
porticus, **-us** *m*: a portico
pretiosus, **-a**, **-um**: precious, expensive
pretium, **-i** *n*: a price
proprius, **-a**, **-um**: special, particular
respondeo, (2): to answer to, correspond to (+ *dat.*)
saepe: (*adv.*) often, many times
sol, solis *m*: sun
solido, (1): to strengthen
splendor, **-oris** *m*: brilliance
totus, **-a**, **-um**: all
varius, **-a**, **-um**: colored, variegated
vehementer: (*adv.*) vehemently, strongly

---

lapide pretioso caesim deminuto: abl. abs., "with a precious jewel having been made smaller by cutting," i.e. made of mosaics
beatos illos: acc. exclamation, "happy are those!"
sine pretio: "without regard to cost," i.e. priceless
massis aureis: abl. means, "strengthened *by golden masses*"
splendore proprio: abl. specification, "glitter *with particular brilliance*"
ut...faciat: pr. subj. in result clause, "gleam *so that* the house *makes*"
sole nolente: abl. abs. with *licet* indicating concession, "even though the sun refuses"
sic...sic...sic: climactic anaphora [see 4.29, 5.9]
Nec setius: "nevertheless"
majestati: dat. after *respondent*, "*to the majesty* of the house"

recte videatur ad conversationem humanam magno Iovi fabricatum caeleste palatium.

Psyche discovers immeasurable wealth in the palace and is informed by a disembodied voice that the wealth and comfort are all for her enjoyment.

[2] Invitata Psyche talium locorum oblectatione propius accessit et paulo fidentior intra limen sese facit, mox prolectante studio pulcherrimae visionis rimatur singula et altrinsecus aedium horrea sublimi fabrica perfecta magnisque congesta gazis conspicit. Nec est quicquam quod ibi non est. Sed praeter ceteram tantarum divitiarum admirationem hoc erat praecipue mirificum, quod nullo

---

accedo, (3), **accessi**, **accessus**: to approach
admiratio, **-onis** *f.* wonder, admiration
aedes, **-is** *f.* a room, house (*pl.*)
altrinsecus: on the other side of (+ *gen.*)
caelestis, **-e**: heavenly
congestus, **-a**, **-um**: piled up, crowded
conspicio, (3): to observe
conversatio, **-onis** *f.* a way of life
divitia, **-ae** *f.* wealth
fabrica, **-ae** *f.* workmanship
fabrico, (1): to build
fidens, **-entis** (*gen.*): confident
gaza, **-ae** *f.* a treasure (royal)
horreum, **-i** *n*: a storehouse
ibi: in that place
intra: within, inside (+ *acc.*)
invito, (1): to invite, entice
limen, **-inis** *n*: a threshold, house
mirificus, **-a**, **-um**: amazing
mox: soon
oblectatio, **-onis** *f.* delighting
palatium, **-i** *n*: a palace
paulo: somewhat more (makes adj. comp.)
perficio, (3), **perfeci**, **perfectus**: to complete
praecipue: especially
praeter: besides (+ *acc.*)
prolecto, (1): to lure
propior, **-ius**: nearer
pulcher, **-ra**, **-rum**: beautiful, illustrious
rimor, (1), **rimatus sum**: to explore
singulus, **-a**, **-um**: every
studium, **-i** *n*: eagerness, enthusiasm
sublimus, **-a**, **-um**: lofty, exalted
videor, (2): seem (+ *inf.*)
visio, **-onis** *f.* a vision

---

ut...videatur: pr. subj. in result clause, "so that it might seem" + inf.
ad conversationem: expressing purp., "for the purpose of human dwelling"
magno Iovi: dat., "constructed *for great Jupiter*"
fabricatum (sc. esse): complementing *videatur*, "seems *to have been constructed*"
oblectatione: abl. means, "enticed *by the delighting*"
prolectante studio: abl. abs., "with eagerness luring"
sese facit: colloquial, "makes herself (go)"
horrea...perfecta...congesta: acc. neut. pl., "observes *storehouses completed and piled up*"
sublimi fabrica: abl. means, "completed *with lofty workmanship*"
magnis...gazis: abl. means, "piled up *with extensive treasures*"
hoc...quod: "*this* was especially amazing, namely *that*"

vinculo, nullo claustro, nullo custode totius orbis thensaurus ille muniebatur. Haec ei summa cum voluptate visenti offert sese vox quaedam, corporis sui nuda, et: "Quid," inquit, "domina, tantis obstupescis opibus? Tua sunt haec omnia. Prohinc cubiculo te refer et lectulo lassitudinem refove et ex arbitrio lavacrum pete. Nos, quarum voces accipis, tuae famulae sedulo tibi praeministrabimus nec corporis curatae tibi regales epulae morabuntur."

---

arbitrium, **-i** *n*: a choice
claustrum, **-i** *n*: a barrier
corpus, -oris *n*: a body
curatus, **-a**, **-um**: well looked-after
custos, **-odis** *m*: a guard
epula, **-ae** *f.* a banquet
famula, **-ae** *f.* a handmaiden
lassitudo, **-inis** *f.* weariness
lavacrum, **-i** *n*: a bath
lectulus, **-i** *m*: a bed, couch
moror, (1), **moratus sum**: to be delayed
munio, (4): to fortify, protect
nudus, **-a**, **-um**: stripped of (+ *gen.*)
obstupesco, (3): to be astounded
offero, **offerre**, **obtuli**, **oblatus**: to present
ops, **opis** *f.* wealth (*pl.*)
orbis, **-is** *m*: world
peto, (3): to ask (for)
praeministro, (1): to administer to (+ *dat.*)
prohinc: so then
quaedam: certain
refero, **referre**, **rettuli**, **relatus**: to retire
refoveo, (2): to refresh
regalis, **-e**: royal
sedulo: (*adv.*) carefully
thensaurus, **-i** *m*: a treasure chamber
vinculum, **-i** *n*: a chain
viso, (3): to look at
voluptas, **-atis** *f.* pleasure

---

nullo vinculo, nullo claustro, nullo custode: anaphora, "with no chain, no barrier, no guard"
totius orbis: gen., "treasure *of the whole world*"
ei...visenti: dat. ind. obj., "offfered *to her looking at*"
tantis...opibus: abl. means, "astounded *by such great wealth*"
cubiculo: dat. with verb of motion, "retire *to the bedroom*"
refer...refove...pete: imper., "retire!...refresh!...ask for!"
tuae famulae: appositive, "We, *as your handmaidens*"
nec...morabuntur: "nor will food be delayed"
corporis: gen. respect, "having been cared for *with respect to your body*"
curatae: dat. agreeing with *tibi*, "delayed for you, *well cared-for*"

Psyche refreshes herself with sleep, a bath, a feast, and music.

[3] Sensit Psyche divinae providentiae beatitudinem, monitusque vocis informis audiens et prius somno et mox lavacro fatigationem sui diluit, visoque statim proximo semirotundo suggestu, propter instrumentum cenatorium rata refectui suo commodum, libens accumbit. Et ilico vini nectarei eduliumque variorum fercula copiosa nullo serviente sed tantum spiritu quodam impulsa subministrantur. Nec quemquam tamen illa videre poterat, sed verba tantum audiebat excidentia et solas voces famulas habebat. Post

---

accumbo, (3): to recline at the table
beatitudo, **-udinis** *f.* beatitude
cenatorius, **-a**, **-um**: of/used for dining
commodum, **-i** *n*: a convenience (+ *dat.*)
copiosus, **-a**, **-um**: plentiful
diluo, (3): to diminish
divinus, **-a.** **-um**: divine
edulia, **-ium** *n*: edibles, food
excido, (3): to fall out
famula, **-ae** *f.* a handmaiden
fatigatio, **-onis** *f.* fatigue
ferculum, **-i** *n*: a course
ilico: (*adv.*) immediately
impello, (3), **impuli**, **impulsus**: to impel, set in motion
informis, **-e**: formless
instrumentum, **-i** *n*: tools
libens, **-entis** *(gen.)*: pleased
monitus, **-us** *m*: a command, advice
mox: next
nectareus, **-a**, **-um**: sweet as nectar
prior, prius: prior, first
providentia, **-ae** *f.* providence
proximus, **-a**, **-um**: nearby
refectus, **-us** *m*: a refreshment, restoration
reor, (2), **ratus sum**: to suppose
semirotundus, **-a**, **-um**: circular
sentio, (4), **sensi**, **sensus**: to feel
servio, (4): to serve
solus, **-a**, **-um**: only
spiritus, **-us** *m*: a breath
subministro, (1): to supply
suggestus, **-us** *m*: a dais
varius, **-a**, **-um**: various, diverse
vinum, **-i** *n*: wine

---

somno...lavacro: abl. means, "she diminishes *by sleep...by a bath*"
viso proximo semirotundo suggestu: abl. abs., "a nearby semi-circular dais having been seen," i.e. a dinner couch
rata: perf. part. deponent of *reor*, "she supposing"
commodum: acc. pred. after *rata*, "supposing (the dais) to be a *convenience* for her own refreshment"
vini nectarei eduliumque variorum: gen. desc. with *fercula*, "courses *of nectar-sweet wine and various foods*"
nullo serviente: abl. abs., "with no one serving"
spiritu quodam: abl. agent, "having been impelled *by some breath*"
impulsa: perf. part. nom. agreeing with *fercula*, "courses *having been impelled*"
illa: "that girl," i.e. Psyche
famulas: acc. pred., "voices *as handmaidens*"

opimas dapes quidam introcessit et cantavit invisus et alius citharam pulsavit, quae videbatur nec ipsa. Tunc modulatae multitudinis conserta vox aures eius affertur, ut, quamvis hominum nemo pareret, chorus tamen esse pateret.

Psyche retires to bed and is joined by her unknown husband, who leaves before dawn.

[4] Finitis voluptatibus vespera suadente, concedit Psyche cubitum. Jamque provecta nocte clemens quidam sonus aures eius accedit. Tunc virginitati suae pro tanta solitudine metuens et pavet et horrescit et quovis malo plus timet quod ignorat. Jamque aderat

---

accedo, (3): to approach
affero, **affere**, **attuli**, **allatus**: to convey
auris, **-is** *f.* an ear
canto, (1): to sing
chorus, **-i** *m*: a choir
cithara, **-ae** *f.* a cithara
clemens, **-entis**: loving, gentle
concedo, (3): to withdraw, retire
consero, (3), **conserui**, **consertus**: to join
cubitus, **-us** *m*: a bed
daps, **dapis** *f.* a feast
finio, (4), **finivi**, **finitus**: to end
horresco, (3): to tremble
ignoro, (1): to not know
introcedo, (3), **introcessi**, **introcessus**: to enter
invisus, **-a**, **-um**: unseen
metuo, (2): to fear for (+ *dat.*)
modulor, (1), **modulatus sum**: to sing
multitudo, **-inis** *f.* a crowd
nemo, **-inis** *n*: no one, nobody
opimus, **-a**, **-um**: rich
pareo, (2): to appear
pateo, (2): to be well known, to be clear
paveo, (2): to be terrified at
plus, **-uris** *(gen.)*: more
provectus, **-a**, **-um**: advanced
pulso, (1): to beat, pulsate
quidam: someone
solitudo, **-inis** *f.* loneliness
sonus, **-i** *m*: a sound
suadeo, (2): to persuade
timeo, (2): to dread
vespera, **-ae** *f.* evening
virginitas, **-atis** *f.* maidenhood

---

ut...pateret: impf. subj. result clause, "*so that it was well known* to be," i.e. "it was clearly there"
quamvis...nemo pareret: impf. subj. concessive, "although no one was appearing"
finitis voluptatibus: abl. abs., "with the delights having been ended"
vespera suadente: abl. abs., "with the evening persuading"
provecta nocte: abl. abs., "with the evening having advanced"
pro tanta solitudine: causal use of *pro*, "because of so much loneliness"
quovis malo: abl. comparison with *plus*, "more than *any evil*"
et...et...et: polysyndeton emphasizing heightened emotion
quod ignorat: rel. clause after *timet*, "fears (that) *which she does not know*"

ignobilis maritus et torum inscenderat et uxorem sibi Psychen fecerat et ante lucis exortum propere discesserat. Statim voces cubiculo praestolatae novam nuptam interfectae virginitatis curant. Haec diutino tempore sic agebantur. Atque ut est natura redditum, novitas per assiduam consuetudinem delectationem ei commendarat et sonus vocis incertae solitudinis erat solacium.

---

ante: earlier than, before
assiduus, **-a**, **-um**: constant
commendo, (1): to recommend, commend
consuetudo, **-inis** *f.* habit, intimacy
curo, (1): to attend to
delectatio, **-onis** *f.* pleasure
discedo, (3), **discessi**, **discessus**: to withdraw
diutinus, **-a**, **-um**: long
exortus, **-us** *m*: a rising
ignobilis, **-e**: unknown
incertus, **-a**, **-um**: unknown
inscendo, (3): to mount, ascend
interficio, (3), **interfeci**, **interfectus**: to destroy, slay
natura, **-ae** *f.* nature
novitas, **-atis** *f.* strangeness, novelty
nupta, **-ae** *f.* a bride
praestolor, (1), **praestolatus sum**: to stand ready for
propere: (*adv.*) quickly
reddo, (3), **reddidi**, **redditus**: to render
solacium, **-i** *n*: solace, relief in sorrow
solitudo, **-inis** *f.* loneliness
sonus, **-i** *m*: a sound
tempus, **-oris** *n*: time
torus, **-i** *m*: a bed
virginitas, **-atis** *f.* maidenhood, virginity

---

et inscenderat et…fecerat et…discesserat: plupf. with polysyndeton indicates acceleration of events after impf., "he was present and *had mounted and had made and had withdrawn*"
uxorem: acc. pred., "made Psyche *his wife*"
cubiculo: abl. place where, "in the bedroom"
interfectae virginitatis: gen. resp. with *novam*, "new *with respect to her slain virginity*"
Haec agebantur: ambigious referent, either the nightly visits of Cupid or the care of the servants, "these things were conducted"
diutino tempore: abl. time within which, "in the course of a long time"
ut est redditum: "*as it is provided* by nature"
delectationem: acc. pred., "commended itself *as a pleasure*"
commendarat: syncopated plupf. (=*commendaverat*), "strangeness *had commended*"
solitudinis: objective gen., "the solace *of loneliness*," i.e. soothed the loneliness

Interea parentes eius indefesso luctu atque maerore consenescebant, latiusque porrecta fama sorores illae majores cuncta cognorant propereque maestae atque lugubres deserto lare certatim ad parentum suorum conspectum adfatumque perrexerant.

Psyche's husband, still unseen, warns her of the potential danger coming with her grieving sisters and advises her against responding to them.

[5] Ea nocte ad suam Psychen sic infit maritus — namque praeter oculos et manibus et auribus eius nihil non sentiebatur: "Psyche dulcissima et cara uxor, exitiabile tibi periculum minatur fortuna saevior, quod observandum pressiore cautela censeo.

---

adfatus, **-us** *m*: speech, conversation
auris, **-is** *f.* an ear
carus, **-a**, **-um**: beloved
cautela, **-ae** *f.* caution
censeo, (2): to recommend
certatim: with rivalry
cognosco, (3), **cognovi**, **cognitus**: to learn
consenesco, (3): to waste away
conspectus, **-us** *m*: sight
cunctus, **-a**, **-um**:all
desero, (3), **deserui**, **desertus**: to forsake
exitiabilis, **-e**: deadly
fama, **-ae** *f.* fame
fortuna, **-ae** *f.* fate
indefessus, **-a**, **-um**: unwearied
infio, **infieri**: begin to speak
lar, **laris** *m*: a household deity
latius (**comp. adv.**): more widely
luctus, **-us** *m*: a lamentation
lugubris, **-e**: grievous
maeror, **-oris** *m*: mourning
maestus, **-a**, **-um**: mournful
major, **majus**: older
minor, (1), **minatus sum**: to threaten
nihil: nothing
observo, (1): to heed
pergo, (3), **perrexi**, **perrectus**: to proceed
periculum, **-i** *n*: peril
porrigo, (3), **porrexi**, **porrectus**: to extend
praeter: before (+ *acc.*)
pressus, **-a**, **-um**: deliberate
propere: (*adv.*) quickly
saevus, **-a**, **-um**: cruel
sentio, (4): to perceive
uxor, **-oris**, *f.* a wife

---

indefesso luctu atque maerore: abl. cause, "wasting away *from unwearied lamentation and mourning*"
porrecta fama: abl. abs., "with fame having extended"
cognorant: syncopated plupf. (=*cognoverant*), "they had learned"
deserto lare: abl. abs, a *Lar* is a household deity used here metonymically for "home" "their own home having been deserted"
Ea nocte: abl. time, referring to the day of the sisters' arrival at their parents' home, "On that night"
manibus et auribus: abl. means, "perceived *with hands and ears*"
nihil non: litotes, "*nothing* of him was *not* perceived," i.e. she was able to sense all of him
Psyche dulcissima et cara uxor: chiasmus, "Psyche sweetest and beloved wife"
observandum: fut. pass. inf. in ind. st., "which I recommend *ought to be heeded*"
pressiore cautela: abl. manner, "with more deliberate caution"

Sorores jam tuae mortis opinione turbatae tuumque vestigium requirentes scopulum istum protinus aderunt, quarum si quas forte lamentationes acceperis, neque respondeas immo nec prospicias omnino; ceterum mihi quidem gravissimum dolorem tibi vero summum creabis exitium." Annuit et ex arbitrio mariti se facturam spopondit, sed eo simul cum nocte dilapso diem totum lacrimis ac plangoribus misella consumit, se nunc maxime prorsus perisse iterans, quae beati carceris custodia septa et humanae conversationis

---

annuo, (3), **annui**: nod assent
arbitrium, **-i** *n*: judgment
beatus, **-a**, **-um**: blessed, sumptuous
carcer, **-eris** *m*: a prison
consumo, (3): to waste
conversatio, **-onis** *f.* association
creo, (1): to bring about
custodia, **-ae** *f.* a prisoner
dilabor, (3), **dilapsus sum**: to pass
dolor, **-oris** *m*: anguish
exitium, **-i** *n*: ruin
forte: by chance
gravis, **-e**: grave
immo: no indeed
itero, (1): to repeat
lamentatio, **-onis** *f.* lamentation
misellus, **-a**, **-um**: wretched
omnino: at all
opinio, **-onis** *f.* rumor
pereo, (4), **perivi**: be ruined
plangor, **-oris** *m*: a shriek
prorsus: (*adv.*) entirely
prospicio, (3): to look out for
protinus: (*adv.*) immediately
requiro (3): see again
respondeo, (2): to answer
sepio, (4), **sepsi**, **septus**: to enclose
simul: at once
spondeo, (2), **spopondi**: pledge
totus, **-a**, **-um**: whole
turbo, (1): to disturb
vestigium, **-i** *n*: a trace

---

opinione: abl. cause, "stirred up *by the rumor*"
si...acceperis: fut. perf. in more vivid protasis, "if you hear"
neque respondeas...nec proscipias: pr. subj. in prohibition, "neither answer nor look towards"
ceterum: for *ceteroquin*, "otherwise"
mihi quidem...tibi vero: idiomatic, "for me, on the one hand...for yourself, on the other hand"
se facturam (sc. esse): fut. act. inf. in ind. st., "promised *that she would act*"
eo...dilapso: abl. abs., "that one having slipped away"
diem totum: acc. duration, "all day long"
lacrimis ac plangoribus: abl. means with *consumit*, "wastes *with tears and shrieks*"
se...perisse: perf. inf. in ind. st. after *iterans*, "repeating *that she had died*"
quae...posset: impf. subj. relative clause of characteristic,"she *who was able* to see"
custodia: nom. appositive, "who *as a prisoner*"
septa...viduata: nom., "a prisoner *enclosed and devoid of*" + abl.

colloquio viduata nec sororibus quidem suis de se maerentibus opem salutarem ferre ac ne videre eas quidem omnino posset. Nec lavacro nec cibo nec ulla denique refectione recreata, flens ubertim decessit ad somnum.

The husband joins Psyche the following night and reprimands Psyche, but eventually he acquiesces to her request that the sisters visit.

[6] Nec mora, cum paulo maturius lectum maritus accubans eamque etiam nunc lacrimantem complexus sic expostulat: "Haecine mihi pollicebare, Psyche mea? Quid jam de te tuus maritus exspecto? Quid spero? Et perdia et pernox, nec inter amplexus

---

accubo, (1): to lie near, recline
amplexus, **-us** *m*: an embrace
cibus, **-i** *m*: food
colloquium, **-i** *n*: a conversation
complector, (3), **complexus sum**: to embrace
decedo, (3), **decessi**: to retire
denique: indeed
expostulo, (1): to remonstrate
exspecto, (1): to expect
fero, **ferre**, **tuli**, **latus**: to bring
fleo, (2): to weep
lacrimo, (1): to weep
lavacrum, **-i** *n*: a bath
lectus, **-i** *m*: a bed
maereo, (2): to mourn
maturus, **-a**, **-um**: early
mora, **-ae** *f*: delay
ops, **opis** *f*: help
paulo: (*adv.*) a little
perdius, **-a**, **-um**: all day long
pernox: (**adj**.) all night long
polliceor, (2), **pollicitus sum**: to promise
recreo, (1): to restore
refectio, **-onis** *f*: refreshment
salutaris, **-e**: saving
spero, (1): to look forward to
ubertim: (*adv.*) copiously
viduatus, **-a**, **-um**: devoid (of) + (*abl.*)

---

colloquio: abl. sep., "devoid of *the conversation* of human association"
sororibus...suis...maerentibus: dat. ind. obj., "bring *to her own sisters mourning*"
nec...ferre ac ne videre: inf. complementing *posset*, "able *neither to bring comfort... nor even to see*"
nec lavacro nec cibo nec ulla...refectione: abl. means, "restored *neither by a bath nor by food nor by any refreshment*"
Nec mora, cum: links with previous events, "Neither (was there) a delay, when"
paulo maturius: "a little earlier (than usual)"
Haecine: acc. neut. pl. *haec* with interrogative ending, "Did you promise *these things*?"
pollicebare: deponent impf., "did you promise?"
Quid...exspecto, quid spero: deliberative quest. where the subjunctive is expected, "What am I to expect? What should I hope for?"
Et perdia et pernox: nom. f. adjectives used as predicates, "you, all day and all night"

conjugales desinis cruciatum. Age jam nunc ut voles, et animo tuo damnosa poscenti pareto! Tantum memineris meae seriae monitionis, cum coeperis sero paenitere." Tunc illa, precibus et dum se morituram comminatur, extorquet a marito cupitis adnuat ut sorores videat, luctus mulceat, ora conferat. Sic ille novae nuptae precibus veniam tribuit et insuper quibuscumque vellet eas auri vel monilium donare concessit, sed identidem monuit ac saepe

---

adnuo, (3): to agree to
ago, (3): to act
animus, **-i** *m*: a heart
aurum, **-i** *n*: gold
coepio, (3), **coepi**, **coeptus**: to begin
comminor, (1), **comminatus sum**: to threaten
concedo, (3), **concessi**: to agree
confero, **-ferre**, **-tuli**, **collatus**: to join
conjugalis, **-e**: marital
cruciatus, **-us** *m*: self-torment
cupitum, **-i** *n*: one's desire
damnosus, **-a**, **-um**: harmful
desino, (3): to cease
dono, (1): to present X (*acc.*) with Y (*abl.*)
extorqueo, (2): to extort
identidem: (*adv.*) repeatedly
insuper: in addition
luctus, **-us** *m*: sorrow
memini, (2): to remember
moneo, (2), **monui**: to warn
monile, **-is** *n*: a jewel
monitio, **-onis** *f*: a warning
morior, (4), **moritus sum**: to die
mulceo, (2): to soothe
nupta, **-ae** *f*: a bride
os, oris, *n*: a face
paeniteo, (2): to repent
pareo, (2): to obey (+ *dat.*)
posco, (3): to ask, demand
saepe: (*adv.*) many times
serius, **-a**, **-um**: serious
sero: (*adv.*) too late
terreo, (2), **terrui**: to frighten
tribuo, (3), **tribui**: grant
velle, volui: wish
venia, **-ae** *f*: favor
volo, velle, volui: wish

---

ut voles: fut. parenthetical, "as you wish"
animo tuo...poscenti: dat. after *pareto*, "obey *your demanding heart*"
pareto: fut. imper., "obey!"
memineris: perf. subj. jussive following *age* and *pareto*, "may you remember" + gen.
meae seriae monitionis: gen. with *memineris*, "remember *my serious warning*"
cum coeperis: fut. perf. in cum temporal clause, "when you will have begun to" + inf.
precibus: abl. means with *extorquet*, "she extorts *with prayers*"
morituram (sc. esse): fut. act. inf. in ind. st. after *comminatur*, "she threatens *that she will die*"
adnuat: pr. subj. result clause after *extorquet* , "extorts *so that he agrees to*" + dat.
ut...videat...mulceat...conferat: pr. subj. in noun clause in apposition to *cupitis*, "her desires, *namely that she might see, might soothe, might join*"
ora conferat: "join faces," i.e. see each other face to face
quibuscumque vellet: impf. subj. in noun clause after *donare*, "he agreed to present them *with whatever she might wish*"
auri vel monilium: partitive gen. with *quibuscumque*, "whatever *of gold or jewels*"

terruit ne quando sororum pernicioso consilio suasa de forma mariti quaerat neve se sacrilega curiositate de tanto fortunarum suggestu pessum dejiciat nec suum postea contingat amplexum. Gratias egit marito jamque laetior animo: "sed prius," inquit, "centies moriar quam tuo isto dulcissimo conubio caream. Amo enim et efflictim te, quicumque es, diligo aeque ut meum spiritum, nec ipsi Cupidini comparo. Sed istud etiam meis precibus, oro, largire

---

aeque: in same manner
ago, (3), **egi**: act, thank (with *gratias*, + *dat.*)
careo, (2): to be without + abl.
centum: one hundred times
comparo, (1): to treat as equal, compare
consilium, **-i** *n*: counsel
contingo, (3): to touch
conubium, **-i** *n*: marriage
curiositas, **-atis** *f*: curiosity
dejicio, (3): to throw down
diligo, (3): to value
efflictim: (*adv.*) passionately
forma, **-ae** *f*: a form
gratia, **-ae** *f*: gratitude
laetus, **-a**, **-um**: glad
largior, (4): to bestow
morior, (4), **moritus sum**: to die
oro, (1): to beg
perniciosus, **-a**, **-um**: pernicious
pessum: (*adv.*) to the lowest part, downward
postea: afterwards
priusquam: before (+ subj.)
quaero, (3): to seek, inquire
quando: when
sacrilegus, **-a**, **-um**: impious
spiritus, **-us** *m*: life
suadeo, (2), **suasi**, **suasus**: to persuade
suggestus, **-us** *m*: a raised platform, height

---

pernicioso consilio: abl. means, "persuaded *by pernicious counsel*"
ne...quaerat: pr. subj. in ind. prohibition after *monuit*, "warned *not to inquire*"
neve...deiciat nec...contingat: pr. subj. in negative purp. clause, "lest she throw down...and never touch"
sacrilega curiositate: abl. cause, "because of her impious curiousity"
de tanto...suggestu: "from such a great height"
marito: dat. after *gratias egit*, "she has thanked the *husband*"
animo: abl. specification, "gladder *in spirit*"
moriar: pr. subj. hortatory, "may I die one hundred times"
prius...quam caream: pr. subj. anticipatory, "before I would be without"
tuo...dulcissimo conubio: abl. sep. after *caream*, "be without *your sweetest marriage*"
ipsi Cupidini: dat. after *comparo*, "compare you *to Cupid himself*"
meis precibus: abl. accordance, "in accordance with my prayers"
oro: parenthetical, "I beg," i.e. "please"
largire: pr. imper., "*bestow* this!"

et illi tuo famulo Zephyro praecipe simili vectura sorores hic mihi sistat," et imprimens oscula suasoria et ingerens verba mulcentia et inserens membra cohibentia haec etiam blanditiis astruit: "mi mellite, mi marite, tuae Psychae dulcis anima." Vi ac potestate veneri susurrus invitus succubuit maritus et cuncta se facturum spopondit atque etiam luce proxumante de manibus uxoris evanuit.

The sisters are carried to Psyche by Zephyr and the three reunite.

[7] At illae sorores percontatae scopulum locumque illum quo fuerat Psyche deserta festinanter adveniunt ibique difflebant oculos et plangebant ubera, quoad crebris earum hejulatibus saxa

---

advenio, (4): to arrive at
anima, **-ae** *f.* a soul
astruo, (3): to add to (+ *dat.*)
blanditia, **-ae** *f.* caresses, flatterings
cohibeo, (2): to confine, compel
creber, **-era**, **-erum**: repeated
desero, (3), **deserui**, **desertus**: to forsake
diffleo, (2): to weep away
evanesco, (3), **evanui**: to vanish
famulus, **-i** *m*: a servant
festinanter: (*adv.*) hurriedly
hejulatus, **-us** *m*: wailing
imprimo, (3): to impress
ingero, (3): to throw in
insero, (3): to insert, entwine
invitus, **-a**, **-um**: reluctant
mellitus, **-a**, **-um**: honey-sweet
membrum, **-i** *n*: a limb
mulceo, (2): to soothe
osculum, **-i** *n*: a kiss
percontor, (1), **percontatus sum**: to inquire
plango, (3): to strike
potestas, **-atis** *f.* power
praecipio, (3): to order
proxumo, (1): to approach
saxum, **-i** *n*: a stone
similis, **-e**: similar
sisto, (3): to set up
spondeo, (2), **spopondi**: to promise
suasorius, **-a**, **-um**: persuasive
succumbo, (3), **succubui**: to surrender
susurrus, **-i** *m*: a whisper
uber, **-eris** *n*: a breast
vectura, **-ae** *f.* transportation
venerus, **-a**, **-um**: amorous
vis, **vis** *f.* force
Zephyrus, **-i** *m*: Zephyr, the west wind

---

illi tuo famulo Zephyro: dat. ind. obj. after *praecipe*, "order *that famous servant of yours, Zephyr*"
simili vectura: abl. means, "that he set up *by a similar transportation*"
sistat: pr. subj. in ind. command after *praecipe*, "order Zephyrus *to set up*"
blanditiis: dat. after *astruit*, "added these words *to the caresses*"
mi mellite, mi marite: alliterative address, "my honey-sweet, my husband"
vi ac potestate: abl. cause, "surrenders *because of the force and power*"
veneri susurrus: gen. specification, "power *of the amorous whispering*"
se facturum (sc. esse): fut. act. inf. in ind. st., "he promised *that he would do*"
luce proxumante: abl. abs., "with daylight approaching"
quo: relative pron., abl. place where, "that place *on which* Psyche had been deserted"
difflebant...plangebant: impf. inceptive, "they began weeping and striking"
crebris...hejulatibus: abl. means, "echo *with repeated wailings*"

cautesque parilem sonum resultarent. Jamque nomine proprio sororem miseram ciebant, quoad sono penetrabili vocis ululabilis per prona delapso amens et trepida Psyche procurrit e domo et: "Quid," inquit "vos miseris lamentationibus necquicquam effligitis? Quam lugetis, adsum. Lugubres voces desinite et diutinis lacrimis madentes genas siccate tandem, quippe cum jam possitis quam plangebatis amplecti." Tunc vocatum Zephyrum praecepti maritalis admonet. Nec mora, cum ille parens imperio statim

---

admoneo, (2): to remind X (*acc.*) of Y (*gen.*)
adsum, -esse: to be near, be present
amens, **-entis** (*gen.*): frantic
amplector, (3), **amplexus sum**: to embrace
cautis, **-is** *f.* a cliff
cieo, (2): to call on by name
delabor, (3), **delapsus sum**: to descend
desino, (3): to abandon, desist
diutinus, **-a**, **-um**: long lasting
effligo, (3): to torment
gena, **-ae** *f.* cheeks
imperium, **-i** *n*: a command
lamentatio, **-onis** *f.* lamentation
lugeo, (2): to mourn
lugubris, **-e**: mourning
madeo, (2), **madui**: be dripping
maritalis, **-e**: of a husband
mora, **-ae** *f.* delay
necquicquam: in vain
pareo, (2): to comply
parilis, **-e**: like (+ *dat.*)
penetrabilis, **-e**: piercing
plango, (3): to lament for
praeceptum, -i *n***:** an order
procurro, (3), **procurri**: to run out ahead
pronus, **-a**, **-um**: leaning forward or downward
proprius, **-a**, **-um**: particular, one's own
quippe: as you see
quoad: until (=ad quo)
resulto, (1): to re-echo
sicco, (1): to dry
sonus, **-i** *m*: a sound
trepido, (1): to be afraid
ululabilis, **-e**: shrieking

---

quoad...resultarent: impf. subj. anticipatory, "*until* the rocks and cliffs *would re-echo*"
crebris...heiulatibus: dat. after *parilem*, "equal to *the wailings*"
nomine proprio: abl. means, "calling *by her own name*"
sono penetrabili...delapso: abl. cause, "frantic *from the piercing sound descending*"
per prona: "downward"
miseris lamentationibus: abl. means, "torment *with distressing lamentations*"
desinite...siccate: pr. imper., "abandon!...dry!"
diutinis lacrimis: abl. specification, "dripping *with long lasting tears*"
cum...possitis: pr. subj. causal clause, "since you are able"
quam plangebatis: relative clause, "her *whom you were lamenting*"
amplecti: pr. inf. deponent after *possitis*, "able *to embrace*"
praecepti: gen. after *admonet*, "he reminds him *of the order*" i.e. the one given above
imperio: dat. after *parens*, "obeying *the command*"

clementissimis flatibus innoxia vectura deportat illas. Jam mutuis amplexibus et festinantibus saviis sese perfruuntur, et illae sedatae lacrimae postliminio redeunt prolectante gaudio. "sed et tectum," inquit, "et larem nostrum laetae succedite et afflictas animas cum Psyche vestra recreate."

Psyche shows the palace to her sisters and tells them that her husband is a young, handsome hunter before sending them back home.

[8] Sic allocuta summas opes domus aureae vocumque servientium populosam familiam demonstrat auribus earum lavacroque pulcherrimo et inhumanae mensae lautitiis eas opipare reficit, ut

---

afflicto, (1): to oppress
alloquor, (3), **allocutus sum**: to speak to
aureus, **-a**, **-um**: golden
auris, **-is** *f.* an ear
clemens, **-entis** *(gen.)*: gentle
demonstro, (1): to reveal
deporto, (1): to carry down
familia, **-ae** *f.* a household
flatus, **-us** *m*: a breeze
gaudium, **-i** *n*: joy
inhumanus, **-a**, **-um**: inhuman
innoxius, **-a**, **-um**: harmless
laetus, **-a**, **-um**: cheerful
Lar, **Laris** *m*: Lares, hearth, home
lautitia, **-ae** *f.* splendor
mensa, **-ae** *f.* a table
mutuus, **-a**, **-um**: mutual
opipare: *(adv.)* splendidly
ops, **opis** *f.* wealth
perfruor, (3), **perfructus sum**: to enjoy (+ *abl.*)
populosus, **-a**, **-um**: populous
postliminium, **-i** *n*: a return home or to one's prior privileges
prolecto, (1): to entice
pulcher, **-chra**, **-chrum**: beautiful
recreo, (1): to restore
reficio, (3): to restore
savium, **-i** *n*: a kiss; sweetheart
sedo, (1): to restrain
servio, (4): to serve
succedo, (3): to advance
tectum, **-i** *n*: a roof, house
vectura, **-ae** *f.* transportation

---

clementissimis flatibus: abl. means, "carries *with the gentlest breezes*"
innoxia vectura: abl. means, "carries *on a harmless transportation*"
mutuis...saviis: abl. means after *perfruuntur*, "they enjoyed *mutual embraces and hurrying kisses*"
postliminio: abl. circum., "with their repatriation," a legal term
prolectante gaudio: abl. abs., "with joy enticing"
succedite et...recreate: imper., "advance and restore!"
vocumque servientium: gen. pl., "household *of serving voices*"
auribus earum: "she presents *to the ears of them*" because they are invisible
lavacro pulcherrimo: abl. means, "restores *with a beautiful bath*"
lautitiis: abl. means, "restores *with splendors*"

illarum prorsus caelestium divitiarum copiis affluentibus satiatae jam praecordiis penitus nutrirent invidiam. Denique altera earum satis scrupulose curioseque percontari non desinit, quis illarum caelestium rerum dominus, quisve vel qualis ipsius sit maritus. Nec tamen Psyche conjugale illud praeceptum ullo pacto temerat vel pectoris arcanis exigit, sed e re nata confingit esse juvenem quendam et speciosum, commodum lanoso barbitio genas inumbrantem, plerumque rurestribus ac montanis venatibus occupatum,

---

affluens, **-entis** (*gen.*): overflowing
alter, **-era**, **-erum**: one (of two)
arcanum, **-i** *n*: a secret
barbitium, **-i** *n*: a beard
caelestis, **-e**: heavenly
commodum: just
confingo, (3): to fabricate
conjugalis, **-e**: marital
copia, **-ae** *f*: plenty
curiose: (*adv.*) curiously
denique: and then
desino, (3): to cease from (+ *inf.*)
divitia, **-ae** *f*: riches
dominus, **-i** *m*: a lord
exigo, (3): to expel
gena, **-ae** *f*: cheeks
inumbro, (1): to cast a shadow, darken
invidia, **-ae** *f*: envy
juvenis, **-is** *m*: a youth
lanosus, **-a**, **-um**: woolly
montanus, **-a**, **-um**: mountainous
nascor, (3), **natus sum**: to be produced spontaneously
nutrio, (4): to nourish
occupatus, **-a**, **-um**: occupied
pactum, **-i** *n*: manner
pectus, **-oris** *n*: a heart
penitus: deep within
percontor, (1), **percontatus sum**: to inquire
plerumque: frequently
praecordium, **-i** *n*: a breast
prorsus: (*adv.*) utterly
res, **-ei** *f*: property
rurestris, **-e**: rustic
satio, (1): to satisfy, satiate
scrupulose: (*adv.*) scrupulously
speciosus, **-a**, **-um**: handsome
temero, (1): to violate
venatus, **-us** *m*: a hunt

---

ut...nutrirent: impf. subj. result clause, "so that they were nourishing"
satiatae: perf. part., "they, *having been satiated*"
praecordiis: abl. place, "nourishing *in their breasts*"
quis...sit: pr. subj. in ind. quest. after *percontari*, "to ask *who is* lord...or who or what kind *is*..."
ullo pacto: abl. manner, "in any manner"
arcanis: abl. sep. after *exigit*, "expel *from the secrets*"
e re nata: idiomatic, "in the circumstances; on the spur of the moment," literally "from the thing produced spontaneously"
esse iuvenem: ind. st. after *confingit*, "she fabricates *that he is a young man*"
lanoso barbitio: abl. means, "darkening *with a woolly beard*"
venatibus: abl. means, "occupied *by hunts*"

Et ne qua sermonis procedentis labe consilium tacitum proderetur, auro facto gemmosisque monilibus onustas eas statim vocato Zephyro tradit reportandas.

The sisters grow envious, and the first whines about her old husband.

[9] Quo protenus perpetrato sorores egregiae domum redeuntes jamque gliscentis invidiae felle fraglantes multa secum sermonibus mutuis perstrepebant. Sic denique infit altera: "En, orba et saeva et iniqua Fortuna! Hocine tibi complacuit, ut utroque parente prognatae germanae diversam sortem sustineremus? Et nos

---

alter, **-era**, **-erum**: one (of two)
aurum, **-i** *n*: gold
complaceo, (2), **complacui**: to be acceptable to
consilium, **-i** *n*: intention
denique: (*adv.*) finally
diversus, **-a**, **-um**: different
egregius, **-a**, **-um**: extraordinary
fel, **fellis** *n*: bitterness
fortuna, **-ae** *f*: fate
fraglans, **-antis** (*gen*): flaming
gemmosus, **-a**, **-um**: full of gems
germana, **-ae** *m*: a sister
glisco, (3): to swell
infio: to begin to speak
iniquus, **-a**, **-um**: unjust
labes, **-is** *f*: a disaster
monile, **-is** *n*: a necklace
onustus, **-a**, **-um**: laden
orbus, **-a**, **-um**: bereft of sight, blind
perpetro, (1): to accomplish
perstrepo, (3): to screech
procedo, (3): to advance
prodo, (3): to disclose, betray
prognatus, **-a**, **-um**: descended
protenus: (*adv.*) immediately
reporto, (1): to carry back
saevus, **-a**, **-um**: cruel
sermo, **-onis** *m*: a discussion
sors, **sortis** *f*: a lot
sustineo, (2): to put up with
tacitus, **-a**, **-um**: secret
trado, (3): to hand over
uterque, **-traque**, **-trumque**: each
voco, (1): to summon

---

ne ... proderetur: impf. subj. in negative purp. clause, "*lest* her secret *be betrayed*"
qua…labe: abl. of means, "by some lapse"
auro facto gemmosisque monilibus: abl. means after *onustas*, "laden *with wrought gold and with necklaces*"
vocato Zephyro: dat. ind. obj., "hands *to Zephyr having been summoned*"
reportandas: gerundive agreeing with *eas* expressing purp., "she hands them to Zephyr *in order to be carried back*"
Quo…perpetrato: abl. abs., "Which having been accomplished"
felle…multa: abl. specification, "seething *with great bitterness*"
sermonibus mutuis: abl. means, "began screeching *in mutual discussions*"
Hocine: interrogative, "Has *this* pleased?"
ut…sustineremus: impf. subj. in noun clause in apposition to *hoc*, "this, *namely that we would put up with*"
utroque parente: abl. source, "descended *from each* [i.e. *the same*] *parent*"

quidem quae natu maiore sumus maritis advenis ancillae deditae extorres et lare et ipsa patria degamus longe parentum velut exulantes, haec autem novissima, quam fetu satiante postremus partus effudit, tantis opibus et deo marito potita sit, quae nec uti recte tanta bonorum copia novit? Vidisti, soror, quanta in domo jacent et qualia monilia, quae praenitent vestes, quae splendicant gemmae,

---

advenus, **-a**, **-um**: ignorant, foreign
ancilla, **-ae** *f.* a slave girl
bonum, **-i** *n*: wealth
copia, **-ae** *f.* abundance
dedo, (3), **dedidi**, **deditus**: to give up
dego, (3): to endure
domus, **-i** *f.* a house
effundo, (3), **effudi**: to drop out, pour forth
extorris, **-e**: exiled
exulo, (1): to be banished
fetus, **-us** *m*: a bearing (of offspring)
gemma, **-ae** *f.* a jewel
jaceo, (2): to be situated
Lar, **Laris** *m*: Lares; hearth
longe: distant
monile, **-is** *n*: a necklace
natus, **-us** *m*: age
nosco, (3), **novi**, **notus**: to know how to (+ *inf.*)
novus, **-a**, **-um**: young
ops, **opis** *f.* power, wealth, riches
partus, **-us** *m*: a birth
patria, **-ae** *f.* a fatherland
postremus, **-a**, **-um**: last, worst
potior, (3), **potitus sum**: to obtain, possess (+ *abl.*)
praeniteo, (2): to shine forth
satio, (1): to satisfy, sate
splendico, (1): to sparkle
utor, (3), **usus sum**: to enjoy (+ *abl.*)
velut: as if
vestis, **-is** *f.* a garment
video, (2), **vidi**: to see

---

nos quidem...haec autem: "are we, on the one hand...while she, on the other"
natu maiore: abl. desc., "with greater age," i.e. "older"
ancillae: nom. pred., "given away *as servants*"
et lare et ipsa patria: abl. sep., "both from the hearth and from the fatherland itself"
degamus: pr. subj. in deliberative quest., "are we to endure?"
parentum: gen. after *longe*, "far *from our parents*"
velut exulantes: pr. part., "as though being exiled"
fetu satiante: abl. abs., "with bearing being satiated," i.e. when the process of childbearing and fertility were near their end
tantis opibus: dat. after *potita sit*, "obtains *such great riches*"
marito: dat. pred., "obtains a god *as a husband*"
haec autem...potita sit: perf. subj. in second part of deliberative quest., "is she to have obtained?"
uti: pr. inf. after *novit*, "she does not know how *to use*" + abl.
quanta...iacent et qualia...quae praenitent...quae splendicant...quantum... calcatur: vivid indicative in ind. quest. after *vidisti*, "you see *how many and what sort of* necklaces *are situated...what* clothes *shine forth...what* jewels *sparkle...how much* gold *is trampled under foot*"

quantum praeterea passim calcatur aurum. Quodsi maritum etiam tam formonsum tenet ut affirmat, nulla nunc in orbe toto felicior vivit. Fortassis tamen procedente consuetudine et adfectione roborata deam quoque illam deus maritus efficiet. Sic est, hercules, sic se gerebat ferebatque. Jam jam sursum respicit et deam spirat mulier, quae voces ancillas habet et ventis ipsis imperat. At ego misera primum patre meo seniorem maritum sortita sum, dein cucurbita calviorem et quovis puero pusilliorem, cunctam domum seris et catenis obditam custodientem."

---

adfectio, **-onis** *f.* affection
affirmo, (1): to assert
calco, (1): to spurn, trampled under foot
calvus, **-a**, **-um**: bald
catena, **-ae** *f.* a chain
consuetudo, **-inis** *f.* intimacy
cucurbita, **-ae** *f.* a pumpkin
cunctus, **-a**, **-um**: whole of
custodio, (4): to guard
dein: next
deus, **-i** *m*: a god
efficio, (3): to make
felix, **-icis** *(gen.)*: lucky, happy
fero, **ferre**, **tuli**, **latus**: to bear
formonsus, **-a**, **-um**: handsome
fortassis: perhaps
gero, (3): to carry
Hercules, **-is** *m*: Hercules
impero, (1): to command (+ *dat.*)
maritus, **-i** *m*: a husband
mulier, **-eris** *f.* a wife
obdo, (3), **obdidi**, **obditus**: to fasten
orbis, **-is** *m*: a circle
passim: everywhere
praeterea: besides
procedo, (3): to proceed
pusillus, **-a**, **-um**: small
quodsi: but if
quoque: likewise
respicio, (3): to consider
roboro, (1): to reinforce
senior, **-ius**: older
sera, **-ae** *f.* a bar
sortior, (4), **sortitus sum**: to obtain by lot
spiro, (1): to breath, live
sursum: upward
tam: such a degree
teneo, (2): to posses
totus, **-a**, **-um**: whole
ventus, **-i** *m*: wind
vivo, (3): to live

---

procedente consuetudine et adfectione roborata: abl. abs., "with intimacy proceeding and with affection having been reinforced"
deam: acc. pred., "will make her *a goddess*"
Sic...sic: climactic anaphora [see 4.29, 5.1]
deam: acc. pred., "she lives *as a goddess*"
patre meo: abl. comparison after *seniorem*, "a husband older *than my father*"
cucurbita: abl. comparison after *calviorem*, "balder *than a pumpkin*"
quovis puero: abl. comparison after *pusilliorem*, "smaller *than any boy*"
seris et catenis: abl. means, "fastened *with bars and chains*"
custodientem: pr. part. with *maritum*, "a husband *guarding*"

The second sister complains about her invalid husband and suggests plotting against Psyche.

[10] Suscipit alia: "ego vero maritum articulari etiam morbo complicatum curvatumque, ac per hoc rarissimo Venerem meam recolentem sustineo, plerumque detortos et duratos in lapidem digitos eius perfricans, fomentis olidis et pannis sordidis et faetidis cataplasmatibus manus tam delicatas istas adurens, nec uxoris officiosam faciem sed medicae laboriosam personam sustinens. Et tu quidem soror videris quam patienti vel potius servili — dicam enim libere quod sentio — haec perferas animo: enimvero ego

aduro, (3): to scorch
animus, **-i** *m*: spirit, pride
articularis, **-e**: arthritic
cataplasma, **-atis** *n*: a poultice
complico, (1): to bend at joint
curvo, (1): to make stoop
delicatus, **-a**, **-um**: delicate
detorqueo, (2), **detorsi**, **detortus**: to twist
dico, (3): to declare
digitus, **-i** *m*: a finger, toe
duro, (1): to harden
enimvero: upon my word
facies, **-ei** *f*: an appearance
faetidus, -a, -um: having an offensive odor
fomentum, **-i** *n*: a poultice
laboriosus, **-a**, **-um**: laborious
lapis, **-idis** *m*: a stone
libere: (*adv.*) freely
medica, **-ae** *f*: a healer, nurse
morbus, **-i** *m*: an illness, weakness
officiosus, **-a**, **-um**: dutiful
olidus, **-a**, **-um**: stinking
pannus, **-i** *m*: rags
patiens, **-entis** (*gen.*): patient, long-suffering
perfero, **-ferre**, **-tuli**, **-latus**: to endure to the end
perfrico (1): to rub all over
persona, **-ae** *f*: a mask, role
plerumque: (*adv.*) frequently
potius: rather
rarus, **-a**, **-um**: infrequent
recolo, (3): to cultivate afresh, renew
sentio, (4): to feel
servilis, **-e**: servile
sordidus, **-a**, **-um**: filthy
suscipio, (3): to support, take up in turn
sustineo, (2): to sustain, tolerate

articulari...morbo: abl. cause, "bent and stooped *from arthritic weakness*"
per hoc: "on account of this"
Venerem meam: metonymy, "my sexual passion"
rarissimo: abl. time, "very infrequently"
in lapidem: "hardened *into stone*"
fomentis olidis et pannis sordidis et faetidis cataplasmatibus: abl. means, "scorching my hands *with stinking poultices and filthy rags and odorous poultices*"
nec...faciem sed...personam: acc. obj. of *sustinens*, "not taking on the appearance, but the role"
videris: fut. perf. jussive instead of pr. subj., "you should see"
quam...perferas: pr. subj. in ind. quest. after *videris*, "see *how you may endure*"
patienti vel...servili...animo: abl. manner, "with patient or with servile spirit"

nequeo sustinere ulterius tam beatam fortunam allapsam indignae. Recordare enim quam superbe, quam adroganter nobiscum egerit et ipsa jactatione immodicae ostentationis tumentem suum prodiderit animum deque tantis divitiis exigua nobis invita projecerit confestimque, praesentia nostra gravata, propelli et efflari exsibilarique nos jusserit. Nec sum mulier nec omnino spiro, nisi eam pessum de tantis opibus dejecero. Ac si tibi etiam, ut par est, inacuit nostra contumelia, consilium validum requiramus ambae. Jamque

---

adroganter: (*adv.*) arrogantly
ago, (3), **egi**: to act
allabor, (3), **allapsus sum**: to fall towards (+ *dat.*)
ambo, **-ae**, **-o**: both
beatus, **-a**, **-um**: happy
confestim: (*adv.*) hastily
consilium, **-i** *n*: a strategy
contumelia, **-ae** *f*: indignity
dejicio, (3), **dejeci**: overthrow
divitia, **-ae** *f*: wealth (*pl.*)
efflo, (1): to blow out
exiguus, **-a**, **-um**: meager, scanty
exsibilo, (1): to hiss away
gravor, (1), **gravatus sum**: to show annoyance
immodicus, **-a**, **-um**: excessive
inacuo, (3), **inacui**: provoke
indignus, **-a**, **-um**: unworthy
invitus, **-a**, **-um**: reluctant
jactatio, **-onis** *f*: boasting
jubeo, (2), **jussit**: to order
mulier, **-eris** *f*: a woman
nequeo: to be unable, cannot (+ *inf.*)
omnino: at all
ops, **opis** *f*: wealth (*pl.*)
ostentatio, **-onis** *f*: a display
par, **paris** *f*: reasonable
pessum *(adv.)*: to the lowest part
praesentia, **-ae** *f*: presence
prodo, (3), **prodidi**: to reveal
projicio, (3), **projeci**: to throw down
propello, (3): to drive off
recordor, (1), **recordatus sum**: to remember
spiro, (1): to breathe, live
superbe: (*adv.*) proudly
sustineo, (2): to sustain, put up with
tumeo, (2): to be swollen with conceit
ulterius *(adv.)*: further
validus, **-a**, **-um**: strong

---

indignae: dat. after *allapsam*, "falling toward *an unworthy one*"
recordare: pr. imper., "remember!"
jactatione: abl. means, "she has revealed *with boasting*"
quam...egerit: perf. subj. in ind. quest. after *recordare, "how* haughtily *she acted"*
prodiderit...proiecerit...iusserit: perf. subj. also in ind. quest., "how *she has revealed...has thrown down...has ordered*"
tumentem: pr. part. agreeing with *animum*, "her mind *swelling*"
exigua: acc. neut. pl., "she threw *small amounts*"
invita: nom. f. with adverbial force, "she *reluctantly*"
praesentia: abl. means, "annoyed *by our presence*"
propelli: pr. inf. pass. in ind. command, "ordered us *to be driven off*"
dejecero: fut. perf., "I shall have overthrown"
requiramus: pr. subj. hortatory, "let us seek"

ista, quae ferimus, non parentibus nostris ac nec ulli monstremus alii, immo nec omnino quicquam de eius salute norimus. Sat est quod ipsae vidimus quae vidisse paenitet, nedum ut genitoribus et omnibus populis tam beatum eius differamus praeconium. Nec sunt enim beati quorum divitias nemo novit. Sciet se non ancillas sed sorores habere majores. Et nunc quidem concedamus ad maritos, et lares pauperes nostros sed plane sobrios revisamus, diuque

---

concedo, (3): to depart
differo, **-ferre**, **distuli**, **dilatus**: to spread
divitia, **-ae** *f*: wealth
fero, **ferre**, **tuli**, **latus**: to bear, carry
genitor, **-oris** *m*: a father, parent
immo: no indeed
Lar, **Laris** *m*: Lares; hearth, home
monstro, (1): to reveal, show
nedum: while not, much less
nemo, **-inis** *n*: no one
nosco, (3), **novi**: to know, get to know
omnino: (*adv.*) entirely
paeniteo, (2): to displease
pauper, **-eris** *(gen.)*: meager
plane: (*adv.*) completely
praeconium, **-i** *n*: a proclamation, report
reviso, (3): to revisit
sat: enough
scio, (4): to understand
sobrius, **-a**, **-um**: sober, respectable

---

ista: acc. pl., "*these things* which we carry"
non...monstremus: pr. subj. hortatory, "let us not show" where *ne* is expected
nec...norimus: sync. (=*noverimus*), perf. subj. hortatory, "*let us not know* anything"
non...nec...immo nec omnino: note the climactic use of negative
quae: (=quibus) attracted into the case of *ipsae* for the dat. after paenitet, "*to whom* it is displeasing"
vidisse: perf. inf. after *paenitet*, "displeasing *to have seen*"
nedum ut...differamus: subj. in jussive clause contrasting with *sat est*, "much less let us spread"
genitoribus: dat. ind. obj., "to her parents"
quorum...novit: syncopated (=*noverit*) perf. subj. in relative clause of characteristic, "*whose* wealth no one *knows*"
sciet: pr. subj. jussive, "let her know"
se...habere: pr. inf. in ind. st. after *sciet*, "that she has"
concedamus: subj. hortatory, "let us depart"
revisamus: subj. hortatory, "let us revisit"

cogitationibus pressioribus instructae ad superbiam poeniendam firmiores redeamus."

The sisters are pleased at their plotting. Meanwhile, Psyche's husband again warns her of the sisters and informs her that she is pregnant.

[11] Placet pro bono duabus malis malum consilium totisque illis tam pretiosis muneribus absconditis comam trahentes et proinde ut merebantur ora lacerantes simulatos redintegrant fletus. Ac sic parentes quoque redulcerato prorsum dolore raptim deserentes vesania turgidae domus suas contendunt dolum scelestum, immo vero parricidium, struentes contra sororem insontem.

---

abscondeo, (2), **abscondui**, **absconditus**: to hide
bonum, **-i** *n*: a good thing
cogitatio, **-onis** *f*: a plan
coma, **-ae** *f*: hair
consilium, **-i** *n*: a plan
contendo, (3): to hasten
desero, (3): to desert, forsake
dolor, **-oris** *m*: anguish
dolus, **-i** *m*: fraud
firmus, **-a**, **-um**: secure
fletus, **-us** *m*: weeping
immo: nay more
insons, **-ontis** (*gen.*): innocent
instructus, **-a**, **-um**: prepared
lacero, (1): to mangle
mereo, (2): to merit
munus, **-eris** *n*: a gift
os, oris *n*: a face
parricidium, **-i** *n*: family murder
placet, (2): it is pleasing to (+ *dat.*)
poenio, (4): to punish
pressus, **-a**, **-um**: deliberate
pretiosus, **-a**, **-um**: precious
proinde: in the same degree
prorsum: (*adv.*) utterly
raptim: (*adv.*) hurriedly
redintegro, (1): to renew
redulcero, (1): to cause to fester again
scelestus, **-a**, **-um**: wicked
simulo, (1): to simulate
struo, (3): to construct
superbia, **-ae** *f*: haughtiness, pride
totus, **-a**, **-um**: all
traho, (3): to drag
turgidus, **-a**, **-um**: inflamed with passion
vesania, **-ae** *f*: madness

---

cogitationibus pressioribus: abl. means, "prepared *with more deliberate plans*"
ad poeniendam: gerundive expressing purp., "*in order that* her pride *be punished*"
redeamus: pr. subj. hortatory, "let us return"
pro bono: here not "for the good" but "as if it were good"
duabus malis: (sc. *sororibus*): dat. after *placet*, "pleasing *to those two bad sisters*"
totis illis pretiosis muneribus absconditis: abl. abs., "with all those precious gifts having been hidden"
proinde ut merebantur: impf. pass., parenthetical, "just as they deserved," referring to the mangling they inflict on their faces
parentes: acc. obj. of *deserentes*, "leaving *their parents*"
redulcerato…dolore: abl. abs., "with the anguish having been caused to fester again"
vesania: abl. specification with *turgidae*, "swollen *with madness*"
domus suas: acc. place to which, "to their own homes"

Interea Psychen maritus ille quem nescit rursum suis illis nocturnis sermonibus sic commonet: "Videsne quantum tibi periculum? Velitatur Fortuna eminus, ac nisi longe firmiter praecaves mox comminus congredietur. Perfidae lupulae magnis conatibus nefarias insidias tibi comparant, quarum summa est ut te suadeant meos explorare vultus, quos, ut tibi saepe praedixi, non videbis si videris. Ergo igitur si posthac pessimae illae lamiae noxiis animis armatae venerint — venient autem, scio — neque omnino sermonem conferas, et si id tolerare pro genuina simplicitate proque animi tui

---

anima, **-ae** *f.* spirit
armatus, **-a**, **-um**: equipped
comminus: hand to hand
commoneo, (2): to warn
comparo, (1): to prepare
conatus, **-us** *m*: endeavor
confero, **-ferre**, **-tuli**, **collatus**: to join in, connect
congredior, (3), **congressus sum**: to approach
eminus *(adv.)*: at a distance
exploro, (1): to investigate
firmiter: (*adv.*) firmly
genuinus, **-a**, **-um**: innate
insidia, **-ae** *f.* a trap
lamia, **-ae** *f.* a witch
longe *(adv.)*: by far
lupula, **-ae** *f.* a little whore
mox: soon
nefarius, **-a**, **-um**: wicked
nescio, (4): to not know
nocturnus, **-a**, **-um**: nocturnal
noxius, **-a**, **-um**: criminal
omnino: at all (after neg.)
perfidus, **-a**, **-um**: treacherous
pessimus, **-a**, **-um**: most disloyal
posthac: hereafter
praecaveo, (3): to guard (against)
praedico, (3), **praedixi**: warn
quantum: how much
saepe: (*adv.*) often
simplicitas, **-atis** *f.* simplicity
suadeo, (2): to induce, persuade
summa, **-ae** *f.* chief point
tolero, (1): to endure
velitor, (1), **velitatus sum**: to fight
vultus, **-us** *m*: looks

---

suis illis nocturnis sermonibus: abl. means, "warns *with these his own nocturnal speeches*"
nisi...praecaves: fut. in fut. more vivid protasis, "unless you guard"
congredietur: fut. in fut. more vivid apodosis, "she will approach"
lupulae: *lupa*, "she-wolf," is a popular expression for a prostitute; the diminutive here could allude to the idea of preying on the helpless.
magnis conatibus: abl. means, "prepare *with great endeavors*"
ut...suadeant: pr. subj. purp. clause, "in order that they might persuade"
te...explorare: ind. st. after *suadeant*, "they persuade *you to investigate*"
si videris: fut. perf. in more vivid protasis, "if you (will) have seen"
noxiis animis: abl. manner, "equipped *with criminal spirits*"
si...venerint: fut. perf. in fut. more vivid protasis, "if they shall have come"
neque...conferas: pr. subj. prohibition, "*don't join* in speech!"

teneritudine non potueris, certe de marito nil quicquam vel audias vel respondeas. Nam et familiam nostram jam propagabimus et hic adhuc infantilis uterus gestat nobis infantem alium, si texeris nostra secreta silentio, divinum, si profanaveris, mortalem."

Psyche rejoices at the news of her pregnancy. Her husband again warns her to disregard her approaching sisters.

[12] Nuntio Psyche laeta florebat et divinae subolis solacio plaudebat et futuri pignoris gloria gestiebat et materni nominis dignitate gaudebat. Crescentes dies et menses exeuntes anxia

---

adhuc: besides
anxius, **-a**, **-um**: anxious
cresco, (3): to increase
dignitas, **-atis** *f.* honor
exeo, **-ire**, **-ivi**, **-itum**: to pass
familia, **-ae** *f.* family
floreo, (2): to blossom
futurus, **-a**, **-um**: about to be, future
gaudeo, (2): to rejoice
gestio, (4): to be eager
gesto, (1): to carry
gloria, **-ae** *f.* glory
infans, **-antis** *n*: an infant
infantilis, **-e**: infantile
laetus, **-a**, **-um**: joyful
maternus, **-a**, **-um**: maternal
mensis, **-is** *m*: a month
nuntium, **-i** *n*: an announcement
pignus, **-oris** *n*: a pledge
plaudeo, (2): to express approval
profano, (1): to desecrate
propago, (1): to increase
respondeo, (2): to answer
secretum, **-i** *n*: a secret
silentium, **-i** *n*: silence
solacium, **-i** *n*: comfort
suboles, **-is** *f.* offspring
tego, (3), **texi**: to defend
teneritudo, **-inis** *f.* tenderness
uterus, **-i** *m*: a womb

---

si...non potueris: fut. perf. in fut. more vivid protasis, "if you shall be unable to" + inf.
vel audias vel respondeas: pr. subj. jussive in fut. more vivid apodosis, "either you should hear or answer"
si texeris...si profanaveris: fut. perf. in fut. more vivid protasis, "if you will have defended...if you will have desecrated"
silentio: abl. means, "defended *with silence*"
divinum...mortalem: acc. agreeing with *infantem*, "a *divine* infant if you defend, a *mortal* infant if you desecrate"
nuntio...solacio...gloria...dignitate: abl. cause, "she blossomed *because of the announcement*...expressed approval *because of the solace*...was eager *because of the glory*...rejoiced *because of the honor*"

numerat et sarcinae nesciae rudimento miratur de brevi punctulo tantum incrementulum locupletis uteri. Sed jam pestes illae taeterrimaeque Furiae anhelantes vipereum virus et festinantes impia celeritate navigabant. Tunc sic iterum momentarius maritus suam Psychen admonet: "dies ultima et casus extremus et sexus infestus et sanguis inimicus jam sumpsit arma et castra commovit et aciem direxit et classicum personavit; jam mucrone destricto jugulum tuum nefariae tuae sorores petunt. Heu quantis urguemur cladibus,

---

acies, **-ei** *f.* a battle line
admoneo, (2): to admonish
anhelo, (1): to breathe out
armum, **-i** *n*: arms (*pl.*)
brevis, **-e**: brief
castrum, **-i** *n*: a camp (*pl.*)
casus, **-us** *m*: an emergency
celeritas, **-atis** *f.* speed
clades, **-is** *f.* bane
classicum, **-i** *n*: a war-trumpet
commoveo, (2), **commovi**: to move
destringo, (3), **destrinxi**, **destrictus**: to draw
dirigo, (3), **direxi**: to mark
extremus, **-a**, **-um**: farthest
festino (1): to hasten
Furiae, **-arum** *f.* Furies
impius, **-a**, **-um**: wicked
incrementulum, **-i** *n*: a small growth
infestus, **-a**, **-um**: hostile
inimicus, **-a**, **-um**: unfriendly
iterum: again
jugulus, **-i** *m*: a throat
locuples, **-pletis** *(gen.)*: fertile, rich
maritus, **-i** *m*: a husband
miror, (1), **miratus sum**: to wonder
momentarius, **-a**, **-um**: quick
mucro, **-onis** *m*: a sword
navigo, (1): to sail
nefarius, **-a**, **-um**: evil
nescius, **-a**, **-um**: unknowing
numero, (1): to count
persono, (1): to resound
pestis, **-is** *f.* a plague
peto, (3): to attack
punctulum, **-i** *n*: a small pin prick
rudimentum, **-i** *n*: a first lesson, experience
sanguis, **-uinis** *m*: blood, blood relation
sarcina, **-ae** *f.* a burden
sexus, **-us** *m*: sex, gender
sumo, (3), **sumpsi**: to take up
taeter, **-tra**, **-trum**: to foul
ultimus, **-a**, **-um**: last
urgueo, (2): to press upon, beset
uterus, **-i** *n*: a womb
vipereus, **-a**, **-um**: of a viper
virus, **-i** *n*: venom

---

sarcinae nesciae: transferred epithet, "of her ignorant burden," i.e. her ignorance of birth
rudimento: abl. cause, "wonders *because of the first experience*"
illae: i.e. the sisters
impia celeritate: abl. manner, "with wicked speed"
muctone destricto: abl. abs., "with a sword drawn"
quantis…cladibus: abl. means, "beset *with how many banes*"

Psyche dulcissima! Tui nostrique miserere religiosaque continentia domum maritum teque et istum parvulum nostrum imminentis ruinae infortunio libera. Nec illas scelestas feminas, quas tibi post internecivum odium et calcata sanguinis foedera sorores appellare non licet, vel videas vel audias, cum in morem Sirenum scopulo prominentes funestis vocibus saxa personabunt."

Psyche entreats her husband to allow the visit of her sisters, and, again, he consents against his better judgment.

[13] Suscipit Psyche singultu lacrimoso sermonem incertans: "Jam dudum, quod sciam, fidei atque parciloquio meo perpendisti

---

appello, (1): to call
calco, (1): to trample upon
continentia, **-ae** *f.* self-control
dudum: little while ago
fides, **-ei** *f.* faith
foedus, **-eris** *n*: a bond
funestus, **-a**, **-um**: destructive
immineo, (2): to threaten
incerto, (1): to render inaudible, blur
infortunium, **-i** *n*: misfortune
internecivus, **-a**, **-um**: murderous
lacrimosus, **-a**, **-um**: tearful
libero, (1): to free
licet, (2): it is permitted
misereo, (2): to pity
mos, **moris** *m*: manner
odium, **-i** *n*: hate
parciloquium, **-i** *n*: a discretion, reserve in conversation
parvulus, **-i** *m*: an infant
perpendo, (3), **perpendi**: to weigh carefully
persono, (1): to cause X (*acc.*) to resound
promineo, (2): to lean out
religiosus, **-a**, **-um**: scrupulous
ruina, **-ae** *f.* catastrophe
saxum, **-i** *n*: a stone
scelestus, **-a**, **-um**: accursed
singultus, **-us** *m*: sobbing
Siren, **-enis** *f.* Siren
suscipio, (3): to accept
video, (2): to see, consider

Tui nostrique: gen. after miserere, "have pity *on yourself and me*"
miserere: imper., "pity!" + gen.
religiosa continentia: abl. means, "free *with scrupulous self-control*"
infortunio: abl. sep. after *libera*, "free *from misfortune*"
libera: pr. imper., "free!"
Nec...vel videas vel audias: pr. subj. in prohibition, "don't consider or accept!"
quas...appellare non licet: impersonal, "whom it is not permitted to call"
in morem Sirenum: "in the manner of the Sirens" the temptresses of *Odyssey* 12
cum...personabunt: fut., "when they will call"
scopulo: abl. place, "call *from the rock*"
funestis vocibus: abl. means, "call *with destructive voices*"
singultu lacrimoso: abl. means, "blurring her speech *with tearful sobbing*"
quod (=quoad) sciam: pr. subj. in relative clause of proviso, "as far as I know"
fidei atque parciloquio: dat. with *documenta* where we would expect the gen., "proof *for my faith and discretion*"

documenta, nec eo setius adprobabitur tibi nunc etiam firmitas animi mei. Tu modo Zephyro nostro rursum praecipe fungatur obsequio, et in vicem denegatae sacrosanctae imaginis tuae redde saltem conspectum sororum. Per istos cinnameos et undique pendulos crines, tuos per teneras et teretis et mei similes genas, per pectus nescio quo calore fervidum, sic in hoc saltem parvulo cognoscam faciem tuam: supplicis anxiae piis precibus erogatus

adprobo, (1): to prove
anxius, **-a**, **-um**: anxious
calor, **-oris** *m*: warmth
cinnameus, **-a**, **-um**: smelling of cinnamon
cognosco, (3): to learn
conspectus, **-us** *m*: a view
crinis, **-is** *m*: a tress
denego, (1): to deny
documentum, **-i** *n*: proof
erogo, (1): to successfully implore, win over
facies, **-ei** *f*: a face
fervidus, **-a**, **-um**: glowing
firmitas, **-atis** *f*: strength
fungor, (3), **functus sum**: to discharge (+ *abl.*)
gena, **-ae** *f*: cheeks (*pl.*)
imago,**-inis** *f*: an image
modo (*adv.*): merely
nescius, **-a**, **-um**: unfamiliar
obsequium, **-i** *n*: obligation
pectus, **-oris** *n*: a heart
pendulus, **-a**, **-um**: hanging down
pius, **-a**, **um**: devoted
praecipio, (3): to instruct (+ *dat.*)
reddo, (3): to render
sacrosanctus, **-a** , **-um**: venerable
saltem (*adv.*): at least
setius (*adv.*): less
similis, **-e**: resembling
supplex, **-icis** *m*: a suppliant
tener, **-era**, **-erum**: tender
teres, **-etis** *(gen.)*: smooth
undique: everywhere
vicis, **-is** *f*: a repayment, exchange

eo: abl. specification, "neither less *in this*," i.e. "the same in this as before"
praecipe: imper., "instruct!!"
fungatur: pr. subj. in ind. command after *praecipe*, "instruct him *to discharge*" + abl.
in vicem: "in the place of" + gen.
denegatae: perf. part. gen. f., "*of the denied* image"
Per…per…per: note anaphora
nescio quo calore: abl. means, "glowing *with some unfamiliar warmth*"
cognoscam: pr. subj. hortatory, "let me learn"
piis precibus: abl. means, "win over *by devoted prayers*"
erogatus: here an intensive of *rogo*, "(you) having been won over"

germani complexus indulge fructum et, tibi devotae dicataeque, Psychae animam gaudio recrea. Nec quicquam amplius in tuo vultu requiro, jam nil officiunt mihi nec ipsae nocturnae tenebrae: teneo te, meum lumen." His verbis et amplexibus mollibus decantatus maritus lacrimasque eius suis crinibus detergens facturum spopondit et praevertit statim lumen nascentis diei.

---

amplexus, **-us** *m*: an embrace
amplius (*adv.*): further
complexus, **-us** *m*: an embrace
crinis, **-is** *m*: a tress
decanto, (1): to enchant
detergeo, (2): to wipe
devotus, **-a**, **-um**: devoted
dicatus, **-a**, **-um**: dedicated
fructus, **-us** *m*: enjoyment
gaudium, **-i** *n*: joy
germanus, **-a**, **-um**: kindred
indulgeo, (2): to grant
lacrima, -ae *f.* a tear
mollis, **-e**: tender
nascor, (3), **natus sum**: to be born
nocturnus, **-a**, **-um**: nocturnal
officio, (3): to impede
praeverto, (3), **-verti**: to outrun, leave before
recreo, (1): to restore
requiro, (3): to ask
spondeo, (2), **spopondi**: to promise
tenebra, **-ae** *f.* a shadow, concealment
teneo, (2): to hold, possess
vultus, -us *m*: a face

---

germani complexus: gen. specification, "enjoyment *of a kindred embrace*"
indulge...recrea: imper., "grant!...restore!"
tibi: dat. with *devotae*, "devoted *to you*"
Psychae animam: note the bilingual pun, "soul of Soul"
gaudio: abl. manner, "restore *with joy*"
in tuo vultu: abl. respect, "with respect to your face"
his verbis et amplexibus mollibus: abl. means, "enchanted *by these words and by tender embraces*"
suis crinibus: abl. means, "wiping *with his own tresses*"
facturum (sc. esse): fut. act. inf. in ind. st., "promised *that he would do it*"
nascentis diei: gen., "light *of the dawning day*"

Zephyr again carries down the conspiring sisters, who feign joy at Psyche's coming baby.

[14] Jugum sororium consponsae factionis, ne parentibus quidem visis, recta de navibus scopulum petunt illum praecipiti cum velocitate nec venti ferentis oppertae praesentiam licentiosa cum temeritate prosiliunt in altum. Nec immemor Zephyrus regalis edicti, quamvis invitus, susceptas eas gremio spirantis aurae solo reddidit. At illae incunctatae statim conferto vestigio domum penetrant complexaeque praedam suam sorores nomine mentientes

---

altum, **-i** *n*: the deep
aura, **-ae** *f.* a breeze
complector, (3), **complexus sum**: to embrace
confertus, **-a**, **-um**: densely packed
consponsus, **-a**, **-um**: bound by mutual pledges
edictum, **-i** *n*: an edict
factio, **-onis** *f.* a faction
fero, **ferre**, **tuli**, **latus**: to bear
gremium, **-i** *n*: a lap
immemor, **-oris**: heedless of (+ *gen.*)
incunctatus, **-a**, **-um**: not hesitating
invitus, **-a** , **-um**: unwilling
jugum, **-i** *n*: a team
licentiosus, **-a**, **-um**: unrestrained
mentior, (4), **mentitus sum**: to imitate
navis, **-is** *f.* a ship
opperior, (4), **oppertus sum**: to wait
penetro, (1): to penetrate
peto, (3): to make for
praeceps, **-ipitis** (*gen.*): precipitous
praeda, **-ae** *f.* prey
praesentia, **-ae** *f.* presence
prosilio, (4), **prosilivi**: to leap forward
recta: (*adv.*) directly
reddo, (3), **reddidi**: to return
regalis, **-e**: royal
solum, **-i** *n*: ground
sororius, **-a**, **-um**: sisterly
spiro, (1): to blow
suscipio, (3), **suscepi**, **susceptus**: to take up
temeritas, **-atis** *f.* rashness
velocitas, **-atis** *f.* speed
ventus, **-i** *m*: wind
vetigium, **-i** *n*: a footstep
viso, (3), **visi**, **visus**: to visit

---

ne...quidem: "not even"
parentibus visis: abl. abs., "parents having been visited"
petunt...oppertae: pl. although the subject is actually *iugum*, "the team *seeks*, not *having waited for*"
praecipiti cum velocitate: abl. manner, "seek *with precipitous speed*"
venti ferentis: "presence *of a carrying wind*," i.e. a favorable wind
licentiosa cum temeritate: abl. manner, "with unrestrained rashness"
gremio: abl. place where, "in the lap"
susceptas: perf. part., "them *having been picked up*"
solo: abl. place where, "on the ground"
conferto vestigio: abl. manner, "penetrate *in a packed step*," i.e. like a formation of soldiers
complexae: perf. part., "the sisters *embracing*"
nomine: abl. specification, "sisters *in name*"

thensaurumque penitus abditae fraudis vultu laeto tegentes sic adulant: "Psyche, non ita ut pridem parvula, et ipsa jam mater es. Quantum, putas, boni nobis in ista geris perula! Quantis gaudiis totam domum nostram hilarabis! O nos beatas quas infantis aurei nutrimenta laetabunt! Qui si parentum, ut oportet, pulchritudini responderit, prorsus Cupido nascetur."

Psyche lavishes her sisters with refreshments, but when they ask about her husband she forgets her earlier tale and invents a middle-aged merchant for a husband.

[15] Sic adfectione simulata paulatim sororis invadunt animum. Statimque eas lassitudine viae sedilibus refotas et

abditus, **-a**, **-um**: hidden
adfectio, **-onis** *f.* affection
adulo, (1): to flatter
aureus, **-a**, **-um**: golden
beatus, **-a**, **-um**: blissful
bonum, **-i** *n*: good
fraus, **fraudis** *f.* deceit
gaudium, **-i** *n*: joy
gero, (3): to bear
hilaro, (1): to gladden
infans, **-antis** *n*: an infant
invado, (3): to invade
laeto, (1): to cheer
laetus, **-a**, **-um**: pleasing
lassitudo, **-inis** *f.* weariness
nutrimentum, **-i** *n*: nourishment
oportet, (2): (*impers.*) it ought
parvulus, **-a**, **-um**: very small
paulatim (*adv.*): little by little
penitus: (*adv.*) thoroughly
perula, **-ae** *f.* a pouch
pridem: (*adv.*) previously
prorsus (*adv.*): by all means, utterly
pulchritudo, **-inis** *f.* beauty
puto, (1): to think
refoveo, (2), **refovi**, **refotus**: to refresh
respondeo, (2): to answer
sedile, **-is** *n*: a chair
simulo, (1): to pretend
tego, (3): to cover
thensaurus, **-i** *m*: a vault
via, **-ae** *f.* a journey
vultus, **-us** *m*: an expression

vultu laeto: abl. means, "hiding *with a pleasing expression*"
Quantum...boni: "how much of good"
nobis: dat. of reference, "you bear *for us*"
quantis glaudiis: abl. means, "gladdened *with how many joys*"
si...responderit: fut. perf., "if he will have answered to" + dat.
nascetur: fut. more vivid apodosis, "a Cupid *will be born*"
adfectione simulata: abl. abs., "with affection having been simulated"
lassitudine: abl. sep., "refreshed *from weariness*"
sedilibus: abl. means, "refreshed *with chairs*"

balnearum vaporosis fontibus curatas pulcherrime triclinio mirisque illis et beatis edulibus atque tuccetis oblectat. Jubet citharam loqui: psallitur; tibias agere: sonatur; choros canere: cantatur. Quae cuncta nullo praesente dulcissimis modulis animos audientium remulcebant. Nec tamen scelestarum feminarum nequitia vel illa mellita cantus dulcedine mollita conquievit, sed ad destinatam fraudium pedicam sermonem conferentes dissimulanter occipiunt

---

ago, (3): to perform
audiens, **-entis** *m*: a listener
balnea, **-ae** *f*: a bath
cano, (3): to sing
canto, (1): to sing
cantus, **-us** *m*: a song
chorus, **-i** *m*: a choir
cithara, **-ae** *f*: a cithara
confero, **-ferre**, **-tuli**, **collatus**: to confer, direct (a conversation)
conquiesco, (3), **conquievi**: to settle
cunctus, **-a**, **-um**: all
curo, (1): to attend to
destinatus, **-a**, **-um**: determined
dissimulanter: (*adv.*) dissemblingly
dulcedo, **-inis** *f*: charm
edulia, **-ium** *n*: food
jubeo, (2): to request
loquor, (3), **locutus sum**: to speak
mellitus, **-a**, **-um**: honey-sweet
mirus, **-a**, **-um**: wonderful
modulus, **-i** *m*: little measure
mollio, (4), **mollivi**, **mollitus**: to soften
nequitia, **-ae** *f*: evil ways
nullus, **-i** *m*: no one
oblecto, (1): to delight
occipio, (3): to begin (+ *inf.*)
pedica, **-ae** *f*: snare
praesens, **-entis** (*gen.*): present
psallo, (3): to play on the cithara
pulcherrime: (*adv.*) most nobly
remulceo, (2): to stroke
scelestus, **-a**, **-um**: wicked
sono, (1): to be heard
tibia, **-ae** *f*: a flute
triclinium, **-i** *n*: a dining room
tuccetum, **-i** *n*: a sausage
vaporosus, **-a**, **-um**: steaming

---

vaporosis fontibus: abl. means, "cared for them *with steaming waters*"
triclinio: abl. place where, "in the dining room"
mirisque illis et beatis edulibus atque tuccetis: abl. means, "delights *with those wonderful and sumptuous foods and sausages*"
nullo praesente: abl. abs., "with no one present"
dulcissimis modulis: abl. means, "stroked *with sweetest little measures*"
illa mellita dulcedine: abl. means, "softened *by that honey-sweet charm*"

sciscitari qualis ei maritus et unde natalium, secta cuia proveniret. Tunc illa simplicitate nimia pristini sermonis oblita novum commentum instruit atque maritum suum de provincia proxima magnis pecuniis negotiantem jam medium cursum aetatis agere interspersum rara canitie. Nec in sermone isto tantillum morata rursum opiparis muneribus eas onustas ventoso vehiculo reddidit.

---

aetas, **-atis** *f.* age
canities, **-ei** *f.* gray hair
commentum, **-i** *n*: fabrication
cuius, **-a**, **um**: whose? which?
cursus, **-us** *m*: a course
instruo, (3): to construct
interspersus, **-a**, **-um**: sprinkled
medius, **-a**, **-um**: middle
moror, (1), **moratus sum**: to delay
munus, **-eris** *n*: a gift
natales, **-ium** *m*: parentage
negotio, (1): to trade
nimius, **-a**, **-um**: excessive
obliviscor, (3), **oblitus sum**: to forget (+ *gen.*)
onustus, **-a**, **-um**: laden
opiparus, **-a**, **-um**: splendid
pecunia, **-ae** *f.* money
pristinus, **-a**, **-um**: original
provenio, (4): to grow up, flourish
provincia, **-ae** *f.* a province
rarus, **-a**, **-um**: rare
reddo, (3), **reddidi**: return
sciscitor, (1), **sciscitatus sum**: to question
secta, **-ae** *f.* a path
sermo, **-onis** *m*: rumor
simplicitas, **-atis** *f.* simplicity
tantillus, **-a**, **-um**: so small
unde: whence
vehiculum, **-i** *n*: a carriage
ventosus, **-a**, **-um**: windy

---

qualis...unde: ind. quest. after *sciscitari* with verb understood, "to question *what sort he was...and whence*"
natalium: gen. pred., "whence was *his parentage*"
cuia proveniret: impf. subj. in ind. quest. after *sciscitari*, where we would expect the pr. or perf. tense, "to question *on what path he grew up*"
simplicitate nimia: abl. cause, "because of excessive simplicity"
oblita: deponent perf. part., "having forgetten" + gen.
negotiantem: circum. part. agreeing with *maritum*, "the husband who was *trading*"
magnis pecuniis: abl. means, "trading *with great money*"
agere: pr. inf. in ind. st., "*that* her husband *was conducting* the middle course of age"
rara canitie: abl. desc., "sprinkled *with a rare gray hair*"
tantillum: acc. extent, "not delayed *a so small amount*"
opiparis muneribus: abl. means, "laden *with splendid gifts*"

The sisters conclude that Psyche must not know the identity of her husband and that he must therefore be a god. They reconfirm their desire to bring about Psyche's ruin.

[16] Sed dum Zephyri tranquillo spiritu sublimatae domum redeunt, sic secum altercantes: "quid, soror, dicimus de tam monstruoso fatuae illis mendacio? Tunc adolescens modo florenti lanugine barbam instruens, nunc aetate media candenti canitie lucidus. Quis ille quem temporis modici spatium repentina senecta reformavit? Nil aliud reperies, mi soror, quam vel mendacia istam pessimam feminam confingere vel formam mariti sui nescire; quorum

---

adolescens, **-entis** *m*: a youth
alterco, (1): to quarrel
barba, **-ae** *f*: a beard
candeo, (2): to gleam
canities, **-ei** *f*: white hair
confingo, (3): to invent
dico, (3): to say
fatua, **-ae** *f*: a fool
floreo, (2): to blossom
forma, **-ae** *f*: a form
instruo, (3): to construct, build
lanugo, **-inis** *f*: down
lucidus, **-a**, **-um**: shining
mendacium, **-i** *n*: a lie
modicus, **-a**, **-um**: short, small
modo: just now
monstruosus, **-a**, **-um**: monstrous
nescio, (4): to not know
pessimus, **-a**, **-um**: wickedest
reformo, (1): to transform
repentinus, **-a**, **-um**: sudden
reperio, (4): to discover
senecta, **-ae** *f*: old age
spatium, **-i** *n*: an interval
spiritus, **-us** *m*: a breath
sublimo, (1): to raise
tempus, **-oris** *n*: time
tranquillus, **-a**, **-um**: calm

---

tranquillo spiritu: abl. means, "raised up *by the calm breath*"
quid...dicimus: deliberative quest. where subj. is expected, "what are we to say?"
Tunc...nunc: "earlier...but now"
florenti lanugine: abl. desc., "with blossoming down"
aetate media: abl. time, "in middle age"
candenti canitie: abl. desc., "with shining white hair"
Quis ille quem: "who (is) that one whom?"
repentina senecta: abl. manner, "transformed *with sudden old age*"
Nil aliud...quam: "nothing other than"
confingere...nescire: pr. inf. in ind. st. after *reperies*, "you will discover *that she is inventing...that she does not know*"
quorum utrum: "*whichever of which* is true"

utrum verum est, opibus istis quam primum exterminanda est. Quodsi viri sui faciem ignorat, deo profecto denupsit et deum nobis praegnatione ista gerit. Certe si divini puelli — quod absit— haec mater audierit, statim me laqueo nexili suspendam. Ergo interim ad parentes nostros redeamus et exordio sermonis huius quam concolores fallacias adtexamus."

---

absum: be absent
adtexo, (3): to weave in
concolor, **-oris**: agreeing with (+ *dat.*)
denubo, (3), **denupsi**, **denuptus**: to marry
exordium, **-i** *n*: a beginning (of a speech)
extermino, (1): to banish
facies, **-ei** *f.* an appearance
fallacia, **-ae** *f.* deceit
gero, (3): to bear
ignoro, (1): to be ignorant of
interim: meanwhile
laqueum, **-i** *n*: a noose
nexilis, **-e**: woven together
ops, **opis** *f.* wealth
praegnatio, **-onis** *f.* being pregnant, pregnancy
profecto: (*adv.*) surely
puellus, **-i** *m*: a boy
quodsi: but if
suspendo, (3): to hang up
uter, **-tra**, **-trum**: whichever
verus, **-a**, **-um**: true

---

opibus istis: abl. sep., "banished *from that wealth*"
exterminanda est: pass. periphrastic, "she must be banished"
deo: dat. after compound verb, "she has married *a god*"
praegnatione ista: abl. means, "carries *with that pregnancy of hers*"
quod absit: pr. subj. jussive, "which let it be absent," i.e. "god forbid"
si...audierit: fut. perf. in more vivid protasis, "if she shall have heard"
mater: nom. pred., "heard to be *mother*," i.e. if she is called a mother
suspendam: fut., "I will hang" or hortatory subj., "may I hang"
laqueo nexili: abl. means, "with a woven noose"
redeamus...adtexamus: subj. hortatory, "let us return...let us weave in"
exordio: dat. with *concolores*, "agreeing *with the beginning*"
quam concolores: "agreeing as closely as possible with" + dat.

The sisters visit their parents once more, the return to Psyche and inform her that her husband is a monstrous serpent, fitting with the oracle of Apollo.

[17] Sic inflammatae, parentibus fastidienter appellatis et nocte turbatis, vigiliis perditae matutino scopulum pervolant et inde solito venti praesidio vehementer devolant, lacrimisque pressura palpebrarum coactis hoc astu puellam appellant: "tu quidem felix et ipsa tanti mali ignorantia beata sedes incuriosa periculi tui, nos autem, quae pervigili cura rebus tuis excubamus, cladibus tuis misere cruciamur. Pro vero namque comperimus nec te, sociae scilicet doloris casusque tui, celare possumus, immanem colubrum

---

appello, (1): to address, to call upon
astus, **-us** *m*: cunning
beatus, **-a**, **-um**: blissful
clades, **-is** *f.* reverse, devastation
cogo, (3), **coegi**, **coactus**: to force
comperio, (4), **comperi**: to discover
crucio, (1): to torment
cura, **-ae** *f.* concern
devolo, (1): to fly down
excubo, (1): to be attentive to (+ *dat.*)
fastidienter: (*adv.*) disdainfully
felix, **-icis** (*gen.*): happy
ignorantia, **-ae** *f.* ignorance
incuriosus, **-a**, **-um**: unsuspecting
inflammatus, **-a**, **-um**: inflamed
matutinus, **-a**, **-um**: early
misere: (*adv.*) wretchedly
palpebra, **-ae** *f.* an eyelid
perditus, **-a**, **-um**: reckless
periculum, **-i** *n*: a danger
pervigil, **-ilis** (*gen.*): sleepless
pervolo, (1): to move rapidly
praesidium, **-i** *n*: help
pressura, **-ae** *f.* a pressing together
sedeo, (2): to sit
socia, **-ae** *f.* companion
solitus, **-a**, **-um**: customary
turbo, (1): to disturb
vehementer: (*adv.*) vehemently
ventus, **-i** *m*: wind
verum, **-i** *n*: truth
vigilia, **-ae** *f.* wakefulness

---

parentibus appellatis et turbatis: abl. abs., "with the parents having been called upon and disturbed"
vigiliis: abl. means, "the sisters exhausted *by wakefulness*"
matutino: abl. time, "in the early morning"
solito...praesidio: abl. means, "flying down *by the customary help*"
lacrimis coactis: abl. abs., "*with tears having been forced*"
pressura: abl. means, "forced *by a pressing together* of the eyelids"
hoc astu: abl. manner, "with this cunning"
Tu quidem...nos autem: "you, on the one hand...but we, on the other"
ipsa...ignorantia: abl. cause, "blessed *because of ignorance itself*"
pervigili cura: abl. manner, "attentive *with sleepless concern*"
cladibus tuis: abl. means, "tormented *by your devastations*"
comperimus: perf., "we have discovered"
te: abl. sep., "to hide *from you*"
sociae: nom. appositive, "we, *who are companions*"

multinodis voluminibus serpentem, veneno noxio colla sanguinantem hiantemque ingluvie profunda, tecum noctibus latenter adquiescere. Nunc recordare sortis Pythicae, quae te trucis bestiae nuptiis destinatam esse clamavit. Et multi coloni quique circumsecus venantur et accolae plurimi viderunt eum vespera redeuntem e pastu proximique fluminis vadis innatantem.

---

accola, **-ae** *m*: a neighbor
adquiesco, (3): to lie with (with cum)
bestia, **-ae** *f.* a beast
casus, **-us** *m*: plight
celo, (1): to conceal
circumsecus (*adv.*): in the region around
clamo, (1): to proclaim
collum, **-i** *n*: a neck
colonus, **-i** *m*: a farmer
coluber, **-i** *m*: a serpent
destino, (1): to intend
dolor, **-oris** *m*: suffering
flumen, **-inis** *n*: a river
hio, (1): to be greedy for
immanis, **-e**: monstrous
ingluvies, **-i** *f.* gluttony
innato, (1): to swim
latenter: (*adv.*) secretly
multinodus, **-a**, **-um**: many-knotted
noxius, **-a**, **-um**: noxious
pastus, **-us** *m*: a feeding ground
plurimus, **-a**, **-um**: very many
profundus, **-a**, **-um**: insatiable
Pythieus, -a, -um: of Delphi
recordor, (1), **recordatus sum**: to remember
sanguino (1): to be bloodthirsty
scilicet: of course
serpo, (3): to creep
sors, sortis *f.* an oracular response
trux, **-ucis** (*adv.*): wild
vadum, **-i** *n*: a stream
venenum, **-i** *n*: poison
venor, (1), **venatus sum**: to hunt
vespera, **-ae** *f.* evening
volumen, **-inis** *n*: a fold

---

colubrum...adquiescere: ind. st. after *comperimus*, "discovered *that a snake lies* with you"
multinodis voluminibus: abl. desc., "with many-knotted folds"
veneno noxio: abl. specification, "red *with noxious poison*"
ingluvie profunda: abl. specification, "gaping *with insatiable gluttony*"
noctibus: abl. time, "in nights"
recordare: pr. imper., "remember!" + gen.
te trucis...destinatam esse: ind. st. after *clamavit*, "that you had been destined"
nuptiis: dat. purp., "for marriage"
redeuntem...innatantem: pr. part. circumstantial after *viderunt*, "they saw him *returning and swimming*"
vadis: abl. place where, "swimming *in the streams*"

They continue, convincing Psyche that her husband will soon devour her.

[18] nec diu blandis alimoniarum obsequiis te saginaturum omnes adfirmant, sed cum primum praegnationem tuam plenus maturaverit uterus, opimiore fructu praeditam devoraturum. Ad haec jam tua est existimatio, utrum sororibus pro tua cara salute sollicitis adsentiri velis et declinata morte nobiscum secura periculi vivere an saevissimae bestiae sepeliri visceribus. Quodsi te ruris huius vocalis solitudo vel clandestinae Veneris faetidi periculosique

---

adfirmo, (1): to assert
adsentior, (4), **adsensus sum**: to comply with (+ *dat.*)
alimonia, **-ae** *f.* nourishment
blandus, **-a**, **-um**: flattering
carus, **-a**, **-um**: precious
clandestinus, **-a**, **-um**: secret
declino, (1): to avoid
devoro, (1): to devour
diu: for a long time
existimatio, **-onis** *f.* judgment
faetidus, **-a**, **-um**: stinking, offensive
fructus, **-us** *m*: fruit
maturo, (1): to ripen
mors, mortis *m*: death
obsequium, **-i** *n*: compliance
opimus, **-a**, **-um**: rich
periculosus, **-a**, **-um**: dangerous
periculum, **-i** *m*: danger
plenus, **-a**, **-um**: plump
praeditus, **-a**, **-um**: provided with
praegnatio, **-onis** *f.* pregnancy
quodsi: but if
rus, ruris *n*: country
saevus, **-a**, **-um**: savage
sagino, (1): to lavish
salus, **-utis** *f.* salvation
securus, **-a**, **-um**: free from care
sepelio, (4): to bury
solitudo, **-inis** *f.* solitude
sollicitus, **-a**, **-um**: concerned
uterus, **-i** *m*: a womb
utrum...an: whether...or
viscer, **-eris** *n*: entrails
vivo, (3): to live
vocalis, **-e**: voice-filled, able to speak
volo, **velle**, **volui**: to wish

---

blandis...obsequiis: abl. means, "lavish *with flattering compliances*"
saginaturum: fut. act. inf. in ind. st. after *adfirmant*, "*that he will lavish* you"
cum primum...maturaverit: fut. perf. in temporal clause, "*as soon as* your womb *has ripened*"
opimiore fructu: abl. specification, "provided *with a richer fruit*"
devoraturum: fut. act. inf. in ind. st. after *adfirmant*, "*that he will devour* you"
utrum...adsentiri velis: pr. subj. in ind. quest., "whether you wish to comply"
sororibus...sollicitis: dat. after *adsentiri*, "to comply *with the concerned sisters*"
declinata morte: abl. abs., "with death having been avoided"
vivere: also complementing *velis*, "and you wish *to live* securely"
an...sepeliri (sc. velis): ind. quest., "or whether (you wish) to be buried"
visceribus: abl. place where, "buried *in the entrails*"
te: acc. dir. obj. of *delectant*, "they please *you*"
faetidi periculosique concubitus: nom. pl., "the stinking and dangerous couplings"

concubitus et venenati serpentis amplexus delectant, certe piae sorores nostrum fecerimus." Tunc Psyche misella, utpote simplex et animi tenella, rapitur verborum tam tristium formidine: extra terminum mentis suae posita prorsus omnium mariti monitionum suarumque promissionum memoriam effudit et in profundum calamitatis sese praecipitavit tremensque et exsangui colore lurida tertiata verba semihianti voce substrepens sic ad illas ait:

---

aio, (1): to say
amplexus, **-us** *m*: an embrace, coil (snake)
calamitas, **-atis** *f*: disaster
color, **-oris** *n*: complexion
concubitus, **-us** *m*: a coupling
delecto, (1): to please
effundo, (3), **effudi**: to shed
exsanguis, **-e**: pale
extra: beyond (+ *acc.*)
formido, **-inis** *f*: terror
luridus, **-a**, **-um**: ghastly
memoria, **-ae** *f*: memory
mens, **mentis** *f*: mind
misellus, **-a**, **-um**: wretched
monitio, **-onis** *f*: a warning
pius, **-a**, **-um**: faithful
pono, (3), **posui**, **positus**: to set, put
praecipito, (1): to throw headlong
profundum, **-i** *n*: depths
promissio, **-onis** *f*: a promise
prorsus: (*adv.*) entirely
rapio, (3): to carry away
semihians, **-antis** (*gen.*): half-open
serpens, **-entis** *m*: a snake
simplex, **-icis** (*gen.*): simple
substrepo, (3): to mutter confusedly
tenellus, **-a**, **-um**: tender
termenus, **-i**: boundary
tertio, (1): to repeat three times, stammer
tremo, (3): to tremble
tristis, **-e**: sorrowful
utpote: as
venenatus, **-a**, **-um**: venomous
vox, **vocis** *f*: a mouth

---

fecerimus: fut. perf., "*we will have done* our duty"
formidine: abl. means, "is carried away *by the terror*"
posita: perf. part. nom, "she, *having been put* beyond the limit," i.e. driven out of her mind
omnium...promissionum: gen. after *memoriam*, "the memory *of the promises*"
exsangui colore: abl. desc., "ghastly *with a pale complexion*"
semihanti voce: abl. manner, "mutters *with half-open mouth*"

Psyche, fearful and naïve, admits to her ignorance and accepts the help of her sisters.

[19] "Vos quidem, carissimae sorores, ut par erat, in officio vestrae pietatis permanetis, verum et illi qui talia vobis adfirmant non videntur mihi mendacium fingere. Nec enim umquam viri mei vidi faciem vel omnino cuiatis sit novi, sed tantum nocturnis subaudiens vocibus maritum incerti status et prorsus lucifugam tolero, bestiamque aliquam recte dicentibus vobis merito consentio. Meque magnopere semper a suis terret aspectibus malumque grande de vultus curiositate praeminatur. Nunc si quam salutarem opem periclitanti sorori vestrae potestis adferre, jam nunc subsistite; ceterum

---

adfero, **-ferre**, **-tuli**, **-latus**: to convey
adfirmo, (1): to assert
aspectus, **-us** *m*: a sight
carus, **-a**, **-um**: dear
ceterum: for, since
consentio, (4): to agree
cuiatis, cuiatis (*gen.*): whence
curiositas, **-atis** *f.* curiosity
facies, **-ei** *f.* a shape
fingo, (3): to invent
grandis, **-e**: great
incertus, **-a**, **-um**: uncertain, inconstant
lucifuga, **-ae** *m*: one who avoids the light of day
magnopere: (*adv.*) with great effort
mendacium, **-i** *n*: a lie
merito: (*adv.*) rightly
nocturnus, **-a**, **-um**: nocturnal, at night
nosco, (3), **novi**, **notus**: to know
officium, **-i** *n*: duty
omnino: at all
ops, **opis** *f.* help
par, **paris**: right
periclitor, (1), **periclitatus sum**: to endanger
permaneo, (2): to endure
pietas, **-atis** *f.* loyalty
praeminor, (1), **praeminatus sum**: to threaten in advance
salutaris, **-e**: saving
status, **-us** *m*: status
subaudio, (4): to hear a little
subsisto, (3): to halt, stand
terreo, (2): to frighten
tolero, (1): to endure
video, (2): to see; (pass.) seem to (+ *inf.*)
vultus, **-us** *m*: looks

---

cuiatis sit: subj. in ind. quest., "I do not know *whence he may be*;" *cuiatis* is an archaic nominative
nocturnis...vocibus: dat. after *subaudiens*, "hearing *nocturnal voices*"
incerti status: gen. specification, "husband *of uncertain status*"
bestiamque aliquam (sc. esse): ind. st. after *dicibus*, "declaring him to be *some monster*"
dicentibus vobis: dat. after *consentio*, "agree *with you declaring*"
vultus: gen. specification, "because of my curiosity *with regards to his face*"
periclitanti sorori: pr. part. dat., "saving help to your *endangered sister*"
nunc...iam nunc: intensified by repetition, "right now"

incuria sequens prioris providentiae beneficia conrumpet." Tunc nanctae jam portis patentibus nudatum sororis animum facinerosae mulieres, omissis tectae machinae latibulis, destrictis gladiis fraudium simplicis puellae paventes cogitationes invadunt.

The first sister advises Psyche to visit her husband at night with a lamp and a blade so to view him and then kill him, after which the sisters will take her home.

[20] Sic denique altera: "quoniam nos originis nexus pro tua incolumitate ne periculum quidem ullum ante oculos habere compellit, viam quae sola deducit iter ad salutem diu diuque cogitatam monstrabimus tibi. Novaculam praeacutam adpulsu etiam

---

adpulsus, **-us** *m*: impact
alter, **-era**, **-erum**: one (of two)
animus, **-i** *m*: mind
beneficium, **-i** *n*: benefit
cogitatio, **-onis** *f*: thought
cogito, (1): to consider
compello, (3): to compel
conrumpo, (3): to spoil
deduco, (3): to lead, draw
denique: and then
destringo, (3), **destrinxi**, **destrictus**: to draw (sword)
facinerosus, **-a**, **-um**: wicked
gladius, **-i** *m*: a sword
incolumitas, **-atis** *f*: safety
incuria, **-ae** *f*: carelessness
invado, (3): to invade
iter, itineris *n* path
latibulum, **-i** *n*: a hiding-place, den
machina, **-ae** *f*: a scheme
monstro, (1): to reveal, teach
mulier, **-eris** *f*: a woman
nanciscor, (3), **nanctus sum**: to obtain, take possesssion of (+ *acc.*)
nexus, **-us** *m*: an obligation
novacula, **-ae** *f*: a razor
nudo, (1): to leave unprotected
omitto, (3), **omisi**, **omissus**: to lay aside
origo, **-inis** *f*: an origin
pateo, (2): to stand open
paveo, (2): to be terrified at
porta, **-ae** *f*: a gate
praeacutus, **-a**, **-um**: sharpened
prior, **-ius**: prior
providentia, **-ae** *f*: providence
quoniam: because
salus, **-utis** *f*: salvation
sequens, **-entis** (*gen.*): following
simplex, **-icis** (*gen.*): simple
tectus, **-a**, **-um**: covered, secret

---

portis patentibus: abl. abs., "with the gates standing open"
omissis...latibulis: abl. abs., "with hiding places having been set aside"
destrictis gladiis: abl. abs., "with swords having been drawn"
nos...habere: ind. com. after *compellit*, "compells *us to have* not even any danger"
viam...cogitatam: acc. perf. part., "reveal *the way having been considered*"
adpulsu: abl. means, "incited *by the impact*," i.e. so sharp as to cut with only the slightest provocation

palmulae lenientis exasperatam tori qua parte cubare consuesti latenter absconde, lucernamque concinnem completam oleo, claro lumine praemicantem subde aliquo claudentis aululae tegmine, omnique isto apparatu tenacissime dissimulato, postquam sulcatum trahens gressum cubile solitum conscenderit jamque porrectus et exordio somni prementis implicitus altum soporem flare coeperit, toro delapsa nudoque vestigio pensilem gradum paullulatim

---

abscondeo, (2): to conceal
altus, **-a**, **-um**: deep
apparatus, **-us** *m*: preparation
aulula, **-ae** *f*: a small pot
clarus, **-a**, **-um**: bright
claudo, (3): to confine
coepio, (3), **coepi**: to commence
completus, **-a**, **-um**: filled full
concinnis, **-e**: ready for use
conscendo, (3), **conscendi**: to ascend
consuesco, (2), **consuevi**: to be accustomed
cubile, **-is** *n*: a bed
cubo, (1): to rest
delabor, (3), **delapsus sum**: to slip
dissimulo, (1): to hide
exaspero, (1): to incite
exordium, **-i** *n*: a beginning
flo, (1): to breathe
gradus, **-us** *m*: a step
gressus, **-us** *m*: a going, trail
implico, (1): to envelop
latenter: (*adv.*) secretly
lenio, (4): to soften, calm
lucerna, **-ae** *f*: an oil lamp
nudus, **-a**, **-um**: bare
oleum, **-i** *n*: oil
palmula, **-ae** *f*: a palm
pars, **partis** *f*: a part
paullulatim: little by little
pensilis, **-e**: hanging
porrectus, **-a**, **-um**: stretched out
postquam: after
praemico, (1): to glitter forth
premo, (3): to overwhelm
solitus, **-a**, **-um**: usual
somnus, **-i** *m*: sleep
sopor, **-oris** *m*: deep sleep
subdo, (3): to place X (*acc.*) under Y (*abl.*)
sulco, (1): to furrow
tegmen, **-inis** *n*: a covering
tenax, **-acis** (*gen.*): steadfast
torus, **-i** *m*: a bed
traho, (3): to draw
vestigium, **-i** *n*: a footstep

---

qua parte: abl. place where, "*in which part* of the bed"
consuesti: syncopated (=*consuesisti*) perf., "you have been accustomed"
oleo: abl. specification, "filled *with oil*"
claro lumine: abl. manner, "glittering forth *with a bright light*"
omni isto apparatu...dissimulato: abl. abs., "with all that preparation having been hidden"
postquam...conscenderit...coeperit: fut. perf. in temporal clause, "after he will have ascended...will have commenced"
sulcatum trahens gressum: "drawing a furrowed trail," suggesting the movement of a snake
toro: abl. sep., "having slipped *from the bed*"
nudo vestigio: abl. manner, "slipping *with a bare footstep*"

minuens, caecae tenebrae custodia liberata lucerna, praeclari tui facinoris opportunitatem de luminis consilio mutuare, et ancipiti telo illo audaciter, prius dextera sursum elata, nisu quam valido noxii serpentis nodum cervicis et capitis abscide. Nec nostrum tibi deerit subsidium; sed cum primum illius morte salutem tibi feceris, anxie praestolatae advolabimus cunctisque istis opibus tecum relatis votivis nuptiis hominem te jungemus homini."

---

abscido, (3): to cut
advolo, (1): to hasten towards
anceps, **-ipitis** (*gen.*): two-edged
anxie: (*adv.*) anxiously
audaciter: (*adv.*) boldly
caecus, **-a**, **-um**: hidden
cervix, **-icis** *f.* a neck
consilium, **-i** *n*: resolution, determination
cunctus, **-a**, **-um**: all
custodia, **-ae** *f.* guard, protection
desum, **-esse**, **-fui**, **-futurus**: to be lacking
dextera, **-ae** *f.* a right hand
elatus, **-a**, **-um**: raised
facinus, **-oris** *n*: a deed
homo, **-inis** *m*: a human being
jungo, (3): to unite
libero, (1): to free
minuo, (3): to diminish
mutuor, (1): to obtain, procure
nisus, **-us** *m*: a thrust
nodus, **-i** *m*: a node
noxius, **-a**, **-um**: noxious
opportunitas, **-atis** *f.* right time
ops, opis *f*: wealth (*pl.*)
praeclarus, **-a**, **-um**: noble
praestolor, (1), **praestolatus sum**: to stand ready
prior, prius: prior, first
refero, referre, rettuli, relatus: to render
salus, **-utis** *f.* safety
serpens, **-entis** *m*: a snake
subsidium, **-i** *n*: reinforcement
sursum (*adv.*): on high
telum, **-i** *n*: a weapon
tenebra, **-ae** *f.* concealment
validus, **-a**, **-um**: strong
votivus, **-a**, **-um**: offered in fulfillment of a vow

---

opportunitatem...mutuare: imper. deponent, "procure the right moment!"
de luminis consilio: "procure *from the determination of the light*"
ancipiti telo illo: abl. means, "procure *with that two-edged weapon*"
dextera...elata: abl. abs., "with the right hand raised"
nisu: abl. means, "cut *with a thrust*"
quam valido: intensifying, "as strong as possible"
cum primum...feceris: fut. perf., "as soon as you have made"
morte: abl. means, "made safety *by the death*"
cunctis...relatis: abl. abs., "all having been carried back"
hominem te: "we will join *you, a human*"
votivis nuptiis: abl. specification, "will join you *in vowed marriage*"

Psyche's sisters leave her alone, afraid, and determined.

[21] Tali verborum incendio flammata viscera sororis prorsus ardentis deserentes ipsae protinus, tanti mali confinium sibi etiam eximie metuentes, flatus alitis impulsu solito porrectae super scopulum ilico pernici se fuga proripiunt statimque conscensis navibus abeunt. At Psyche relicta sola, nisi quod infestis Furiis agitata sola non est, aestu pelagi simile maerendo fluctuat, et quamvis statuto

---

abeo, **-ire**, **-ivi**, **-itus**: to depart
aestus, **-us** *m*: a tide
agito, (1): to stir
ales, **-itis** (*gen.*): winged
ardeo, (2): to blaze
confinium, **-i** *n*: proximity
conscendo, (3): to board (ship), embark
desero, (3): to desert
eximius, **-a**, **-um**: extraordinary
flammo, (1): to inflame
flatus, **-us** *m*: a breeze
fluctuo, (1): to fluctuate
fuga, **-ae** *f.* an escape
Furiae, **-arum** *f.* Furies, avenging spirits
ilico: (*adv.*) immediately
impulsus, **-um** *m*: blowing
incendium, **-i** *n*: fire
infestus, **-a**, **-um**: hostile
maereo, (2): to grieve, weep
metuo, (3): to fear
navis, **-is** *f.* a ship
pelagus, **-i** *n*: sea
pernix, **-icis** (*gen.*): swift
porrigo, (3), **porrexi**, **porrectus**: to lay before
proripio, (3): to rush or burst forth
prorsus: (*adv.*) already
protinus: (*adv.*) without pause
relinquo, (3), **reliqui**, **relictus**: to leave behind
similis, **-e**: resembling
solitus, **-a**, **-um**: customary
statuo, (3), **statui**, **statutus**: to establish
viscer, **-eris** *n*: innards, heart (*pl.*)

Tali...incendio: abl. means, "inflamed *by such a fire*"
flammata: "her heart *having been inflamed*"
sororis...ardentis: gen. of possession with transferred epithet, "the heart *of the already blazing sister*," i.e. the already blazing heart of the sister
deserentes: nom. pl., agreeing with *ipsae* (sc. *sorores*), "the sisters themselves *deserting*"
impulsu solitu: abl. means, "set down *by the customary blowing*"
se...proripiunt: "they rush themselves forth"
pernici fuga: abl. manner, "with a swift escape"
conscensis navibus: abl. abs., "with the ships having been boarded"
nisi quod: "except for the fact that"
infestis Furiis: abl. means, "stirred *by hostile Furies*"
aestu: an irregular dat. (=*aestui*) found often in Apuleius, after *simile*, "like *the tide* of the sea"
simile: acc. adverbial, "fluctuates *in a similar fashion to*"+ dat.
maerendo: gerund abl. used as a present participle (=*maerens*), "she *weeping*"

consilio et obstinato animo, jam tamen facinori manus admovens adhuc incerta consilii titubat multisque calamitatis suae distrahitur affectibus. Festinat differt, audet trepidat, diffidit irascitur et, quod est ultimum, in eodem corpore odit bestiam, diligit maritum. Vespera tamen jam noctem trahente praecipiti festinatione nefarii sceleris instruit apparatum. Nox aderat et maritus aderat, primusque Veneris proeliis velitatus in altum soporem descenderat.

adhuc: still
admoveo, (2): to apply
adsum, **adesse**, **affui**, **affuturus**: to arrive
affectus, **-us** *m*: emotion
altus, **-a**, **-um**: deep
apparatus, **-us** *m*: supplies
audeo, (2): to have courage
calamitas, **-atis** *f*: disaster
consilium, **-i** *n*: a decision, resolution
descendo, (3), **descendi**: descend
differo, **-ferre**, **distuli**, **dilatus**: to hesitate
diffido, (3): to despair
diligo, (3): to love
distraho, (3): to tear apart
facinus, **-oris** *n*: a deed
festinatio, **-onis** *f*: haste
incertus, **-a**, **-um**: uncertain (+ *gen.*)
instruo, (3): to prepare
irascor, (3), **iratus sum**: to become angry
nefarius, **-a**, **-um**: impious
obstinatus, **-a**, **-um**: resolute
odi, **oditum**: to hate (perf. only)
praeceps, **-ipitis** (*gen.*): precipitous
proelium, **-i** *n*: a battle
scelus, **-eris** *n*: crime
sopor, **-oris** *m*: a deep sleep
titubo, (1): to falter
traho, (3): to draw
trepido, (1): to be afraid
ultimus, **-a**, **-um**: worst, last
velitor, (1), **velitus sum**: to skirmish
vespera, **-ae** *f*: evening

statuo consilio et obstinato animo: abl. abs., "although a decision having been established and her spirit being resolute"
facinori: dat. with compound verb *admovens*, "applying hands *to the deed*"
multis...affectibus: abl. means, "torn apart *by many emotions*"
Festinat...irascitur: note the asyndeton with these three pairs of verbs
Vespera...trahente: abl. abs., "With the evening drawing"
praecipiti festinatione: abl. manner, "with precipitous haste"
descenderat: plupf., "he had descended"

Psyche follows the instructions of her sisters. The lamplight reveals not a monster but none other than the beautiful god Cupid.

[22] Tunc Psyche, et corporis et animi alioquin infirma, fati tamen saevitia subministrante, viribus roboratur et prolata lucerna et adrepta novacula sexum audacia mutatur. Sed cum primum luminis oblatione tori secreta claruerunt, videt omnium ferarum mitissimam dulcissimamque bestiam, ipsum illum Cupidinem formonsum deum formonse cubantem, cuius aspectu lucernae quoque lumen hilaratum increbruit et acuminis sacrilegi novacula paenitebat. At vero Psyche tanto aspectu deterrita et impos animi,

---

acumen, **-inis** *n*: a sharpened point
adripio, (3), **adripui**, **adreptus**: to take hold of
alioquin: in general
aspectus, **-us** *m*: a sight
audacia, **-ae** *f*: boldness
claresco, (3), **clarui**: be illuminated
cubo, (1): to rest
deterreo, (2), **deterrui**, **deterritus**: to be terrified
dulcis, **-e**,: sweet
fatum, **-i** *n*: fate
fera, **-ae** *f*: a wild beast
formonsus, **-a**, **-um**: beautiful
hilaro, (1): to cheer
impos, **-otis** (*gen*.): not in control of (+ *gen.*)
increbresco, (3), **increbrui**: to become stronger
infirmus, **-a**, **-um**: weak
mitis, **-e**: gentle
muto, (1): to change
novacula, **-ae** *f*: a razor
oblatio, **-onis** *f*: a presentation
paeniteo, (2): to repent, be sorry
profero, **-ferre**, **-tuli**, **-latus**: to bring forward
roboro, (1): to strengthen
sacrilegus, **-a**, **-um**: sacrilegious
saevitia, **-ae** *f*: cruelty
secretum, **-i** *n*: a secret
sexus, **-us** *m*: sex, gender
subministro, (1): to supply
torus, **-i** *m*: a bed
vis, **viris** *f*: strength, might

---

et corporis et animi: gen. specification, "usually weak *in body and soul*"
saevitia subministrante (sc. vires): abl. abs., "*with cruelty supplying* (strength)"
viribus: abl. specification, "is strengthened *in might*" i.e. gains strength
prolata lucerna: abl. abs., "the oil lamp having been brought forward"
adrepta novacula: abl. abs., "the razor having been taken hold of"
sexum...mutatur: "she changes her sex," i.e. she acts like a man
audacia: abl. manner, "with boldness" or "boldly"
cum primum...claruerunt: "as soon as the secrets have been illuminated"
oblatione: abl. means, "by the presentation"
aspectu: abl. specification, "*at the sight* of whom"
hilaratum: perf. part., "the light *having been cheered*"
acuminis sacrilegi: gen. quality, "the razor *of sacrilegious sharpness*"
tanto aspectu: abl. means, "terrified *by so great a sight*"

marcido pallore defecta, tremensque desedit in imos poplites et ferrum quaerit abscondere, sed in suo pectore; quod profecto fecisset, nisi ferrum timore tanti flagitii manibus temerariis delapsum evolasset. Jamque lassa, salute defecta, dum saepius divini vultus intuetur pulchritudinem, recreatur animi.

Videt capitis aurei genialem caesariem, ambrosia temulentam, cervices lacteas genasque purpureas, pererrantes crinium globos decoriter impeditos, alios antependulos, alios retropendulos,

---

abscondeo, (2): to hide, bury
ambrosia, **-ae** *f.* food of the gods, ambrosia
antependulus, **-a**, **-um**: hanging down in front
aureus, **-a**, **-um**: golden
caesaries, **-ei** *f.* hair
cervix, **-icis** *f.* a neck
crinis, **-is** *m*: hair
decoriter: (*adv.*) gracefully
deficio, (3), **defeci**, **defectus**: to lack, be bereft of (+ *abl.*); to grow faint
delabor, (3), **delapsus sum**: to fall
desido, (3), **desedi**: to sink down
evolo, (1): to rush out
ferrum, **-i** *n*: a weapon
flagitium, **-i** *n*: shame
gena, **-ae** *f.* cheeks (*pl.*)
genialis, **-e**: delightful
globus, **-i** *m*: a dense mass, tuft
impeditus, **-a**, **-um**: bound
imus, **-a**, **-um**: deepest
intueor, (2), **intuitus sum**: to admire
lacteus, **-a**, **-um**: milk-white
lassus, **-a**, **-um**: weary
marcidus, **-a**, **-um**: weak
pallor, **-oris** *m*: paleness
pectus, **-oris** *n*: a heart
pererro, (1): to roam over
poples, **-itis** *m*: a knee
profecto: (*adv.*) certainly
pulchritudo, **-inis** *f.* beauty
purpureus, **-a**, **-um**: dark red
quaero, (3): to seek
recreo, (1): to restore + *gen.*
retropendulus, **-a**, **-um**: hanging down behind
saepe: (*adv.*) many times
salus, **-utis** *f.* salvation
temerarius, **-a**, **-um**: rash
temulentus, **-a**, **-um**: drunken
timor, **-oris** *m*: fear
tremo, (3): to tremble
vultus, **-us** *m*: a face

---

marcido pallore: abl. desc., "grows faint *with weak paleness*"
fecisset: plupf. subj. in past contrafactual apodosis, "which she would have done"
nisi evolasset: syncopated (=*evolavisset*) plupf. subj. in past contrafactual protasis, "if it had not rushed out"
timore: abl. cause, "*from fear* of such a crime"
manibus temerariis: abl. sep., "having slipped *from the rash hands*"
salute: abl. sep., "bereft *of salvation*"
ambrosia: abl. specification, "drunken *with ambrosia*"
pererrantes...impeditos: part. acc., "globs of hair *wandering...having been bound*"
alios...alios: "*some* (tufts of hair) before...*some* behind"

quorum splendore nimio fulgurante jam et ipsum lumen lucernae vacillabat; per umeros volatilis dei pinnae roscidae micanti flore candicant et, quamvis alis quiescentibus, extimae plumulae tenellae ac delicatae tremule resultantes inquieta lasciviunt; ceterum corpus glabellum atque luculentum et quale peperisse Venerem non paeniteret. Ante lectuli pedes jacebat arcus et pharetra et sagittae, magni dei propitia tela.

---

ala, **-ae** *f.* a wing
arcus, **-us** *m*: a bow
candico, (1): to have white appearance, glow
ceterum: for the rest
delicatus, **-a**, **-um**: delicate
extimus, **-a**, **-um**: farthest
flos, **-oris** *m*: a blossom
fulguro, (1): to flash
glabellus, **-a**, **-um**: without hair, smooth
inquietus, **-a**, **-um**: restless
jaceo, (2): to lie
lascivio, (4): to frisk
lectulus, **-i** *m*: a bed
luculentus, **-a**, **-um**: brilliant
micans, **-antis** (*gen.*): gleaming
nimius, **-a**, **-um**: excessive
paeniteo, (2): to displease
pario, (3), **peperi**: to beget
pes, **pedis** *m*: a foot
pharetra, **-ae** *f.* a quiver
pinna, **-ae** *f.* a feather
plumula, **-ae** *f.* a little feather
propitius, **-a**, **-um**: gracious
quiesco, (3): to rest
resulto, (1): to reverberate
roscidus, **-a**, **-um**: dewy
sagitta, **-ae** *f.* an arrow
splendor, **-oris** *m*: brilliance
telum, **-i** *n*: a weapon
tenellus, **-a**, **-um**: tender
tremulus, **-a**, **-um**: trembling
umerus, **-i** *m*: a shoulder
vacillo, (1): to falter
volatilis, **-e**: equipped to fly

---

splendore...fulgurante: abl. abs. causal, "because of the brilliance flashing"
micanti flore: abl. desc., "glows *like a gleaming blossom*"
alis quiescentibus: abl. abs. concessive, "although *with wings resting*"
tremule: "reverberating *tremulously*"
inquieta: neut. pl. used adverbially, "frolic *restlessly*"
peperisse: perf. inf. after *paeniteret*, "displease *to have begotten*"
quale...non paeniteret: impf. subj. in relative clause of characteristic, "such as would not displease"

Curious, Psyche accidentally pricks herself on one of his arrows and falls madly in love with Cupid, but he wakes and flies away.

[23] Quae dum insatiabili animo Psyche, satis et curiosa, rimatur atque pertrectat et mariti sui miratur arma, depromit unam de pharetra sagittam et, puncto pollicis extremam aciem periclitabunda, trementis etiam nunc, articuli nisu fortiore pupugit altius, ut per summam cutem roraverint parvulae sanguinis rosei guttae. Sic ignara Psyche sponte in Amoris incidit amorem. Tunc, magis magisque cupidine fraglans Cupidinis, prona in eum

---

acies, **-ei** *f.* sharpness, a point
altius (**comp. adv.**): more deeply
amor, **-oris** *m*: love
armum, **-i** *n*: weapons (*pl.*)
articulus, **-i** *m*: a joint, finger
curiosus, **-a**, **-um**: curious
cutis, **-is** *f.* a surface, skin
depromo, (3): to draw out
extremus, **-a**, **-um**: extreme
fortis, **-e**: strong
fraglo (1): to burn
gutta, **-ae** *f.* a drop
ignarus, **-a**, **-um**: unaware
incido, (3), **incidi**, **incasus**: to fall in with
insatiabilis, **-e**: insatiable
magis (*adv.*): more
miror, (1), **miratus sum**: to wonder
nisus, **-us** *m*: push
parvulus, **-a**, **-um**: very small
periclitabundus, **-a**, **-um**: testing (+ *acc.*)
pertrecto, (1): to busy oneself with, study
pharetra, **-ae** *f.* a quiver
pollex, **-icis** *m*: a thumb
pronus, **-a**, **-um**: leaning forward
punctum, **-i** *n*: a prick, puncture
pungo, (3), **pupugi**: prick, puncture
rimor, (1), **rimatus sum**: to examine
roro, (1): to drip, moisten
roseus, **-a**, **-um**: rose-colored
sanguis, **-uinis** *m*: blood
sponte: voluntarily
summus, **-a**, **-um**: top
tremo, (3): to tremble

---

insatiabili animo: abl. manner, "with an insatiable spirit"
satis et curiosa: "and quite curious"
rimatur…miratur: note the anagram
puncto: abl. means, "testing *with a puncturing* of the thumb"
extremam aciem: acc. dir. obj. of *periclitabunda*, "testing *the very point*"
trementis…articuli: gen., "of her trembling finger"
nisu fortiore: abl. means, "pricked *with a stronger push*"
ut…roraverint: perf. subj. in result clause, "*so that* drops *moistened*"
in…amorem: "fell *into love*"
Amoris…amorem: note the pun
cupidine…Cupidinis: another pun, "burning *with desire* for the god *of desire*"

efflictim inhians patulis ac petulantibus saviis festinanter ingestis de somni mensura metuebat. Sed dum, bono tanto percita, saucia mente fluctuat, lucerna illa, sive perfidia pessima sive invidia noxia sive quod tale corpus contingere et quasi basiare et ipsa gestiebat, evomuit de summa luminis sui stillam ferventis olei super umerum dei dexterum. Hem, audax et temeraria lucerna et amoris vile ministerium? Ipsum ignis totius deum aduris, cum te scilicet amator aliquis, ut diutius cupitis etiam nocte potiretur, primus invenerit.

---

aduro, (3): to burn
amator, **-oris** *m*: a lover
audax, **-acis** (*gen.*): presumptuous
basio, (1): to kiss
contingo, (3): touch
cupitum, **-i** *n*: one's desire
dexter, **-era**, **-um**: right
diutius: for a longer time
efflictim: (*adv.*) desperately
evomo, (3), **evomui**: to vomit out
ferveo, (2): to burn
festinanter: (*adv.*) hastily
fluctuo, (1): to be agitated
gestio, (4): to be eager, wish passionately
hem: what's that?
ignis, **-is** *m*: fire, passion
ingero, (3), **ingessi**, **ingestus**: to put upon
inhio, (1): to gape
invenio, (4), **inveni**: to invent
invidia, **-ae** *f.* envy
mens, **mentis** *f.* mind
mensura, **-ae** *f.* length, depth
metuo, (3): to be afraid
ministerium, **-i** *n*: an assistant
noxius, **-a**, **-um**: noxious
oleum, **-i** *n*: oil
patulus, **-a**, **-um**: wide open
percitus, **-a**, **-um**: roused
perfidia, **-ae** *f.* treachery
pessimus, **-a**, **-um**: most disloyal
petulans, **-antis** (*gen.*): wanton
potior, (4), **potitus sum**: to possess (+ *abl.*)
saucius, **-a**, **-um**: wounded, ill
savium, **-i** *n*: a kiss
stilla, **-ae** *f.* a drip
summa, **-ae** *f.* essence
temerarius, **-a**, **-um**: reckless
umerus, **-i** *m*: a shoulder
vilis, **-e**: worthless

---

patulis ac petulantibus saviis ingestis: abl. abs., "with wide open and wanton kisses having been planted"
bono tanto: abl. means, "roused *by such good*"
mente: abl. specification, "wounded *in her mind*," i.e. by Cupid's arrow
perfidia pessima sive invidia noxia: abl. cause, "whether because of most disloyal treachery or noxious envy"
contingere et quasi basiare: pr. inf. after *gestiebat*, "eager *to touch and kiss*"
Hem: an apostrophe to the lamp
ut...potiretur: impf. subj. deponent in purp. clause, "so that he might possess"
cupitis: abl. with *potiretur*, "possess *one's desires*"
nocte: abl. time, "in the night"
invenerit: perf. subj. in concessive clause, "*although* some lover *invented*"

Sic inustus, exiluit deus, visaque detectae fidei colluvie, prorsus ex osculis et manibus infelicissimae conjugis tacitus avolavit.

Psyche follows by holding his leg. Cupid explains his unintended love for Psyche and punishes her by leaving her.

[24] At Psyche statim resurgentis eius crure dextero manibus ambabus adrepto sublimis evectionis adpendix miseranda, et per nubilas plagas, penduli comitatus extrema consequia, tandem fessa delabitur solo. Nec deus amator humi jacentem deserens involavit proximam cupressum deque eius alto cacumine sic eam graviter commotus adfatur: "Ego quidem, simplicissima Psyche, parentis

---

adfor, (1), **adfatus sum**: to address
adpendix, **-icis** *f.* an attachment, hanger on
adripio, (3), **adripui**, **adreptus**: to seize
altus, **-a**, **-um**: high
ambo, **-ae**, **-o**: both
avolo, (1): to fly away
cacumen, **-inis** *n*: the tip of a tree
colluvies, **-ei** *f.* filth
comitatus, **-us** *m*: escort
commoveo, (2), **commovi**, **commotus**: to agitate
conjunx, **-ugis** *f.* a wife
consequia, **-ae** *f.* rear guard
crus, **-uris** *n*: a leg
cupressus, **-us** *f.* a cypress-tree
delabor, (3), **delapsus sum**: to fall
desero, (3): to abandon
detego, (3), **detexi**, **detectus**: to remove
dexter, **-era**, **-um**: right
evectio, **-onis** *f.* ascension
exilio, (4), **exilui**: to leap up
fessus, **-a**, **-um**: exhausted
fides, **-ei** *f.* faith
graviter: (*adv.*) deeply
humus, **-i** *f.* ground
infelix, **-icis** (*gen.*): wretched
inuro, (3), **inussi**, **inustus**: to scorch
involo, (1): to fly into
jaceo, (2): to lie
miserandus, **-a**, **-um**: pitiable
nubilus, **-a**, **-um**: cloudy
osculum, **-i** *n*: lips
pendulus, **-a**, **-um**: hanging
plaga, **-ae** *f.* an open expanse of sky
resurgo, (3): to rise
simplex, **-icis** (*gen.*): simple
solum, **-i** *n*: ground
sublimis, **-e**: lofty
taceo, (2), **tacui**, **tacitus**: to pass over in silence
tandem: after some time

---

visa...colluvie: abl. abs., "with the filth having been seen"
detectae fidei: gen., "filth *of the faith removed*"
crure dextero...adrepto: abl. abs., "his right leg having been seized"
manibus ambabus: abl. means, "seized *with both hands*"
adpendix...consequia: nom. in appos. to Psyche, "she, an attachment...a rear guard"
sublimis evectionis: gen. after *adpendix*, "Psyche, an attachment *to his lofty ascension*"
penduli comitatus: gen. after *consequia*, "Psyche, the rear guard *of his hanging escort*"
solo: abl. place where, "fell *on the ground*"
jacentem: "her *lying* on the ground"

meae Veneris praeceptorum immemor, quae te miseri extremique hominis devinctam cupidine infimo matrimonio addici jusserat, ipse potius amator advolavi tibi. Sed hoc feci leviter, scio, et, praeclarus ille sagittarius, ipse me telo meo percussi teque conjugem meam feci, ut bestia scilicet tibi viderer et ferro caput excideres meum quod istos amatores tuos oculos gerit. Haec tibi identidem semper cavenda censebam, haec benivole remonebam. Sed illae quidem consiliatrices egregiae tuae tam perniciosi magisterii

---

addico, (3): to doom
advolo, (1): to fly to (+ *dat.*)
benivole: (*adv.*) in a spirit of good will
bestia, **-ae** *f.* a beast
caveo, (2): to avoid
censeo, (2): to advise
conjunx, **-ugis** *f.* a wife
consiliatrix, **-icis** *f.* an adviser
cupido, **-inis** *n*: desire
devinctus, **-a**, **-um**: captivated
egregius, **-a**, **-um**: excellent
excido, (3): to cut off
ferrum, **-i** *n*: a sword
gero, (3): to carry
homo, **-inis** *m*: a man
identidem: again and again
immemor, **-oris**: heedless of (+ *gen.*)
infimus, **-a**, **-um**: vilest
jubeo, (2), **jussi**: to order
leviter: (*adv.*) thoughtlessly
magisterium, **-i** *n*: instruction
matrimonium, **-i** *n*: marriage
miser, **-era**, **-um**: wretched
percutio, (3), **percussi**: to pierce
perniciosus, **-a**, **-um**: destructive
potius: rather
praeceptum, **-i** *n*: an order
praeclarus, **-a**, **-um**: famous
remoneo, (2): to warn again
sagittarius, **-i** *m*: an archer
telum, **-i** *n*: a weapon
video, (2): to see; (pass.) seem

---

te...devinctam: perf. part., "you, having been captivated"
cupidine: abl. means, "captivated *by desire*"
infimo matrimonio: dat. after *addici*, "doomed *to the vilest marriage*"
te...addici: inf. pass. in ind. com. after *iusserat*, "who had order *you to be doomed*"
telo meo: abl. means, "I struck myself *with my weapon*"
coniugem meam: acc. pred. after *feci*, "I made you *my wife*"
ut...viderer...excideres: impf. subj. in result clause, "so that I seemed...so that you tried to cut"
ferro: abl. means, "cut *with a sword*"
quod...gerit: "the head *which carries*"
istos amatores: appositive, "those eyes *that are your lovers*"
Haec...cavenda (sc. esse): future passive participle in ind. st. after *censebam*, "I advised *that these things must be avoided*"
egregiae: ironic

dabunt actutum mihi poenas, te vero tantum fuga mea punivero." Et cum termino sermonis pinnis in altum se proripuit.

Psyche attempts to drown herself and is comforted by the god Pan.

[25] Psyche vero humi prostrata et, quantum visi poterat, volatus mariti prospiciens extremis affligebat lamentationibus animum. Sed ubi, remigio plumae raptum, maritum proceritas spatii fecerat alienum, per proximi fluminis marginem praecipitem sese dedit. Sed mitis fluvius in honorem dei, scilicet qui et ipsas aquas urere consuevit, metuens sibi confestim eam innoxio volumine super

---

actutum: (*adv.*) immediately
affligo, (3): to afflict
alienus, **-i** *m*: a stranger
altum, **-i** *n*: a height (of sky)
aqua, **-ae** *f.* water
confestim: (*adv.*) immediately
consuesco, (2), **consuevi**: to be accustomed to (+ *inf.*)
do, (1): to give, pay
flumen, **-inis** *n*: a river
fluvius, **-i** *m*: a river
fuga, **-ae** *f.* flight
honor, **-oris** *m*: honor
humi (*locative*): on the ground
innoxius, **-a**, **-um**: harmless
lamentatio, **-onis** *f.* lamentation
margo, **-inis** *f.* an edge
metuo, (3): to fear
mitis, **-e**: gentle
pluma, **-ae** *f.* plumage
poena, **-ae** *f.* penalty
praeceps, **-ipitis** (*gen.*): headlong
proceritas, **-atis** *f.* great length
proripio, (3), **proripui**: to rush forth
prospicio, (3): to watch for
prosterno, (3), **prostravi**, **prostratus**: to prostrate
punio, (4), **punivi**: to punish
quantum: so much as
rapio, (3), **rapui**, **raptus**: to carry off
remigium, **-i** *n*: rowing, oarage
spatium, **-i** *n*: an intervening space
terminus, **-i** *m*: an end
uro, (3): to burn
viso, (3): to visit, see
volatus, **-us** *m*: flight
volumen, **-inis** *n*: a fold, wave

---

fuga mea: abl. means, "punished *with my flight*"
punivero: fut. perf., "you *I will have punished*"
cum termino: abl. attend. circumstance, a common usage in Apuleius, "and with the end of his speech"
pinnis: abl. means, "rushed forth *on wings*"
visi: pr. inf. pass. of *viso* after *poterat*, "possible *to be seen*"
extremis...lamentationibus: abl. means, "afflicting her mind *with the most extreme lamentations*"
remigio: abl. means, "carried off *by the oarage* of his plumage"
alienum: acc. pred., "made her husband *a stranger*"
dei: i.e. Cupid
innoxio volumine: abl. manner, "put forth *with a harmless surge*"

ripam florentem herbis exposuit. Tunc forte Pan, deus rusticus juxta supercilium amnis sedebat complexus Echo montanam deam eamque voculas omnimodas edocens recinere; proxime ripam vago pastu lasciviunt comam fluvii tondentes capellae. Hircuosus deus sauciam Psychen atque defectam, utcumque casus eius non inscius, clementer ad se vocatam sic permulcet verbis lenientibus: "Puella scitula, sum quidem rusticans et upilio, sed senectutis prolixae beneficio multis experimentis instructus. Verum si recte conjecto,

---

amnis, **-is** *m*: a river
beneficium, **-i** *n*: a benefit
capella, **-ae** *f.* a little goat
casus, **-us** *m*: a fall
clementer: (*adv.*) softly
coma, **-ae** *f.* hair
complector, (3), **complexus sum**: to embrace
conjecto, (1): to guess
defectus, **-a**, **-um**: worn out
Echo, **-us** *f.* Echo, a nymph
edoceo, (2): to teach thoroughly
experimentum, **-i** *n*: experience
expono, (3), **exposui**, **expositus**: to put forth
florens, **-entis** (*gen.*): flowering
fors, **fortis** *f.* chance
herba, **-ae** *f.* an herb
hircuosus, **-a**, **-um**: goat-like
inscius, **-a**, **-um**: ignorant
instructus, **-a**, **-um**: equipped
juxta: near (+ *acc.*)
lascivio, (4): to frisk
lenio, (4): to calm
montanus, **-a**, **-um**: mountainous
omnimodus, **-a**, **-um**: of all sorts
Pan, **Panos** *m*: Greek god of shepherds
pastus, **-us** *m*: fodder, feeding
permulceo, (2): to soothe
prolixus, **-a**, **-um**: ample
recino, (3): to chant back
ripa, **-ae** *f.* a bank
rusticans, **-antis** (*gen.*): rustic
rusticus, **-a**, **-um**: country
saucius, **-a**, **-um**: wounded
scitulus, **-a**, **-um**: elegant
sedeo, (2): to sit
senectus, **-utis** *f.* old age
supercilium, **-i** *n*: an eyebrow
tondeo, (2): to clip, shave
upilio, **-onis** *m*: a shepherd
vagus, **-a**, **-um**: roving
voco, (1): to summon
vocula, **-ae** *f.* a petty speech

---

herbis: abl. after *florentem*, "flowering *with herbs*"
forte: abl. manner, "by chance"
supercilium: "eyebrow," i.e. overhanging ledge or "brow" of the river
Echo: acc. s., "embracing *Echo*" a nymph loved by Pan
eamque...recinere: pr. inf. in ind. st. after *edocens*, "teaching *her to chant back*"
vago pastu: abl. circumstance, "clipping *in a roving feeding*"
casus eius: gen. after *inscius*, "not ignorant *of her situation*"
vocatam: perf. part., "her *having been summoned* to himself "
verbis lenientibus: abl. means, "soothes *with calming words*"
beneficio: abl. cause, "because of *the benefit*"
multis experimentis: abl. means, "equipped *by many experiences*"

quod profecto prudentes viri divinationem autumant, ab isto titubante et saepius vaccillante vestigio deque minio pallore corporis et assiduo suspiritu immo et ipsis marcentibus oculis tuis amore nimio laboras. Ergo mihi ausculta: nec te rursus praecipitio vel ullo mortis accersitae genere perimas. Luctum desine et pone maerorem precibusque potius Cupidinem, deorum maximum, percole et utpote adolescentem delicatum luxuriosumque blandis obsequiis promerere."

---

accersitus, **-a**, **-um**: self-inflicted
adolescens, **-entis** *m*: a young man
assiduus, **-a**, **-um**: incessant
ausculto, (1): to listen (to), obey
autumo, (1): to call
blandus, **-a**, **-um**: flattering
delicatus, **-a**, **-um**: delicate
desino, (3): to cease
divinatio, **-onis** *f.* prophecy
genus, **-eris** *n*: a kind
immo: indeed
laboro, (1): to be sick
luctus, **-us** *m*: mourning
luxuriosus, **-a**, **-um**: luxurious
maeror, **-oris** *m*: sorrow
marceo, (2): to droop, wither
maximus, **-a**, **-um**: greatest
minius, **-a**, **-um**: red
obsequium, **-i** *n*: deference
pallor, **-oris** *m*: paleness
percolo, (3): to honor thoroughly
perimo, (3): to kill
pono, (3): to lay aside
potius (*adv.*): rather, instead
praecipitium, **-i** *n*: a throwing headlong
profecto: (*adv.*) surely
promereor, (2): to propitiate, render favorable
prudens, **-entis** (*gen.*): farseeing
rursus (*adv.*): again
suspiritus, **-us** *m*: a sigh
titubo, (1): to stagger
utpote: inasmuch as
vaccillo (1): to reel, stagger

---

quod...autumant: in apposition to *recte coniecto*, "*which* wise men *call* divination"
ab isto titubante et...vaccillante vestigio: abl. cause, "from that staggering and reeling step"
de minio pallore...et assiduo suspiritu...et ipsis marcentibus oculis tuis: abl. cause, "from the red paleness and incessent sigh and those your drooping eyes"
amore: abl. of cause, "you are sick *from love*"
nec...perimas: pr. subj. in prohibition, "do not kill!"
praecipitio: abl. means, "kill *by throwing headlong*"
ullo...genere: abl. means, "kill *by any kind*"
Luctum desine et pone maerorem: note chiasmus
precibus: abl. means, "honor *with prayers*"
blandis obsequiis: abl. means, "propitiate *with flattering deferences*"
promerere: deponent imper., "render him favorable!"

Psyche takes action, beginning with vengeance against her sisters.

[26] Sic locuto deo pastore nulloque sermone reddito sed adorato tantum numine salutari Psyche pergit ire. Sed cum aliquam multum viae laboranti vestigio pererrasset, inscia quodam tramite jam die labente accedit quandam civitatem, in qua regnum maritus unius sororis eius optinebat. Qua re cognita, Psyche nuntiari praesentiam suam sorori desiderat; mox inducta mutuis amplexibus alternae salutationis expletis percontanti causas adventus sui

---

accedo, (3): to approach
adoro, (1): to honor
adventus, **-us** *m*: an arrival
aliquam: (*adv.*) to a large extent
alternus, **-a**, **-um**: reciprocal
amplexus, **-us** *m*: an embrace
causa, **-ae** *f*: a reason
civitas, **-atis** *f*: a city
cognosco, (3), **cognovi**, **cognitus**: to learn
desidero, (1): to request
eo, **ire**, **ivi**, **itus**: to advance
expleo, (2), **explevi**, **expletus**: to complete
induco, (3), **induxi**, **inductus**: to lead in
inscius, **-a**, **-um**: unknown
labor, (3), **lapsus sum**: to slip
laboro, (1): to be troubled
loquor, (3), **locutus sum**: to speak
mox (*adv.*): soon
mutuus, **-a**, **-um**: mutual
nullus, **-i** *m*: no one
nuntio, (1): to announce
optineo, (2): to hold fast
pastor, **-oris** *m*: a shepherd
percontor, (1), **percontatus sum**: to inquire repeatedly
pererro, (1): to wander through
praesentia, **-ae** *f*: presence
reddo, (3), **reddidi**, **redditus**: to return
regnum, **-i** *n*: royal power
salutaris, **-e**: helpful
salutatio, **-onis** *f*: greeting
trames, **-itis** *m*: track
via, **-ae** *f*: a journey

---

locuto deo pastore: abl. abs., "the shepherd god speaking"
nullo sermone reddito: abl. abs., "with no speech having been returned"
adorato...numine salutari: abl. abs., "with the helpful divinity having been honored"
cum...pererrasset: syncopated plupf. subj. (=*peraverrasset*) in temporal clause, "when she had wandered"
aliquam multum: idiomatic for "*a fair amount* of the way"
laboranti vestigio: abl. manner, "with a laboring step"
inscia quodam tramite: abl. place where, "on an unknown track"
die labente: abl. abs., "with daylight slipping"
Qua re cognita: abl. abs., "which fact having been learned"
nuntiari: pr. inf. pass., "desires her presence *to be announced*"
mutuis amplexibus...expletis: abl. abs., "mutual embraces having been completed"
percontanti: dat. ind. obj., "begins (to speak) *to her (the sister) inquiring*"
adventus sui: gen., "causes *of her (Psyche's) visit*"

sic incipit: "Meministi consilium vestrum, scilicet quo mihi suasistis ut bestiam, quae mariti mentito nomine mecum quiescebat, prius quam ingluvie voraci me misellam hauriret, ancipiti novacula peremerem. Set cum primum, ut aeque placuerat, conscio lumine vultus eius aspexi, video mirum divinumque prorsus spectaculum, ipsum illum deae Veneris filium, ipsum inquam Cupidinem, leni quiete sopitum. Ac dum, tanti boni spectaculo percita et nimia voluptatis copia, turbata fruendi laborarem inopia, casu scilicet

---

aeque (*adv.*): in like manner
anceps, **-ipitis** (*gen.*): two-edged
aspicio, (3), **aspexi**: to behold
bestia, **-ae** *f.* a beast
bonum, **-i** *n*: good
casus, **-us** *m*: an accident
conscius, **-a**, **-um**: conspiratorial
consilium, **-i** *n*: advice
copia, **-ae** *f.* an amount
fruor, (3), **fructus sum**: to enjoy
haurio, (4): to swallow
incipio, (3): to begin
ingluvies, **-ei** *f.* gluttony
inopia, **-ae** *f.* a need
laboro, (1): to be troubled
lenis, **-e**: calm
memini, (2): to remember
mentior, (4), **mentitus sum**: to deceive
mirus, **-a**, **-um**: wonderful
misellus, **-a**, **-um**: poor, miserable
nimius, **-a**, **-um**: too great
novacula, **-ae** *f.* a razor
percio, (4), **percivi**, **percitus**: to excite
peremo, (3): to destroy, kill
placeo, (2), **placui**: to satisfy
prorsus: (*adv.*) utterly
quies, **-etis** *f.* a rest
quiesco, (3): to rest
scilicet: namely
sopio, (4), **sopivi**, **sopitus**: to cause to sleep
spectaculum, **-i** *n*: a spectacle
suadeo, (2), **suasi**: to suggest
turbo, (1): to agitate
voluptas, **-atis** *f.* delight
vorax, **-acis** *m*: voracious devouring

---

ut...peremerem: impf. subj. in jussive noun clause after *suasistis*, "you persuaded me *that I kill*"
mentito nomine: abl. specification, "the husband *with the deceiving name*"
prius quam...hauriret: impf. subj. in anticipatory clause, "before he could drink me"
ingluvie voraci: abl. manner, "drink *with his voracious gluttony*"
ancipiti novacula: abl. means, "kill *with a two-edged razor*"
cum primum...aspexi: "as soon as I saw"
ut aeque placuerat: "as it had been equally pleasing," i.e. as had been agreed
conscio lumine: abl. means, "beheld *by a conspiratorial light*"
inquam: interjection, "I tell you!"
leni quiete: abl. specification, "sleeping *in a calm rest*"
spectaclo: abl. means, "excited *by the spectacle*"
nimia...copia: abl. means, "excited *by too great an amount*"
dum...laborarem: impf. subj. circumstantial, "while...I was troubled"
inopia: abl. means, "agitated *by the scarcity* of enjoying," i.e. by the desire
casu...pessumo: abl. cause, "by the worst accident"

pessumo lucerna fervens oleum rebullivit in eius umerum. Quo dolore statim somno recussus, ubi me ferro et igni conspexit armatam, "Tu quidem," inquit, "ob istud tam dirum facinus, confestim toro meo divorte tibique res tuas habeto. Ego vero sororem tuam" — et nomen quo tu censeris aiebat — "iam mihi confarreatis nuptis conjugabo," et statim Zephyro praecipit ultra terminos me domus eius efflaret."

---

aio, (1): to say
armo, (1): to equip
censeo, (2): to distinguish, be known
confarreo, (1): to contract marriage
confestim: (*adv.*) without delay
conjugo, (1): to join together
conspicio, (3), **conspexi**: to see
dirus, **-a**, **-um**: dire
divorto, (3): to turn away
dolor, **-oris** *m*: pain
efflo, (1): to blow
facinus, **-oris** *n*: a deed
ferrum, **-i** *n*: a weapon
ferveo, (3): to burn
ignis, **-is** *m*: fire
lucerna, **-ae** *f*: an oil lamp
nuptiae, **-arum** *f*: a bride
oleum, **-i** *n*: oil
pessumus, **-a**, **-um**: worst
praecipio, (3): to instruct
rebullio, (4), **rebullivi**: to bubble back
recutio, (3), **recussi**, **recussus**: to strike
terminus, **-i** *m*: a boundary
torus, **-i** *m*: a bed
umerus, **-i** *m*: a shoulder

Quo dolore: abl. means, "*by which pain* having been struck"
somno: abl. sep., "struck *from sleep*"
me...armatam: perf. part. circumstantial, "he saw *me equipped*"
ferro et igni: abl. specification, "equipped *with a weapon and fire*"
toro meo: abl. sep., "turn away *from my bed!*"
divorte...habeto: imper., "*turn away!...keep* your property!" These serve as official formulas for Roman divorce.
quo tu censeris: pr. pass., "the name *by which you are called*"
confarreatis nuptis: abl. abs., "with marriages contracted," referring to the solemn form of marriage reserved for patricians
Zephyro: dat. ind. obj., "orders *Zephyr* "
efflaret: impf. subj. in ind. command after *praecipit*, "he ordered Zephyr *to blow*"

Psyche's two sisters are destroyed.

[27] Necdum sermonem Psyche finierat, et illa, vesanae libidinis et invidiae noxiae stimulis agitata, e re concinnato mendacio fallens maritum, quasi de morte parentum aliquid comperisset, statim navem ascendit et ad illum scopulum protinus pergit et, quamvis alio flante vento, caeca spe tamen inhians, "accipe me," dicens, "Cupido, dignam te conjugem, et tu, Zephyre, suscipe dominam," saltu se maximo praecipitem dedit. Nec tamen ad illum locum vel saltem mortua pervenire potuit. Nam per saxa cautium

---

agito, (1): to drive
ascendo, (3), **ascendi, ascensus**: to embark
caecus, **-a**, **-um**: blind
cautes, **-is** *f.* a cliff
comperio, (4): to learn
concinnatus, **-a**, **-um**: elaborate
conjunx, **-ugis** *f.* a consort
dignus, **-a**, **-um**: deserving of (+ *abl.*)
do, (1), **dedi, datus**: to give
fallo, (3): to deceive
finio, (4): to finish
flo, (1): to blow
inhio, (1): to gape
invidia, **-ae** *f.* jealousy
libido, **-idinis** *f.* desire
locus, -i *m*: a place
maximus, **-a**, **-um**: highest
mendacium, **-i** *n*: a lie
mortuus, **-a**, **-um**: dead
navis, **-is** *f.* a ship
necdum: not yet
noxius, **-a**, **-um**: noxious
pervenio, (4): to arrive
praeceps, **-ipitis** (*gen.*): headlong
protinus: (*adv.*) straight on
quasi: as though
saltem: at the least
saltus, **-us** *m*: a jump
saxum, **-i** *n*: a stone
spes, **-ei** *f.* hope
stimulus, **-i** *m*: a spur
suscipio, (3): to receive, take up
ventus, **-i** *m*: wind
vesanus, **-a**, **-um**: frenzied

---

stimulis: abl. means, "driven *by the spurs*"
concinnato mendacio: abl. means, "deceiving *with an elaborate lie*"
quasi…comperisset: plupf. subj. in past contrafactual protasis, with apodosis suppressed, "as (she would have) if she had learned"
alio flante vento: abl. abs., "although another wind blowing," i.e. a contrary wind
spe: abl. specification, "blind *with hope*"
te: abl. after *dignam*, "worthy *of you*"
saltu maximo: abl. means, "gave herself *with the highest jump*"
Nec…vel saltem: "not…nor at the least"

membris jactatis atque dissipatis, et proinde ut merebatur, laceratis visceribus suis alitibus bestiisque obvium ferens pabulum interiit.

Nec vindictae sequentis poena tardavit. Nam Psyche rursus errabundo gradu pervenit ad civitatem aliam, in qua pari modo soror morabatur alia. Nec setius et ipsa fallacie germanitatis inducta, et in sororis sceleratas nuptias aemula festinavit ad scopulum inque simile mortis exitium cecidit.

---

aemula, **-ae** *f.* a rival
ales, **-itis** *m:* a bird
cado, (3), **cecidi**: to fall
dissipo, (1): to scatter
errabundus, **-a**, **-um**: wandering
exitium, **e-i** *n:* ruin
fallacies, **-ei** *f.* deceit
fero, **ferre**, **tuli**, **latus**: to offer
germanitas, **-atis** *f.* sisterhood
gradus, **-us** *m:* a step, position
induco, (3), **induxi**, **inductus**: to mislead
intereo, **-ire**, **-ivi**, **-itus**: to perish
jacto, (1): to jerk about
lacero, (1): to mangle
membrum, **-i** *n:* a limb
mereor, (2), **meritus sum**: to earn
modus, **-i** *m:* a manner
moror, (1), **moratus sum**: to stay
obvius, **-a**, **-um**: easy
pabulum, **-i** *n:* food
par, **paris** (*gen.*): like
pervenio, (4), **perveni**: to arrive
poena, **-ae** *f.* punishment
proinde: according to
rursus: again
sceleratus, **-a**, **-um**: atrocious
sequor, (3), **secutus sum**: to follow
setius: less
similis, **-e**: similar
tardo, (1): to be late
vindicta, **ae** *f.* an act of revenge
viscer, **-eris** *n:* entrails

---

membris iactatis atque dissipatis: abl. abs., "with limbs having been jerked apart and scattered"
laceratis visceribus suis: abl. abs., "her own entrails having been mangled"
alitibus bestiisque: dat. ind. obj. with *ferens*, "providing *to the birds and beasts*"
errabundo gradu: abl. manner, "with a wandering step"
pari modo: abl. manner, "in like manner"
fallacie: abl. means, "mislead *by the deceit*"
aemula: nom., "the rival," i.e. the second sister

Cupid, lovelorn and pained by his burn, retreats to his mother's house. A gull informs Venus about Cupid and Psyche

[28] Interim, dum Psyche quaestioni Cupidinis intenta populos circumibat, at ille vulnere lucernae dolens in ipso thalamo matris jacens ingemebat. Tunc avis peralba, illa gavia, quae super fluctus marinos pinnis natat, demergit sese propere ad Oceani profundum gremium. Ibi commodum Venerem lavantem natantemque propter assistens, indicat adustum filium eius gravi vulneris dolore maerentem dubium salutis jacere, jamque per cunctorum ora populorum rumoribus conviciisque variis omnem Veneris familiam male

---

aduro, (3), **adussi**, **adustus**: to burn
assisto, (3): to stand before, appear (before)
avis, **-is** *f.* a bird
circumeo, **-ire**, **-ivi**, **-itus**: to wander through
commodum: at this moment
convicium, **-i** *n*: reproof
cunctus, **-a**, **-um**: all
demergo, (3): to plunge
doleo, (2): to be pained
dolor, **-oris** *m*: suffering
dubius, **-a**, **-um**: variable, doubtful of (+ *gen.*)
familia, **-ae** *f.* a household
fluctus, **-us** *m*: a wave
gavia, **-ae**: gull
gravis, **-e**: oppressive
gremium, **-i** *n*: a lap
indico, (1): to reveal
ingemo, (3): to groan
intentus, **-a**, **-um**: intent on (+ *dat.*)
interim: meanwhile
jaceo, (2): to lie
lavo, (1): to bathe
lucerna, **-ae** *f.* an oil lamp
maereo, (2): to grieve
male: (*adv.*) badly
marinus, **-a**, **-um**: marine
nato, (1): to swim
Oceanus, **-i** *m*: Ocean
os, oris *n*: a mouth
peralbus, **-a**, **-um**: pure white
profundus, **-a**, **-um**: deep
propere: (*adv.*) quickly
quaestio, **-onis** *f.* a search for (+ *gen.*)
rumor, **-oris** *m*: rumor
salus, -utis *f.* welfare, safety
thalamus, **-i** *m*: a bedroom
varius, **-a**, **-um**: diverse
vulnus, **-eris** *n*: a wound

---

at ille: "but he," i.e. Cupid
vulnere: abl. cause, "grieving *from the wound*"
pinnis: abl. means, "swims *with his wings*"
filium...iacere: ind. st. after *indicat*, "reports *that her son is lying*"
gravi...dolore: abl. cause, "grieving *from the oppressive suffering*"
rumoribus conviciisque variis: abl. means, "with diverse rumors and reproofs"
familiam male audire: ind. st. after *indicat*, "*reveals that the whole family is hearing badly*," i.e. is being badmouthed

audire, quod ille quidem montano scortatu tu vero marino natatu secesseritis, ac per hoc non voluptas ulla non gratia non lepos, sed incompta et agrestia et horrida cuncta sint; non nuptiae conjugales, non amicitiae sociales, non liberum caritates, sed enormis colluvies et squalentium foederum insuave fastidium. Haec illa verbosa et satis curiosa avis, in auribus Veneris fili lacerans existimationem ganniebat.

At Venus irata solidum exclamat repente: "Ergo jam ille bonus filius meus habet amicam aliquam? Prome agedum, quae sola mihi servis amanter, nomen eius quae puerum ingenuum et investem

---

agedum: come!
agrestis, **-e**: wild
amanter: (*adv.*) lovingly
amica, **-ae** *f.* a mistress
amicitia, **-ae** *f.* friendship
audio, (4): to be able to hear
auris, **-is** *f.* an ear
avis, **-is** *f.* a bird
bonus, **-a**, **-um**: good
caritas, **-atis** *f.* affection
colluvies, **-ei** *f.* muck
conjugalis, **-e**: faithful
curiosus, **-a**, **-um**: meddlesome
enormis, **-e**: shapeless
exclamo, (1): to exclaim
existimatio, **-onis** *f.* reputation
fastidium, **-i** *n*: disgust
foedus, **-eris** *n*: unions
gannio, (4): to speak hostilely
gratia, **-ae** *f.* charm
horridus, **-a**, **-um**: rough
incomptus, **-a**, **-um**: unpolished
ingenuus, **-a**, **-um**: noble
insuavis, **-e**: disagreeable
investis, **-e**: unclothed, infant-like
iratus, **-a**, **-um**: enraged
lacero, (1): to slander
lepos, **-oris** *m*: humor
liber, **-i** *m*: children (*pl.*)
marinus, **-a**, **-um**: of the sea
montanus, **-a**, **-um**: mountainous
natatus, **-us** *m*: swimming
promo, (3): to bring out
repente: (*adv.*) suddenly
scortor, (1): to go whoring
secedo, (3), **secessi**: to withdraw
servio, (4): to serve
socialis, **-e**: allied
solidus, **-a**, **-um**: unbroken
squaleo, (2): to be dirty
verbosus, **-a**, **-um**: verbose
voluptas, **-atis** *f.* pleasure

---

quod...secesseritis: perf. subj. in ind. st., "(alleging) *that you have withdrawn*"
ille quidem...tu vero: "that *that one... but you*"
montano scortatu: abl. supine, "by whoring in the mountains"
marino natatu: abl. supine, "by swimming in the sea"
cuncta sint: pr. subj. in ind. st., "(alleging) *that all are* unpolished"
solidum: adverbial neuter, "unbrokenly"
quae...servis: "you who serve"
quae...sollicitavit: "of her *who seduced*"

sollicitavit, sive illa de Nympharum populo seu de Horarum numero seu de Musarum choro vel de mearum Gratiarum ministerio." Nec loquax illa conticuit avis, sed: "Nescio," inquit "domina: puto puellam, si probe memini, Psyches nomine dici: illam dicitu refflicte cupere." Tunc indignata Venus exclamavit vel maxime: "Psychen, ille meae formae succubam, mei nominis aemulam vere diligit? Nimirum illud incrementum lenam me putavit cuius monstratu puellam illam cognosceret."

---

aemula, **-ae** *f.* a rival
chorus, **-i** *m*: a chorus
cognosco, (3): to become acquainted with
conticesco, (3), **conticui**: to fall silent
cupio, (3): to desire
diligo, (3): to love
efflicte: (*adv.*) desperately
exclamo, (1): to exclaim
forma, **-ae** *f.* beauty
Gratia, **-iae** *f.* grace, the Graces (*pl.*)
Hora, **-ae** *f.* an hour, season, the Horae (*pl.*)
incrementum, **-i** *n*: an offshoot
indignor, (1): to be indignant
lena, **-ae** *f.* a brothel-keeper
loquax, **-acis** (*gen.*): talkative
memini, (2): to remember
ministerium, **-i** *n*: a staff, staff of assistants
monstro, (1): to teach
Musa, **-ae** *f.* a muse, the Muses (*pl.*)
nescio, (4): to not know
nimirum: without doubt
nomen, **-inis** *n*: a title
numerus, **-i** *m*: a number
Nympha, **-ae** *f.* a nymph
probe: (*adv.*) rightly
puto, (1): to think
sollicito, (1): to stir up, seduce
succuba, **-ae** *f.* a succubus, surrogate
vere: truly

Nympharum: minor female nature deities
Horarum: literally the "Hours," three goddesses of the seasons
Musarum: nine goddesses of inspiration of literature, science, and the arts
Gratiarum: goddesses of charm, beauty, nature, human creativity, and fertility
Psyches: gen., "by the name *of Psyche*"
dici: pr. pas. inf. in ind. st. after *puto*: "I think her *to be called*"
dicitur...cupere: personal form of ind. st., "he is said to desire"
efflicte: adverb (=*efflictim*), "desperately"
vel maxime: "rather loudly"
Psychen: acc. obj. of *diligit*, "he loves *Psyche*?"
lenam me (sc. esse): ind. st. after *putavit*, "he thought *me to be a brothel-keeper*"
cuius...cognosceret: impf. subj. in relative clause of characteristic, "by whose instruction *he might come to know*"
monstratu: supine in abl. means, "by instruction"

Venus flies to Cupid in a rage and threatens him.

[29] Haec quiritans, properiter emergit e mari suumque protinus aureum thalamum petit et reperto, sicut audierat, aegroto puero, jam inde a foribus quam maxime boans: "Honesta," inquit, "haec et natalibus nostris bonaeque tuae frugi congruentia, ut primum quidem tuae parentis, immo dominae, praecepta calcares, nec sordidis amoribus inimicam meam cruciares? Verum etiam hoc, aetatis puer, tuis licentiosis et immaturis jungeres amplexibus, ut ego nurum scilicet tolerarem inimicam. Sed utique praesumis, nugo

---

aegrotus, **-a**, **-um**: pining
aetas, **-atis** *f.* age
amplexus, **-us** *m*: an embrace
audio, (4): to hear
aureus, **-a**, **-um**: golden, gleaming
bonus, **-a**, **-um**: noble
boo, (1): to roar
calco, (1): to trample on
congruens, **-entis** (*gen.*): appropriate to (+ *dat.*)
crucio, (1): to torment
emergo, (3): to emerge
foris, **-is** *f.* an entrance
frux, **-ugis** *f.* an honest man
honestus, **-a**, **-um**: honorable
immaturus, **-a**, **-um**: untimely
immo: more correctly
inde: thence
inimica, **-ae** *f.* an enemy
inimicus, **-a**, **-um**: hostile
jungo, (3): to unite
licentiosus, **-a**, **-um**: wanton
mare, **-is** *n*: sea
natalis, **-is** *m*: an origin
nugo, **-onis** *m*: a trifler
nurus, **-us** *f.* a daughter-in-law
peto, (3): to make for
praesumo, (3): to presume
properiter: (*adv.*) quickly
protinus: (*adv.*) immediately
quiritor, (1): to protest
reperio, (4), **repperi**, **repertus**: to discover
sordidus, **-a**, **-um**: vulgar
thalamus, **-i** *m*: a bedroom
tolero, (1): to endure
utique: (*adv.*) assuredly

---

reperto...aegroto puero: abl. abs., "the pining boy having been discovered"
quam maxime: "as loudly as possible"
Honesta...congruentia: nom. pred., "are these things *honorable and appropriate*?"
ut...calcares: impf. subj. in noun clause in apposition to *congruentia*, "appropriate *that that you trample on*"
immo dominae: gen. correcting *parentis*, "of your parent, *or rather of your mistress*"
nec...cruciares: impf. subj. in noun clause after *congruentia*, "appropriate *that you do not torment*"
sordidis amoribus: abl. means, "torment *with vulgur passions*"
tuis licentiosis et immaturis...amplexibus: abl. means, "embrace *with your wanton and untimely embraces*"
jungeres: impf. subj. in noun clause in apposition to *hoc*, "but also this, *namely you would unite*"
nurum: pred. acc., "endure an enemy as a *daughter-in-law*"
ut...tolerarem: impf. subj. in result clause, "so that I endure"

et corruptor et inamabilis, te solum generosum nec me jam per aetatem posse concipere. Velim ergo scias multo te meliorem filium alium genituram, immo ut contumeliam magis sentias aliquem de meis adoptaturam vernulis, eique donaturam istas pinnas et flammas et arcum et ipsas sagittas et omnem meam supellectilem, quam tibi non ad hos usus dederam: nec enim de patris tui bonis ad instructionem istam quicquam concessum est.

---

adopto, (1): to select
arcus, **-us** *m*: a bow
bonum, **-i** *n*: wealth (*pl.*)
concedo, (3), **concessi**, **concessus**: to grant
concipio, (3): to conceive
contumelia, **-ae** *f.* indignity
corruptor, **-oris** *m*: a seducer
do, (1), **dedi**: to give
dono, (1): to bestow
flamma, **-ae** *f.* a flame
generosus, **-a**, **-um**: of noble birth
gigno, (3), **genui**, **genitus**: to bear
immo: nay more
inamabilis, **-e**: disagreeable
instructio, **-onis** *f.* instruction
melior, **-us**: better
multo: by much
sagitta, **-ae** *f.* an arrow
sentio, (4): to realize
solum (*adv.*): only
supellex, **supellectilis** *f.* equipment
usus, **-us** *m*: enjoyment
vernula, **-ae** *f.* a young home-grown slave
volo, **velle**, **volui**: wish

---

generosum: acc. pred. in ind. st. after *praesumis*, "presume that you alone are *of noble birth*"
nec me...posse: inf. in ind. st., "that I am not able to" + inf.
per aetatem: "on account of age"
velim: subj. volitive, "I would like to" + pr. subj.
scias: pr. subj. after *velim*, "I would like *that you know*"
te: abl. comparison after *meliorem*, "much better *than you*"
genituram...adoptaturam...donaturam: fut. act. inf. (sc. *esse*) in ind. st. after *scias*, "know *that I will bear...that I will adopt...that I will bestow*"
ut...sentias: subj. in purp. clause, "so that you realize"
quam...dederam: plupf., "which I had bestowed"
de patris tui: "from your father" i.e. Vulcan

Venus continues raving at Cupid.

[30] Sed male prima a pueritia inductus es et acutas manus habes et majores tuos irreverenter pulsasti totiens et ipsam matrem tuam, me inquam ipsam, parricida denudas cotidie et percussisti saepius et quasi viduam utique contemnis nec vitricum tuum fortissimum, illum maximumque bellatorem, metuis. Quidni? Cui saepius in angorem mei paelicatus puellas propinare consuesti. Sed jam faxo te lusus huius paeniteat et sentias acidas et amaras istas nuptias. — sed nunc inrisui habita, quid agam? Quo me

acidus, **-a**, **-um**: sour
acutus, **-a**, **-um**: sharp, severe
amarus, **-a**, **-um**: bitter
angor, **-oris** *m*: vexation
bellator, **-oris** *m*: a warrior
consuesco, (3), **consuevi**: to be accustomed
contemno, (3): to scorn
cotidie (*adv.*): every day
denudo, (1): to expose, betray
fortis, **-e**: powerful
induco, (3), **induxi**, **inductus**: to influence
inrisus, **-us** *m*: mockery
irreverens, **-entis** (*gen.*): disrespectful
lusus, **-us** *m*: amusement
major, **majoris** *m*: an elder, ancestors (*pl.*)
male: (*adv.*) wickedly
maximus, **-a**, **-um**: greatest
metuo, (3): to fear
paelicatus, **-us**, *m*: a sexual rival, liason
paeniteo, (2): to cause to repent
parricida, **-ae** *m*: parricide, traitor
percutio, (3), **percussi**: to strike
propino, (1): to hand over
pueritia, **-ae** *f*: childhood
pulso, (1): to beat
quidni: why not?
saepius: (*adv.*) often
sentio, (4): to feel
totiens (*adv.*): so many times
utique: (*adv.*) certainly
viduus, **-a**, **-um**: widowed
vitricus, **-i** *m*: a stepfather

inductus es et...habes et...pulsasti...et...denudas...et...percussisti...et contemnis et...metuis: all main verbs in a list of offenses with polysyndeton, "you have been influenced...and you have...and you have beaten...and you bare...and you have struck...and you have feared"
parricida: vocative, "you traitor!"
vitricum tuum: "your stepfather," i.e. Mars, the lover of Venus
consuesti: perf. syncopated (=*consuevisti*), "you are accustomed to" + inf.
paelicatus: acc. pl. in apposition to *puellas*, "girls as *rivals*"
faxo: archaic fut., "I will bring it about that" + subj.
paeniteat: subj. after *faxo*, "that it causes you to repent," i.e. that you repent
sentias: pr. subj. also after *faxo*, "that you feel"
habita: perf. part., "I, now *having been considered*"
inrisui: dat. pred. of *habita* (sc. *esse*), "considered (to be) *a laughing stock*"
quid agam: subj. in deliberative quest., "what am I to do?

conferam? Quibus modis stelionem istum cohibeam? Petamne auxilium ab inimica mea Sobrietate, quam propter huius ipsius luxuriam offendi saepius? At rusticae squalentisque feminae conloquium prorsus horresco. Nec tamen vindictae solacium, undeunde, spernendum est. Illa mihi prorsus adhibenda est nec ulla alia, quae castiget asperrime nugonem istum, pharetram explicet et sagittas dearmet, arcum enodet, taedam deflammet, immo et ipsum corpus eius acrioribus remediis coerceat. Tunc injuriae meae litatum

---

acer, **acris**, **acre**: sharp
adhibeo, (2), **adhibui**, **adhibitus**: to summon
arcus, **-us** *m*: a bow
aspere: (*adv.*) severely
auxilium, **-i** *n*: help
castigo, (1): to chasten, punish
coerceo, (2): to curb, subdue
cohibeo, (2): to repress
confero, **-ferre**, **-tuli**, **collatus**: to direct
conloquium, **-i** *n*: a discussion
dearmo, (1): to disarm
deflammo, (1): to extinguish
enodo, (1): to unstring
explico, (1): to disentangle, undo
horresco, (3): to dread
immo: more correctly
inimica, **-ae** *f*: an enemy
injuria, **-ae** *f*: abuse
lito, (1): to make recompense for (+ *dat.*)
luxuria, **-ae** *f*: extravagance
modus, **-i** *m*: a method
nugo, **-onis** *m*: a trifler
offendo, (3), **offendi**: to offend
peto, (3): to beg
pharetra, **-ae** *f*: a quiver
prorsus (*adv.*): utterly
remedium, **-i** *n*: a remedy
rusticus, **-a**, **-um**: homely
saepe: (*adv.*) often
sobrietas, **-atis** *f*: sobriety
solacium, **-i** *n*: consolation
sperno, (3), **sprevi**, **spretus**: to spurn
squaleo, - (2): be dirty
stelio, **-onis** *m*: a reptile, treacherous person
taeda, **-ae** *f*: a pine torch
undeunde: from wherever
vindicta, **-ae** *f*: vengeance

Quo conferam: subj. in deliberative quest., "*whither am I to direct* myself?"
cohibeam: subj. in deliberative quest., "by what *am I to repress*?"
Petamne: subj. in deliberative quest., "must I beg?"
huius ipsius: i.e. of Cupid
undeunde: adverb (=*undelibet*), "from wherever"
nec...spernendum est: pass. periphrastic, "the consolation *should not be spurned*"
illa: i.e. Sobrietas
adhibenda est: pass. periphrastic, "she must be summoned"
quae...castiget...explicet...dearmet...enodet...deflammet...coerceat: pr. subj. in relative clause of purp., "no other than she *to chasten...disentangle...disarm...unstring...extinguish...subdue*"
acrioribus remediis: abl. means, "subdue *with sharper punishments*"

crediderim, cum eius comas quas istis manibus meis subinde aureo nitore perstrinxi deraserit, pinnas quas meo gremio nectarei fontis infeci praetotonderit."

Venus meets Juno and Ceres, who attempt to placate her without insulting Cupid.

[31] Sic effata foras sese proripit, infesta et stomachata biles venerias. Sed eam protinus Ceres et Juno continantur visamque vultu tumido quaesiere cur truci supercilio tantam venustatem micantium oculorum coerceret. At illa: "Opportune," inquit,

---

bilis, **-is** *f.* bile, wrath
Ceres, **-eris** *f.* Ceres, goddess of grain/fruits
coerceo, (2): to restrain
coma, **-ae** *f.* hair
continor, (1), **continatus sum**: to encounter
credo, (3), **credidi**: to consider
cur: why?
derado, (3), **derasi**: to shave, clip
effatus, **-a**, **-um**: determined
foras: (*adv.*) out, forth
gremium, **-i** *n*: a womb, lap
infestus, **-a**, **-um**: angry
inficio, (3), **infeci**: to color
Juno, **-onis** *f.* Juno, goddess, wife of Jupiter
mico (1): to sparkle
nectareus, **-a**, **-um**: sweet as nectar
nitor, **-oris** *m*: a sheen
opportune: (*adv.*) conveniently
perstringo, (3), **perstrinxi**: to bind together, braid (hair)
praetondeo, (2), **praetotondi**: to thoroughly clip
proripio, (3): to rush forth
protinus: (*adv.*) immediately
quaero, (3), **quaesivi**: to ask
stomachor, (1), **stomachatus sum**: to cause to boil
subinde: (*adv.*) repeatedly
supercilium, **-i** *n*: a frown
trux, **-ucis** (*gen.*): fierce
tumidus, **-a**, **-um**: swollen
Venerius, **-a**, **-um**: of Venus
venustas, **-atis** *f.* attractiveness, charm

Tunc...crediderim: perf. subj. in less vivid apodosis, "then I would believe"
litatum (sc. esse): ind. st. after *crediderim*, "believe him *to have made recompense for*" + dat.
cum...deraserit: perf. subj. in circumstantial clause serving as a less vivid protasis, "when (i.e. if) she should have shaved"
istis manibus meis: abl. means, "braided *with my own hands*"
aureo nitore: abl. desc., "braided *with a golden sheen*"
cum...praetotonderit: perf. subj. in a circumstantial clause also in a less vivid protasis, "when (if) she were to have thoroughly clipped"
meo gremio: abl. place where, "in my own lap"
vultu tumido: abl. desc., "with a swollen face"
quaesiere: perf. syncopated (=*quaesiverunt*), "they asked"
truci supercilio: abl. means, "restrain *with a fierce frown*"
cur...coerceret: impf. subj. in ind. quest. after *quaesiere*, "asked *why she would restrain*"

"ardenti prorsus isto meo pectori, violentiam scilicet perpetraturae venitis. Sed totis, oro, vestris viribus, Psychen illam fugitivam volaticam mihi requirite. Nec enim vos utique domus meae famosa fabula et non dicendi filii mei facta latuerunt." Tunc illae, non ignarae quae gesta sunt, palpare Veneris iram saevientem sic adortae: "quid tale, domina, deliquit tuus filius ut animo pervicaci voluptates illius impugnes et, quam ille diligit, tu quoque perdere gestias? Quod autem, oramus, isti crimen si puellae lepidae libenter adrisit? An ignoras eum masculum et juvenem esse, vel certe jam

---

adorior, (4), **adortus sum**: to undertake
adrideo, (2), **adrisi**: to smile at (+ *dat.*)
an: can it be that…?
ardeo (2): to burn
crimen, **-inis** *n*: crime
delinquo, (3), **deliqui**: to do wrong
dico, (3): to name
diligo, (3): to love
fabula, **-ae** *f.* a story
factum, **-i** *n*: an act
famosus, **-a**, **-um**: infamous
fugitivus, **-a**, **-um**: fugitive
gero, (3), **gessi**, **gestus**: to carry on
gestio, (4): to wish passionately + *inf.*
ignarus, **-a**, **-um**: ignorant
ignoro, (1): to not know
impugno, (1): to attack
ira, irae *f.* anger
juvenis, **-e**: young
lateo, (2), **latui**: to escape notice
lepidus, **-a**, **-um**: delightful
libenter: (*adv.*) gladly
masculus, **-a**, **-um**: male
oro, (1): to beg, beseech
palpo, (1): to flatter
pectus, **-oris** *n*: a heart
perdo, (3): to destroy
perpetro, (1): to perpetrate, carry out
pervicax, **-acis** (*gen.*): stubborn
saevio, (4): to rage
totus, **-a**, **-um**: all
utique: (*adv.*) certainly
violentia, **-ae** *f.* violence
vis, viris *f.* (*pl.*) might
volaticus, **-a**, **-um**: flighty
voluptas, **-atis** *f.* delight

---

ardenti…isto meo pectori: dat. advantage, "on behalf of my burning heart"
perpetraturae: fut. act. part. expressing purp., "you have come *to carry out*"
totis…vestris viribus: abl. manner, "seek *with all your might*"
non dicendi: gerundive gen., "deeds of my son *not to be mentioned*"
animo pervicaci: abl. manner, "attack *with a stubborn spirit*"
ut impugnes et…gestias: subj. in result clause, "what did he do *so that you attack and…wish passionately*" + inf.
Quod…crimen: "What crime (is it)?"

quot sit annorum oblita es? An, quod aetatem portat bellule, puer tibi semper videtur? Mater autem tu et praeterea cordata mulier filii tui lusus semper explorabis curiose et in eo luxuriem culpabis et amores revinces et tuas artes tuasque delicias in formonso filio reprehendes? Quis autem te deum, quis hominum patietur passim cupidines populis disseminantem, cum tuae domus amores amare coerceas et vitiorum muliebrium publicam praecludas officinam?" Sic illae metu sagittarum patrocinio gratioso Cupidini quamvis absenti blandiebantur. Sed Venus, indignata ridicule tractari

---

absens, **-entis** (*gen.*): absent
aetas, **-atis** *f.* age
amare: (*adv.*) bitterly
annus, **-i** *m*: a year
ars, **artis** *f.* art
bellule: (*adv.*) prettily
blandior, (4): coax, flatter (+ *dat.*)
coerceo, (2): to limit
cordatus, **-a**, **-um**: sensible
culpo, (1): to condemn
curiose: (*adv.*) in a meddlesome manner
delicia, **-ae** *f.* charm
dissemino, (1): to disseminate
exploro, (1): to investigate
formonsus, **-a**, **-um**: beautiful
gratiosus, **-a**, **-um**: agreeable
homo, **-inis** *m*: a man
indignor, (1), **indignatus sum**: to be indignant
lusus, **-us** *m*: amusement
luxuries, **-ei** *f.* extravagance
metus, **-us** *m*: fear
muliebris, **-e**: feminine
mulier, **-eris** *f.* a woman
obliviscor, (3), **oblitus sum**: to forget (+ *gen.*)
officina, **-ae** *f.* a workshop, factory
passim (*adv.*): everywhere
patior, (3), **passus sum**: to suffer
patrocinium, **-i** *n*: defence
porto, (1): to carry
praecludo, (3): to block
praeterea: in addition
publicus, **-a**, **-um**: common
quot: how many?
reprehendo, (3): to blame
revinco, (3): to crush
ridicule: (*adv.*) in ridiculous manner
tracto, (1): to treat
video, (2): to (pass.) seem
vitium, **-i** *n*: vice

---

quot sit: subj. in ind. quest. after *oblita es*, "have you forgotten *how many* of years *he is*"
puer: nom. pred., "does he seem to be *a boy*"
te...disseminantem: pr. part. circumstantial after *patietur*, "endure *you disseminating*"
populis: dat. ind. obj., "disseminating *among the peoples*"
cum...coerceas et...praecludas: pr. subj. in circumstantial clause, "when you limit and...you block"
metu: abl. cause, "from fear"
patrocinio gratioso: abl. means, "flatter *with an agreeable defence*"
Cupidini quamvis absenti: dat. advantage "flatter *Cupid, although absent*"
tractari suas iniurias: ind. st. after *indignata*, "indignant *that her injuries were treated*"

suas injurias praeversis illis, alterorsus concito gradu pelago viam capessit.

Psyche wanders in search of her husband. She comes to a disordered temple and arranges the offerings.

[6.1] Interea Psyche variis jactabatur discursibus, dies noctesque mariti vestigationibus inquieta, animo tanto cupidior iratum licet si non uxoriis blanditiis lenire certe servilibus precibus propitiare. Et prospecto templo quodam in ardui montis vertice: "unde autem," inquit, "scio an istic meus degat dominus?" et ilico

---

alterorsus (*adv.*): in another direction
an: whether
arduus, **-a**, **-um**: lofty
blanditia, **-ae** *f.* a caress
capesso, (3): to undertake
concitus, **-a**, **-um**: rapidly-moving
cupidus, **-a**, **-um**: longing for
dego, (3): to spend one's time in, live
discursus, **-us** *m*: a running about
dominus, **-i** *m*: a master
gradus, **-us** *m*: a step
ilico: (*adv.*) on the spot, immediately
injuria, **-ae** *f.* injury
inquietus, **-a**, **-um**: restless
iratus, **-a**, **-um**: furious
istic: (*adv.*) in that place
jacto, (1): toss about, drive
lenio, (4): to placate
licet: it is permitted, although (+ subj.)
mons, **montis** *m*: a mountain
pelagus, **-i** *n*: sea
preverto, (3), **preverti**, **preversus**: to turn away from
propitio, (1): to soothe (feelings)
prospicio, (3), **prospexi**, **prospectus**: to see far off
servilis, **-e**: servile
templum, **-i** *n*: a temple
uxorius, **-a**, **-um**: wifely
varius, **-a**, **-um**: various
vertex, **-icis** *m*: a peak
vestigatio, **-onis** *f.* a seeking after (+ *gen.*)
via, **-ae** *f.* a way

---

praeversis illis: abl. abs, "with those having been turned away from," i.e. having turned away from them
concito gradu: abl. manner, "with a rapidly-moving step"
variis...discursibus: abl. specification, "tossed about *in various runnings about*"
vestigationibus: abl. cause, "restless *from tracking down*"
animo tanto: abl. manner, "longing *with so much spirit*"
iratum licet: concessive, "although him being furious"
uxoriis blanditiis: abl. means, "if not to placate *with wifely caresses*"
lenire...propitiare: inf. epexegetic after *cupidior*, "desirous *to placate...to soothe*"
servilibus precibus: abl. means, "surely to soothe *with servile prayers*"
prospecto templo quodam: abl. abs., "a certain temple having been seen far off"
unde scio: "whence do I know?" i.e. how do I know?
an...degat: pr. subj. in ind. quest., "whether he is living"

dirigit citatum gradum, quem defectum prorsus adsiduis laboribus spes incitabat et votum. Jamque naviter emensis celsioribus jugis pulvinaribus sese proximam intulit. Videt spicas frumentarias in acervo et alias flexiles in corona et spicas hordei videt. Erant et falces et operae messoriae mundus omnis, sed cuncta passim jacentia et incuria confusa et, ut solet aestu, laborantium manibus projecta. Haec singula Psyche curiose dividit et discretim semota rite

---

acervus, **-i** *m*: a cluster
adsiduus, **-a**, **-um**: unremitting
aestus, **-us** *m*: summer heat
celsus, **-a**, **-um**: high
citatus, **-a**, **-um**: quickened
confundo, (3), **confudi**, **confusus**: to disorder
corona, **-ae** *f.* a wreath
cunctus, **-a**, **um**: to all
curiose: (*adv.*) attentively
deficio, (3), **defeci**, **defectus**: to falter, be weak
dirigo, (3): to direct
discretim: (*adv.*) distinctly, separately
divido, (3): to distinguish
emetior, (4), **emensus sum**: to pass through
falx, **falcis** *f.* a sickle
flexilis, **-e**: pliable
frumentarius, **-a**, **-um**: grain-producing
gradus, **-us** *m*: a step
hordeum, **-i** *n*: barley
incito, (1): to urge on
incuria, **-ae** *f.* neglect
infero, **-ferre**, **-tuli**, **-latum**: to import, bring in
jaceo, (2): to lie
jugum, **-i** *n*: a ridge (mountain)
laboro, (1): to labor
messorius, **-a**, **-um**: reaping
mundus, **-i** *m*: equipment
naviter: (*adv.*) diligently
opera, **-ae** *f.* work
projicio, (3), **projeci**, **projectus**: to abandon
prorsus (*adv.*): forwards
pulvinar, **pulvinaris** *n*: couch for a deity, seat
rite: (*adv.*) duly
semoveo, (2), **semovi**, **semotus**: to separate
singulus, **-a**, **-um**: one-by-one
soleo, (2), **solitus sum**: to be in the habit of
spes, **-ei** *f.* hope
spica, **-ae** *f.* an ear of cereal
votum, **-i** *n*: a vow

---

quem defectum: perf. part. concessive, "which, *although weakened*"
adsiduis larboribus: abl. manner, "urged on *with unremitting exertions*"
spem et votum: hendiadys, "the hope and a prayer," i.e. the hope of a prayer
emensis celsioribus jugis: abl. abs., "the higher ridges having been passed through"
pulvinaribus: dat. after *proximat*, "she brings herself near *to the seats*"
Videt spicas...spicas hordei videt: note the chiasmus, "she sees ears...ears she sees"
operae messoriae: dat. purp., "sickles *for harvest work*"
incuria: abl. manner, "disordered *with neglect*"
ut solet: parenthetical, "as is the habit"
aestu: abl. circumstance, "in the summer heat"
manibus: abl. means, "abandoned *by the hands* of the laborers"

componit, rata scilicet nullius dei fana caerimoniasve neglegere se debere sed omnium benivolam misericordiam corrogare.

Ceres appears to Psyche, who beseeches the goddess for help.

[2] Haec eam sollicite seduloque curantem Ceres alma deprehendit et longum exclamat protinus: "ain, Psyche miseranda? Totum per orbem Venus anxia disquisitione tuum vestigium furens animi requirit teque ad extremum supplicium expetit et totis numinis sui viribus ultionem flagitat: tu vero rerum mearum tutelam nunc geris et aliud quicquam cogitas nisi de tua salute?" Tunc Psyche pedes eius advoluta et uberi fletu rigans deae vestigia humumque verrens

---

advolvo, (3), **advolvi**, **advolutus**: to prostrate oneself
aio, (1): to speak
almus, **-a**, **-um**: nourishing, kind
anxius, **-a**, **-um**: uneasy, anxious
benivolus, **-a**, **-um**: benevolent
caerimonia, **-ae** *f.* a ritual
Ceres, **-eris** *f.* Ceres, goddess of grain/fruits
cogito, (1): to consider
compono, (3): to organize
corrogo, (1): to entreat by offering
curo, (1): to arrange
debeo, (2): to be obliged to
deprehendo, (3): to discover
disquisitio, **-onis** *f.* inquiry
exclamo, (1): to call out
expeto, (3): to ask for
fanum, **-i** *n*: sanctuary
flagito, (1): to demand
fletus, **-us** *m*: tears
furo, (3): to rage
gero, (3): to bear
humus, **-i** *f.* ground
miserandus, **-a**, **-um**: pitiable
misericordia, **-ae f.**, sympathy
neglego, (3): to neglect
nullus, **-a**, **-um**: no
orbis, **-is** *m*: a region, world
pes, **pedis** *m*: a foot
reor, (2), **ratus sum**: to believe
rigo, (1): to moisten
salus, **-utis** *f.* safety
sedulo: (*adv.*) carefully
sollicite: (*adv.*) anxiously
supplicium, **-i** *n*: punishment
totus, **-a**, **-um**: total
tutela, **-ae** *f.* guardianship
uber, **-eris** (*gen.*): abundant
ultio, **-onis** *f.* revenge
verro, (3): to sweep
vis, **viris** *f.* force

---

se debere: ind. st. after *rata*, "thinking that she ought to" + inf.
eam...curantem: pr. part. circum. after *deprehendit*, "she discovers *her caring for*"
Ain: (=*aisne*?) indicating surprise, "do you speak?" i.e. "is it really you?"
anxia disquisitione: abl. manner, "seeks *with uneasy inquiry*"
animi: gen. respect, "raging *with respect to the mind*"
totis...viribus: abl. manner, "demands *with all her strength*"
uberi fletu: abl. means, "moistening *with abundant tears*"

crinibus suis multijugis precibus editis veniam postulabat: "per ego te frugiferam tuam dexteram istam deprecor, per laetificas messium caerimonias, per tacita secreta cistarum, et per famulorum tuorum draconum pinnata curricula et glebae Siculae sulcamina et currum rapacem et terram tenacem et inluminarum Proserpinae nuptiarum demeacula et luminosarum filiae inventionum remeacula et cetera quae silentio tegit Eleusinis Atticae sacrarium, miserandae Psyches, animae supplicis tuae subsiste. Inter istam spicarum congeriem

---

Attica, **-ae** *f.* Attica, region of Athens
caerimonia, **-ae** *f.* a ceremony
cista, **-ae** *f.* a box for sacred ceremonial objects
congeries, **-ei** *f.* a heap
crinis, **-is** *m*: a tress
curriculum, **-i** *n*: a chariot
currus, **-us** *m*: a chariot
demeaculum, **-i** *n*: a passage down, descent
deprecor, (1), **deprecatus sum**: to beseech
dextera, **-ae** *f.* a right hand
draco, **-onis** *m*: a dragon, snake
edo, (3), **edidi**, **editus**: to pronounce
Eleusinus, **-i** *m*: a native of Eleusis in Attica, site of a famous shrine to Demeter
famulus, **-a**, **-um**: servile
frugifer, **-a**, **-um**: fertile
gleba, **-ae** *f.* turf
inluminarus, **-a**, **-um**: unlighted
inventio, **-onis** *f.* a discovery
laetificus, **-a**, **-um**: luxuriant
luminosus, **-a**, **-um**: bright, illuminated
messis, **-is** *m*: harvest
miserandus, **-a**, **-um**: pitiable
multijugus, **-a**, **-um**: manifold
pinnatus, **-a**, **-um**: winged
postulo, (1): to pray for
Proserpina, **-ae** *f.* Proserpina
rapax, **-acis** (*gen.*): rapacious
remeaculum, **-i**, *n*: ascent
sacrarium, **-i** *n*: a shrine
secretum, **-i** *n*: a secret, mystic rite
Siculus, **-a**, **-um**: Sicilian
silentium, **-i** *n*: silence
spica, **-ae** *f.* an ear of grain
subsisto, (3): to come to the aid of (+ *dat.*)
sulcamina, **-ae** *f.* a furrow
supplex, **-icis**: suppliant
tacitus, **-a**, **-um**: silent
tego, (3): to protect
tenax, **-acis**: tenacious
venia, **-ae** *f.* favor

---

crinibus suis: abl. means, "sweeping *with her own tresses*"
multijugis precibus editis: abl. abs., "with manifold prayers having been pronounced"
Per ego te: formulaic for prayers, "I (beseech) you by" + acc.
per...pinnata curricula: "by the winged chariots," with which Ceres searched the earth for Proserpina
Siculae: "furrows *of Sicilian* turf," the site of Proserpina's rape
terram tenacem: "the tenacious earth" in the sense that one cannot return from the dead
demeacula...remeacula: note the rhyming clauses, "the descents...the ascents"
luminosarum: "ascents of the *illuminated* discoveries," referring to the torches that Demeter held while searching for Proserpina
silentio: abl. manner, "protects *in silence*"
Atticae: locative, "in Attica," the site of a famous Eleusinian sanctuary to Demeter
animae: dat. after *subsiste*, "aid *the soul*!"

patere vel pauculos dies delitescam, quoad deae tantae saeviens ira spatio temporis mitigetur vel certe meae vires diutino labore fessae quietis intervallo leniantur."

Ceres refuses aid out of respect to Venus, and Psyche moves on and finds a temple of Juno.

[3] Suscipit Ceres: "tuis quidem lacrimosis precibus et commoveor et opitulari cupio, sed cognatae meae, cum qua etiam foedus antiquum amicitiae colo, bonae praeterea feminae, malam gratiam subire nequeo. Decede itaque istis aedibus protinus, et

---

aedis, **-is** *f.* temple, house (*pl.*)
amicitia, **-ae** *f.* friendship
antiquus, **-a**, **-um**: time-honored
bonus, **-a**, **-um**: noble
cognata, **-ae** *f.* a kinswoman
colo, (3): to maintain
commoveo, (2): to upset
cupio, (3): to want
decedo, (3): to depart
delitesco, (3): to hide
dies, **-i** *m*: a day
diutinus, **-a**, **-um**: long
fessus, **-a**, **-um**: wearied
foedus, **-eris** *n*: a bond
gratia, **-ae** *f.* favor
intervallum, **-i** *n*: respite
ira, **-ae** *f.* wrath
lacrimosus, **-a**, **-um**: tearful, causing tears
lenio, (4): to mitigate
mitigo, (1): to lighten
nequeo, **-ire**, **-ivi**, **-itus**: to be unable
opitulor, (1), **opitulatus sum**: to help
patior, (3), **passus sum**: to allow
pauculus, **-a**, **-um**: a few
praeterea: addition
protinus: (*adv.*) at once
quies, **-etis** *f.* peace
quoad: until
saevio, (4): to rave
spatium, **-i** *n*: an interval
subeo, **-ire**, **-ivi**, **-itus**: to endure
suscipio, (3): to undertake, reply
tempus, **-oris** *n*: time
vis, **viris** *f.* strength (*pl.*)

---

delitescam: pr. subj. in noun clause after *patere*, "Allow *that I may hide!*"
vel...vel certe: "*either* for a few days...*or at least*," emphasizing the second alternative
spatio: abl. means, "lightened *by an interval*"
quoad...mitigetur: pr. subj. in general temporal clause, "until it may be lightened (whenever that may be)"
diutino labore: abl. means, "wearied *by long toil*"
intervallo: abl. means, "lightened *by a respite*"
quoad...leniantur: pr. subj. in general temporal clause, "until it may be mitigated"
Tuis...lacrimosis precibus: abl. means, "moved *by your tearful prayers*"
cognatae meae...bonae praeterea feminae: gen. source, "disfavor *from my kinswoman...also a noble woman*"
malam gratiam: "bad favor," i.e. disfavor
Decede...consule: imper., "depart!...consider!"
istis aedibus: abl. sep., "depart *from this house*"

quod a me retenta custoditaque non fueris optimi consule."

Contra spem suam repulsa Psyche et afflicta duplici maestitia, iter retrorsum porrigens inter subsitae convallis sublucidum lucum prospicit fanum sollerti fabrica structum, nec ullam, vel dubiam, spei melioris viam volens omittere sed adire cuiscumque dei veniam sacratis foribus proximat. Videt dona pretiosa et lacinias auro litteratas ramis arborum postibusque suffixas, quae cum

---

adeo, **-ire**, **-ivi**, **-itus**: to approach
affligo, (3), **afflixi**, **afflictus**: to afflict, humble
arbor, **-oris** *f.* a tree
consulo, (3): to consider
contra: contrary to (+ *acc.*)
convallis, **-is** *f.* a valley
custodio, (4), **custodivi**, **custoditus**: to restrain
donum, **-i** *n*: a gift
dubius, **-a**, **-um**: doubtful, dangerous
duplex, **-icis** (*gen.*): twofold
fabrica, **-ae** *f.* workmanship
fanum, **-i** *n*: a temple
foris, **-is** *f.* a gate
iter, **itineris** *n*: a journey
lacinia, **-ae** *f.* a strip of cloth
litteratus, **-a**, **-um**: inscribed with letters
lucus, **-i** *m*: a grove
maestitia, **-ae** *f.* grief
melior, -ius: better
omitto, (3): to disregard
porrigo, (3): to extend
postis, **-is** *m*: a doorpost
pretiosus, **-a**, **-um**: costly
prospicio, (3): to see far off
proximo, (1): to approach (+ *dat.*)
ramus, **-i** *m*: a branch
repello (3), -puli, pulsus: to reject
retineo (2), **-ui**, **retentus**: to retain
retrorsum: backwards
sacratus, **-a**, **-um**: hallowed
sollers, **-ertis** (*gen.*): expert
spes, **-ei** *f.* expectation, hope
struo, (3), **struxi**, **structus**: to build
sublucidus, **-a**, **-um**: somewhat light
subsino, (3), **sivi**, **situs**: to allow beneath
suffigo, (3), **suffixi**, **suffixus** (3): to fix, attach
ullus, -a, -um: any
venia, **-ae** *f.* kindness

---

quod...non fueris: perf. subj. in noun clause after *consule*, "consider *that you have not been*"
optimi: gen. value, "consider it *best*," i.e. consider it a favor
duplici maestitia: abl. means, "afflicted by twofold grief"
sollerti fabrica: abl. manner, "built *with expert workmanship*"
nec ullam...viam: acc., "to omit *not any way*"
sacratis foribus: dat. after *proximat*, "she approaches *the hallowed gates*"
auro: abl. desc., "inscribed *with gold*"
ramis: abl. place where, "on the branches"
postibus: abl. place where, "on the doorposts"

gratia facti nomen deae cui fuerant dicata testabantur. Tunc genu nixa et manibus aram tepentem amplexa detersis ante lacrimis sic adprecatur:

Psyche prays to Juno for aid, but Juno also sends the girl away out of respect for Venus.

[4] "Magni Iovis germana et conjuga, sive tu Sami, quae sola partu vagituque et alimonia tua gloriatur, tenes vetusta delubra, sive celsae Carthaginis, quae te virginem vectura leonis caelo commeantem percolit, beatas sedes frequentas, seu prope ripas Inachi,

---

adprecor, (1), **adprecatus sum**: to beseech
alimonium, **-i** *n*: nurture
amplector, (3), **amplexus sum**: to embrace
ante: (*adv.*) first
ara, **-ae** *f.* an altar
beatus, **-a**, **-um**: happy, fortunate
caelum, **-i** *n*: heavens
Carthago, **-inis** *f.* Carthage
celsus, **-a**, **-um**: lofty, noble
commeo, (1): to travel
conjuga, **-ae** *f.* a wife
delubrum, **-i** *n*: sanctuary
detergeo, (2), **detersi**, **detersus**: to wipe away
dico, (1): to dedicate
factum, **-i** *n*: a deed
frequento, (1): to visit repeatedly
genu, **-us** *n*: a knee
germana, **-ae** *m*: a sister
glorior, (1), **gloriatus sum**: to pride oneself in (+ *abl.*)
gratia, **-ae** *f.* gratitude
leo, **-onis** *m*: a lion
nitor, (3), **nixus sum**: to advance, bent
partus, **-us** *m*: a birth
percolo, (3): to worship completely
prope: near (+ *acc.*)
ripa, **-ae** *f.* a bank
sedes, **-is** *f.* a seat
teneo, (2): to hold, keep
tepeo, (2): to be lukewarm
testor, (1), **testatus sum**: to testify
vagitus, **-us** *m*: infant crying
vectura, **-ae** *f.* a carriage
vetustus, **-a**, **-um**: ancient

---

facti: objective gen. after *gratia*, "with gratitude *for the deed*"
fuerant dicata: plupf. pass., "to whom *they had been dedicated*"
genu nixa: abl. abs. "with knee bent"
detersis…lacrimis: abl. abs., "with tears having been wiped away"
germana et conjuga: "sister and wife," i.e. Juno
sive tu…tenes, sive…frequentas, seu…praesides: "*whether you stay* in Samos…*or you frequent* your seats in Carthage…*or you guard* the walls of the Argives"
Sami…Carthaginis…Argivorum: locatives, "at Samos…Carthage…Argos," all sites sacred to Juno
partu vagituque et alimonia tua: abl. specification, "which prides itself in *your birth and crying and nurture*"
vectura: abl. means, "come *on the carriage*"
caelo: abl. place from which, "traveling *from the heavens*"
Inachi: "banks *of the Inachus*," a river in Argos

qui te jam nuptam Tonantis et reginam deorum memorat, inclitis Argivorum praesides moenibus, quam cunctus oriens Zygiam veneratur et omnis occidens Lucinam appellat, sis meis extremis casibus Juno Sospita meque, in tantis exanclatis laboribus defessam, imminentis periculi metu libera. Quod sciam, soles praegnatibus periclitantibus ultro subvenire."

Ad istum modum supplicanti statim sese Juno cum totius sui numinis angusta dignitate praesentat et protinus: "Quam vellem,"

---

angustus, **-a**, **-um**: lofty
appello, (1): to address
Argivi, -orum *m*: Argives
casus, **-us** *m*: a calamity
defessus, **-a**, **-um**: exhausted
dignitas, **-atis** *f*: dignity
exanclo, (1): to endure
extremus, **-a**, **-um**: extreme
immineo, (2): to threaten
inclitus, **-a**, **-um**: celebrated
Juno, **-onis** *f*: Juno
libero, (1): to free
Lucina, **-ae** *f*: Lucina, goddess of childbirth
memoro, (1): to remember
metus, **-us** *m*: dread
modus, **-i** *m*: a manner
moene, **-is** *n*: town walls (*pl.*)
nupta, **-ae** *f*: a bride
occidens, **-entis** *m*: the west
oriens, **-entis** *m*: the east
periclitor, (1), **periclitatus sum**: to endanger
praegnas, **-antis** (*gen.*): pregnant
praesento, (1): to present oneself, appear
praesideo, (2): to preside over, guard (+ *dat.*)
protinus: (*adv.*) without pause
regina, **-ae** *f*: a queen
soleo, (2): to become accustomed to (+ *inf.*)
sospita, **-ae** *f*: a female preserver
subvenio, (4): to assist
supplico, (1): to pray
tono, (1): to thunder
totus, **-a**, **-um**: entire
ultro: voluntarily
veneror (1), **veneratur**: worship
Zygia, **-ae** *f*: Zygia, goddess of marriage

Tonantis: pr. part. gen., "of the thundering one," i.e. Jupiter
inclitis...moenibus: dat. after *prasides*, "watch over *the celebrated walls*"
Zygiam...Lucinam: acc. pred., "honor you *as Zygia...as Lucina*," cult names referring to marriage and childbearing
sis: pr. subj. jussive, "may you be"
in tantis exanclatis laboribus: *in* with instrumental force, "exhausted with so many labors having been endured"
extremis casibus: abl. circumstance, "in my harshest calamities"
metu: abl. sep., "free me *from the dread*
Quod (=quoad) sciam: subj. in relative clause of proviso, "as far as I know"
praegnatibus periclitantibus: dat. ind. obj., "assist *endangered pregnant women*"
Ad istum modum: "praying *in this manner*"
supplicanti: dat. ind. obj., "presents herself *to her, praying*"
cum angusta dignitate: abl. circumstance, "appears *with lofty dignity*"
Quam vellem: volitive subj., "how I would be willing" + inf.

inquit, "per fidem, nutum meum precibus tuis accommodare. Sed contra voluntatem Veneris, nurus meae, quam filiae semper dilexi loco, praestare me pudor non sinit. Tunc etiam legibus quae servos alienos profugos invitis dominis vetant suscipi prohibeor."

In despair, Psyche decides to surrender herself to Venus.

[5] Isto quoque fortunae naufragio Psyche perterrita, nec indipisci jam maritum volatilem quiens, tota spe salutis deposita, sic ipsa suas cogitationes consuluit: "Iam quae possunt alia meis aerumnis temptari vel adhiberi subsidia, cui nec dearum quidem,

---

accommodo, (1): to apply, adapt
adhibeo, (2): to apply
aerumna, **-ae** *f.* trouble
cogitatio, **-onis** *f.* a thought
consulo, (3), **consului**: consult
contra: against (+ *acc.*)
depono, (3), **-posui:** to set aside
diligo, (3), **dilexi**: love
domina, **-ae** *f.* an owner
fides, **-ei** *f.* faith
fortuna, **-ae** *f.* fate
indipiscor, (3): to overtake
invitus, **-a**, **-um**: unwilling
lex, **legis** *f.* law
naufragium, **-i** *n*: a shipwreck
nurus, **-us** *f.* a daughter-in-law
nutus, **-us** *m*: will
perterreo, (2), **perterrui**, **perterritus**: to frighten greatly
praesto, (1): to show favor
profugus, **-a**, **-um**: fugitive
prohibeo, (2): to forbid
pudor, **-oris** *m*: decency
queo, (4), **-ivi** **-itus**: to be able (+ *inf.*)
salus, **-utis** *f.* salvation
servus, **-i** *m*: a slave
sino, (3): to permit (+ *inf.*)
spes, **-ei** *f.* hope
subsidium, **-i** *n*: relief
suscipio, (3): to support
tempto, (1): to try
veto, (1): to prohibit
volatilis, **-e**: equipped to fly, winged
voluntas, **-atis** *f.* will

---

per fidem: a colloquial interjection, "by my faith!" "I assure you!"
precibus tuis: dat. after **accommodare**. "accomodate my will *to your prayers*"
loco: abl., "*in the place of* a daughter" i.e. like a daughter
legibus: abl. means, "forbidden *by laws*"
invitis dominis: abl. abs., "with the masters unwilling"
suscipi: pr. inf. pass. after *vetant*, "prohibit slaves *to be received*"
Isto...naufragio: abl. means, "frightened *by that shipwreck*"
indipisci: pr. inf. deponent after *quiens*, "being able *to overtake*"
spe ... deposita: abl. abs., "hope ... having been set aside"
quae alia...subsidia: neut. nom. pl., "*what other relief* is possible?"
meis aerumnis: dat. purp., "relief *for my troubles*"

quanquam volentium, potuerunt prodesse suffragia? Quo rursum itaque tantis laqueis inclusa vestigium porrigam quibusque tectis vel etiam tenebris abscondita magnae Veneris inevitabiles oculos effugiam? Quin igitur masculum tandem sumis animum et cassae speculae renuntias fortiter et ultroneam te dominae tuae reddis et vel sera modestia saevientes impetus eius mitigas? Qui scias an etiam quem diu quaeritas illic in domo matris reperias?" sic ad dubium obsequium, immo ad certum exitium, praeparata principium futurae secum meditabatur obsecrationis.

---

abscondeo, (2), **abscondui**, **absconditus**: to hide
animus, **-i** *m*: spirit, courage
cassus, **-a**, **-um**: hollow, useless
certus, **-a**, **-um**: certain
diu: for a long time
dubius, **-a**,**-um**: uncertain
effugio, (3): to escape
exitium, **-i** *n*: destruction
fortiter: (*adv.*) boldly
futurus, **-a**, **-um**: future
illic: there
immo: no indeed, rather
impetus, **-us** *m*: an assault, charge
includo, (3), **inclusi**, **inclusus**: to enclose
inevitabilis, **-e**: unavoidable
laqueus, **-i** *m*: trap
masculus, **-a**, **-um**: masculine
meditor, (1), **meditatus sum**: to rehearse
mitigo, (1): to soothe
modestia, **-ae** *f*: discipline, modesty
obsecratio, **-onis** *f*: supplication
obsequium, **-i** *n*: deference
porrigo, (3): to extend
praeparo, (1): to prepare
principium, **-i** *n*: a beginning
prosum, **prodesse**: to be useful
quaerito, (1): to seek
quanquam: although
quin: why not
reddo, (3): to return
renuntio, (1): to reject
reperio, (4): to find
saevio, (4): to rage
serus, **-a**, **-um**: at a late hour
specula, **-ae** *f*: a glimmer of hope
suffragium, **-i** *n*: vote, prayer
sumo, (3): to take up, assume
tectum, **-i** *n*: a roof
tenebra, **-ae** *f*: darkness (*pl.*)
ultroneus, **-a**, **-um**: voluntary

---

volentium: pr. part. gen. concessive agreeing with *dearum*, "gods, although *willing*"
Quo...porrigam: subj. in deliberative quest., "Whither should I extend my step?"
quibus tectis... effugiam: pr. subj. in delib. quest., "to what roofs should I escape?"
tantis laqueis: abl. means, "surrounded *by such large traps*"
quibus tectis vel...tenebris: abl. place where, "escape to *what roofs or darkness*?"
Quin...sumis: "why do you not assume?"
cassae speculae: dat. after *renuntias*, "reject *the hollow glimmer* of hope"
sera modestia: abl. means, "soothe *with discipline at a late hour*"
impetus eius: "the assaults of her," i.e. of Venus
Qui scias: pr. subj. potential, "how can you know?" *qui* is an archaic ablative
an...reperias: pr. subj. in ind. quest., "whether you will find"
quem diu quaeritas: "him *whom you seek for a long time*"

Venus meanwhile prepares her journey into the heavens.

[6] At Venus terrenis remediis inquisitionis abnuens caelum petit. Jubet instrui currum, quem ei Vulcanus aurifex subtili fabrica studiose poliverat et ante thalami rudimentum nuptiale munus obtulerat, limae tenuantis detrimento conspicuum et ipsius auri damno pretiosum. De multis quae circa cubiculum dominae stabulant, procedunt quattuor candidae columbae et hilaris incessibus, picta colla torquentes, jugum gemmeum subeunt susceptaque domina laetae subvolant. Currum deae prosequentes gannitu

---

abnuo, (3), **abnui**, **abnuitus**: to refuse, rule out
aurifex, **-icis** *m*: a goldsmith
aurum, **-i** *n*: gold
caelum, **-i** *n*: heaven
candidus, **-a**, **-um**: bright, spotless
collum, **-i** *n*: a neck
columba, **-ae** *f*: a dove
conspicuus, **-a**, **-um**: conspicuous
cubiculum, **-i** *n*: a bedroom
currus, **-us** *m*: a chariot
damnum, **-i** *n*: physical loss
detrimentum, **-i** *n*: diminishment
fabrica, **-ae** *f*: workmanship
gannitus, **-us** *m*: chirping
gemmeus, **-a**, **-um**: bejewelled
hilarus, **-a**, **-um**: lively
incessus, **-us** *m*: a procession
inquisitio, **-onis** *f*: a search
instruo, (3): to prepare
jubeo, (2): to order
jugum, **-i** *n*: a yoke
laetus, **-a**, **-um**: joyful
lima, **-ae** *f*: a file (carpenter's)
munus, **-eris** *n*: a gift
offero, **offerre**, **obtuli**, **oblatus**: to present, bestow
peto, (3): to make for
pictus, **-a**, **-um**: embellished
polio, (4), **polivi**: smooth
pretiosus, **-a**, **-um**: precious
procedo, (3): to proceed
prosequor, (3), **prosecutus sum**: to escort
remedium, **-i** *n*: remedy
rudimentum, **-i** *n*: a beginning
stabulo, (1): to be housed
studiose: (*adv.*) attentively
subeo, **-ire**, **-ivi**, **-itus**: to move into, submit to
subtilis, **-e**: exact
subvolo, (1): to fly upwards
suscipio, (3), **suscepi**, **susceptus**: to take up
tenuo, (1): to wear down
terrenus, **-a**, **-um**: earthly
thalamus, **-i** *m*: marriage
torqueo, (2): to twist, whirl
Vulcanus, **-i** *m*: Vulcan, god of fire

---

terrenis remediis: abl. sep. after *abnuens*, "refusing *earthly remedies*"
subtili fabrica: abl. manner, "smoothed *with an exact workmanship*"
quem...poliverat...obtulerat: plupf., "which he had smoothed...he had bestowed"
nuptiale munus: acc. pred., "presented *as a wedding gift*"
detrimento: abl. cause, "conspicuous *because of the diminishment of*" + gen.
damno: abl. cause, "precious *because of the loss of*" + gen.
hilaris incessibus: abl. circumstance, "proceed *with lively processions*"
suscepta domina: abl. abs., "the mistress having been taken up"
gannitu constrepenti: abl. manner, "escorting *with resounding chirping*"

constrepenti, lasciviunt passeres et ceterae quae dulce cantitant aves melleis modulis suave resonantes adventum deae pronuntiant. Cedunt nubes et Caelum filiae panditur et summus Aether cum gaudio suscipit deam, nec obvias aquilas vel accipitres rapaces pertimescit magnae Veneris canora familia.

At Jupiter's citadel, Venus solicits the help of Mercury to bribe the people to turn in Psyche.

[7] Tunc se protinus ad Iovis regias arces dirigit et petitu superbo Mercuri, dei vocalis, operae necessariam usuram postulat. Nec rennuit Iovis caerulum supercilium. Tunc ovans ilico, comitante etiam Mercurio, Venus caelo demeat eique sollicite serit verba:

accipiter, **-tris** *m*: a hawk
adventus, **-us** *m*: an approach
Aether, -eris, *n*: Aether, upper air
aquila, **-ae** *f*: an eagle
arx, **arcis** *f*: a citadel
avis, **-is** *f*: a bird
Caelum, **-i** *n*: Heaven
caerulus, **-a**, **-um**: sky-dark
canorus, **-a**, **-um**: harmonious
cantito, (1): to sing
cedo, (3): to make way
comito, (1): to accompany
constrepo, (3): to resound
demeo, (1): to descend
dirigo, (3): to direct
familia, **-ae** *f*: household of slaves
gaudium, **-i** *n*: joy
ilico: (*adv.*) immediately
lascivio, (4): to frisk, frolic
melleus, **-a**, **-um**: of honey
Mercurius, -i *m*: Mercury, messenger god
modulus, **-i** *m*: a little measure
necessarius, -a, -um: indispensable
nubes, **-is** *f*: a cloud
obvius, **-a**, **-um**: hostile
opera, **-ae** *f*: service
ovo, (1): to rejoice
pando, (3): to spread out
passer, **-eris** *m*: a sparrow
pertimesco, (3): to become very scared (of)
petitus, **-us**, *m*: entreaty, begging
postulo, (1): to demand
pronuntio, (1): to proclaim
protinus: (*adv.*) at once
rapax, **-acis** (*gen.*): rapacious
regius, **-a**, **-um**: regal
rennuo, (3): to refuse (by nodding)
resono, (1): to resound
sero, (3): to compose
sollicite: (*adv.*) anxiously
suavis, **-e**: charming
superbus, **-a**, **-um**: haughty
supercilium, **-i** *n*: an eyebrow
suscipio, (3): to accept
usura, **-ae** *f*: use
vocalis, **-e**: tuneful

melleis modulis: abl. specification, "sing *with honeyed little measures*"
Caelum: Caelum (=Grk *Ouranos*) was god of the sky and "father" of Venus by way of his castration at the hands of his son Juppiter
filiae: dat. advantage, "for his daughter"
Aether: the personification of the upper air of the gods
petitu superbo: abl. manner, "demanded *with a haughty begging*"
comitante...Mercurio: abl. abs., "with Mercury accompanying"
caelo: abl. motion after *demeat*, "Venus descends *from heaven*"

"Frater Arcadi, scis nempe sororem tuam Venerem sine Mercuri praesentia nil unquam fecisse, nec te praeterit utique quanto jam tempore delitescentem ancillam nequiverim reperire. Nil ergo superest quam tuo praeconio praemium investigationis publicitus edicere. Fac ergo mandatum matures meum et indicia, qui possit agnosci, manifeste designes, ne, si quis occultationis illicitae crimen subierit, ignorantiae se possit excusatione defendere;"

---

agnosco, (3): to recognize
ancilla, **-ae** *f.* a slave girl
crimen, **-inis** *n*: a charge
defendo, (3): to defend
delitesco, (3): to hide
designo, (1): to describe
edico, (3): to declare
excusatio, **-onis** *f.* excuse
frater, **fratris** *m*: a brother
ignorantia, **-ae** *f.* ignorance
illicitus, **-a**, **-um**: forbidden
indicium, **-i** *n*: information, proof
investigatio, **-onis** *f.* a search
mandatum, **-i** *n*: a command
manifestus, **-a**, **-um**: clear, plainly guilty
maturo, (1): to hasten
nempe: of course
nequeo, (4), **-ivi**, **-itus**: to be unable
nil: nothing
occultatio, **-onis** *f.* concealment
praeconium, **-i** *n*: a proclamation
praemium, **-i** *n*: a reward
praesentia, **-ae** *f.* presence
praetereo, **-ire**, **-ivi**, **-itus**: to pass by
publicitus: (*adv.*) publicly
reperio, (4): to find
scio, (4): to know
subeo, **-ire**, **-ivi**, **-itus**: to be placed under
supersum, **-esse**: to be remaining
tempus, **-oris** *n*: time
unquam: ever
utique: (*adv.*) certainly

Frater Arcadi: vocative referring to Mercury, born on Mount Cyllene in Arcadia
sororem...fecisse: perf. inf. in ind. st. after *scis*, "you know *that your sister has done*"
quanto....nequiverim: perf. subj. in ind. quest., "know *how long I have been unable*"
quam...edicere: "nothing remaining *other than to declare*"
tuo praeconio: abl. means, "declare *by your proclamation*"
investigationis: gen. specification, "a reward *for the search*"
matures: pr. subj. in noun clause after *fac*, "make *so that that you hasten*"
qui: an archaic interrogative pronoun (=*quibus*), "marks *by which*"
qui possit: pr. subj. in relative clause of characteristic, "marks *by which she can*" + inf.
designes: pr. subj. also after *fac*, "make *so that you declare*"
si...subierit: syncopated fut. perf. (=*subiverit*) in fut. more vivid protasis, "*if anyone undertakes* the crime"
ne...possit: pr. subj. in jussive noun clause after *designes*, "declare *that he will not be able*," the clause also serves as a future more vivid apodosis
excusiatione: abl. means, "defend *with the excuse*"

et simul dicens libellum ei porrigit ubi Psyches nomen continebatur et cetera. Quo facto, protinus domum secessit.

Mercury spreads the message, but Psyche turns herself in and is found by Venus' servant.

[8] Nec Mercurius omisit obsequium. Nam per omnium ora populorum passim discurrens, sic mandatae praedicationis munus exsequebatur: "si quis a fuga retrahere vel occultam demonstrare poterit fugitivam regis filiam, Veneris ancillam, nomine Psychen, conveniat retro metas Murtias Mercurium praedicatorem, accepturus indicivae nomine ab ipsa Venere septem savia suavia et unum blandientis adpulsu linguae longe mellitum."

---

accipio, (3), **accepi**, **acceptus**: to receive
adpulsus, **-us** *m*: an impact
blandio, (4): to please
contineo, (2): to contain
convenio, (4): to approach
demonstro, (1): to point out
discurro, (3): to wander
exsequor, (3), **exsecutus sum**: to execute, accomplish
fuga, **-ae** *f*: flight
fugitivus, **-a**, **-um**: fugitive
indiciva, **-ae** *f*: an informer's reward
libellus, **-i** *m*: a little book, defamatory publication
lingua, **-ae** *f*: a tongue
mando, (1): to entrust, command
mellitus, **-a**, **-um**: honey-sweet
meta, **-ae** *f*: a turning post
munus, **-eris** *n*: duty
nomen, **-inis** *n*: a name, payment
obsequium, **-i** *n*: compliance
occulo, (3), **occului**, **occultus**: to conceal
omitto, (3), **omisi**: to disregard
passim (*adv.*): here and there
porrigo, (3): to stretch out, extend
praedicatio, **-onis** *f*: an announcement
praedicator, **-oris** *m*: a herald, proclaimer
retraho, (3): to bring back
retro: behind (+ *acc.*)
savium, **-i** *n*: a kiss
secedo, (3): to withdraw
simul: at same time
suavis, **-e**: sweet

---

et cetera: nom. with *nomen*, i.e. "the name was contained *and the rest* was contained"
Quo facto: abl. abs., "this having been done"
per omnium ora populorum passim…praedicationis: note alliteration and assonance
nomine: abl. specification, "by name"
conveniat: pr. subj. jussive, "let him approach"
metas Murtias: "the Murtian posts," turning posts at the Circus Maximus
accepturus: fut. part. indicating purp., "in order to receive"
nomine: abl. specification, "*for payment* of the reward"
adpulsu: abl. cause, "honey-sweet because of *the lingering impact*," because of the impact of her loving tongue

Ad hunc modum pronuntiante Mercurio, tanti praemii cupido certatim omnium mortalium studium adrexerat. Quae res nunc vel maxime sustulit Psyches omnem cunctationem. Jamque fores ei dominae proximanti occurrit, una de famulitione Veneris, nomine Consuetudo, statimque (quantum maxime potuit) exclamat: "tandem, ancilla nequissima, dominam habere te scire coepisti? An pro cetera morum tuorum temeritate istud quoque nescire te fingis quantos labores circa tuas inquisitiones sustinuerimus? Sed bene, quod meas potissimum manus incidisti et inter Orci cancros jam

---

adrigo, (3), **adrexi**, **adrectus**: to excite
bene: (*adv.*) well
cancer, **cri** *m*: a barrier
certatim: in competition
coepio, (3), **coepi**: to begin
Consuetudo, **-inis** *f.* Habit
cunctatio, **-onis** *f.* hesitation
cupido, **-inis** *n*: greed
exclamo, (1): to exclaim
famulatio, -onis *f.* the servants of a house
fingo, (3): to pretend
foris, **-is** *f.* a gate
incido, (3), **incidi**, **incasus**: to happen, fall into (+ *acc.*)
inquisitio, **-onis** *f.* search
Mercurius, **-i** *m*: Mercury
modus, **-i** *m*: a manner
mos, moris *m*: custom, habit
nequissimus, **-a**, **-um**: worst, most wicked
nescio, (4): to not know
occurro, (3), **occucurri**: to run to meet
Orcus, **-i** *m*: god of the underworld, Dis
potissimum (*adv.*): before all
praemium, **-i** *n*: reward
pronuntio, (1): to announce
proximo, (1): to draw near
quantum: so much as
studium, **-i** *n*: zeal
suffero, (3), **sustuli**: remove
sustineo, (2), **sustinui**: to sustain, endure
temeritas, **-atis** *f.* rashness

---

pronuntiante Mercurio: abl. abs., "with Mercury announcing"
adrexerat: plupf., "the desire *had excited*"
ei...proximanti: dat. after *occurrit*, "rushed up to *her* (i.e. Psyche) *as she was nearing* the doors"
nomine: abl. specification, "Habit *by name*"
quantum maxime potuit: "as greatly as she could," i.e. "as loudly as she could"
habere te: ind. st. after *scire*, "understand *that you have*"
nescire te: ind. st. after *fingis*, "you pretend *that you do not know*"
quantos labores...sustinuerimus: perf. subj. in ind. quest., "how many labors we have endured"
quod...incidisti et...haesisti: perf. in noun clause, "*that you have fallen into and... have become stuck* is a good thing"
Orci: Orcus, a god of the underworld, punisher of broken oaths

ipso haesisti datura scilicet actutum tantae contumaciae poenas."

Venus insults and tortures Psyche, scorning her as the potential mother of Venus' grandchild.

[9] Et audaciter in capillos eius inmissa manu trahebat eam nequaquam renitentem. Quam ubi primum inductam oblatamque sibi conspexit Venus, latissimum cachinnum extollit et qualem solent furenter irati, caputque quatiens et ascalpens aurem dexteram: "Tandem," inquit, "dignata es socrum tuam salutare? An potius maritum, qui tuo vulnere periclitatur, intervisere venisti? Sed esto secura, jam enim excipiam te ut bonam nurum condecet;"

actutum: (*adv.*) without delay
an: can it be that…?
ascalpo, (3): to scratch
audaciter: (*adv.*) boldly
auris, **-is** *f.* an ear
bonus, **-a**, **-um**: good
cachinnus, **-i** *m*: a derisive laugh, guffaw
capillus, **-i** *m*: hair
condecet, (2): it is fitting
conspicio, (3), **conspexi**: to catch in sight of
contumacia, **-ae** *f.* stubbornness
dexter, **-era**, **-erum**: right
dignor, (1), **dignatus sum**: to deign to (+ *inf.*)
excipio, (3): to receive
extollo, (3): to raise
furenter: (*adv.*) furiously
haereo, (2), **haesi**, **haesus**: to stick
induco, (3), **induxi**, **inductus**: to lead in
inmitto, (3), **inmisi**, **inmissus**: to throw in
interviso, (3): to visit
iratus, **-a**, **-um**: made angry, raging
latus, **-a**, **-um**: extensive
nequaquam: by no means
nurus, **-us** *f.* a daughter-in-law
offero, **offerre**, **obtuli**, **oblatus**: to present
periclitor, (1), **periclitatus sum**: to put in peril
poena, **-ae** *f.* penalty
potius (*adv.*): more likely, rather
quatio, (3): to shake
renitor, (3), **renisus sum**: to struggle
saluto, (1): to greet
securus, **-a**, **-um**: untroubled
socrus, **-us** *f.* a mother-in-law
soleo, (2), **solitus sum**: to be in the habit of, become accustomed to
traho, (3): to haul, drag
venio, (4), **veni**: to come
vulnus, **-eris** *n*: a wound

iam ipso: abl., "at this very moment"
datura: fut. act. part., "you who are about to pay"
inmissa manu: abl. abs., "*with the hand thrown into* her hair""
Quam…inductam oblatamque: "whom, having been led in and presented"
ubi primum: idiomatic, "when first," i.e. as soon as
qualem: acc. s. agreeing with *cachinnum*, "a guffaw extensive *and of the sort*"
tuo vulnere: abl. means, "put in peril *by your wound*"
periclitatur: deponent verb with passive meaning, "who is put in peril"
intervisere: pr. inf. of purpose, "come *to visit*"
esto: fut. imper., "you must be!"

et: "Ubi sunt," inquit, "Sollicitudo atque Tristities, ancillae meae?" quibus intro vocatis torquendam tradidit eam. At illae sequentes erile praeceptum Psychen misellam flagellis afflictam et ceteris tormentis excruciatam iterum dominae conspectui reddunt. Tunc rursus sublato risu Venus: "et ecce!" inquit. "nobis turgidi ventris sui lenocinio commovet miserationem, unde me praeclara subole aviam beatam scilicet faciat. Felix vero ego quae ipso aetatis meae flore vocabor avia et vilis ancillae filius nepos Veneris audiet.

---

aetas, **-atis** *f.* age
affligo, (3), **afflixi**, **afflictus**: to afflict
avia, **-ae** *f.* a grandmother
beatus, **-a**, **-um**: happy
commoveo, (2): to provoke
conspectus, **-us** *m*: a sight, contemplation
ecce: behold!
erilis, **-e**: of a master or mistress
excrucio, (1): torment
felix, **-icis** (*gen.*): happy
flagellum, **-i** *n*: a whip
flos, **-oris** *m*: youthful prime
intro (*adv.*): in, inside
iterum (*adv.*): a second time
lenocinium, **-i** *n*: enticement
misellus, **-a**, **-um**: poor
miseratio, **-onis** *f.* compassion
nepos, **-otis** *m*: a grandson
praeclarus, **-a**, **-um**: noble
reddo, (3): to return
risus, **-us** *m*: laughter
rursus (*adv.*): again
sequor, (3), **secutus sum**: to obey
Sollicitudo, **-inis** *f.* Anxiety
sublatus, **-a**, **-um**: elated
suboles, **-is** *f.* offspring
tormentum, **-i** *n*: a torture device
torqueo, (2): to torture
trado, (3), **tradidi**: to deliver
Tristities, **-ei** *f.* Sadness
turgidus, **-a**, **-um**: swollen
venter, **ventris** *m*: a womb
vilis, **-e**: common
voco, (1): to call, summon

---

ancillae meae: appositive, "Anxiety and Sadness, *my servants*"
Quibus...vocatis: abl. abs., "who having been summoned in"
torquendam: fut. pass. part. indicating purpose, "delivered her *in order to be tortured*"
flagellis: abl. means, "afflicted *with whips*"
ceteris tormentis: abl. means, "tormented *with other torture devices*"
sublato risu: abl. manner, "with elated laughter"
lenocinio: abl. means, "provokes *with the enticement*"
praeclara subole: abl. means, "*with noble offspring*," note sarcasm
unde...faciat: pr. subj. in relative clause of characteristic, "whence (i.e. from the child to be born) she may make"
aviam beatam: acc. pred., "make me *a blessed grandmother*"
ipso...flore: abl. circumstance, "*in the very prime* of life"
filius...audiet: "the son will hear 'grandson,'" i.e. he will be acknowledged as a legitimate grandson

Quanquam inepta ego quae frustra filium dicam; impares enim nuptiae et praeterea in villa sine testibus et patre non consentiente factae legitimae non possunt videri ac per hoc spurius iste nascetur, si tamen partum omnino perferre te patiemur."

Venus sets a task for Psyche: she must sort a disorganized heap of grains before night. A little ant gathers all the ants to perform the task for the overwhelmed Psyche.

[10] His editis involat eam vestemque plurifariam diloricat capilloque discisso et capite conquassato graviter affligit, et accepto frumento et hordeo et milio et papavere et cicere et lente et faba

---

accipio, (3), **accepi**, **acceptus**: to grasp
affligo, (3): to throw down
capillus, **-i** *m*: hair
cicer, **-eris** *n*: chickpea
conquasso, (1): to shake violently
consentio, (4): to consent
dilorico, (1): to tear apart
discindo, (3), **discidi**, **discissus**: to cut in two, tear
edo, (3), **edidi**, **editus**: to declare
faba, **-ae** *f*: bean
frumentum, **-i** *n*: grain
frustra (*adv.*): in vain
graviter: (*adv.*) violently
hordeum, **-i** *n*: barley
impar, **-aris** (*gen.*): unequal (in rank)
ineptus, **-a**, **-um**: foolish
involo, (1): to fly at, attack
legitimus, **-a**, **-um**: lawful
lens, **lentis** *f*: lentil
milium, **-i** *n*: millet
nascor, (3), **natus sum**: to be born
omnino (*adv.*): altogether, at all
papaver, **-eris** *n*: poppy-seed
partus, **-us** *m*: offspring
patior, (3), **passus sum**: to allow
perfero, **-ferre**, **-tuli**, **-latus**: to carry through; bear
plurifariam (*adv.*): extensively
quanquam: yet
spurius, **-i** *m*: a bastard
testis, **-is** *m*: a witness
vestis, **-is** *f*: a garment
video, (2): to see, seem good (pass.)
villa, **-ae** *f*: a country home

---

quae...dicam: pr. subj. in relative clause of characteristic with force of a fut. less vivid protasis, "I am foolish, *if I were to call him*"
impares nuptiae: marriages between people of unequal status were forbidden under Roman law
patre non consentiente: abl. abs., "with no father consenting"
factae legitimae: pred. nom., "able to be viewed *as having been made legitimate*"
si...patiemur: fut. more vivid protasis, "if we allow you" + inf.
His editis: abl. abs., "With these having been declared"
capillo discisso et capite conquassato: abl. abs., "with the hair having been torn and with the head having been violently shaken"
accepto frumento: abl. abs., "with grain having been grasped"
hordeo et milio et papavere et cicere et lente et faba commixtis...confusisque: abl. abs., "with barley and millet and poppy-seed and chickpea and lentil and bean having been combined and having been jumbled," note polysyndeton

commixtisque acervatim confusisque in unum grumulum sic ad illam: "videris enim mihi tam deformis ancilla nullo alio sed tantum sedulo ministerio amatores tuos promereri: jam ergo et ipsa frugem tuam periclitabor. Discerne seminum istorum passivam congeriem singulisque granis rite dispositis atque sejugatis ante istam vesperam opus expeditum approbato mihi."

Sic assignato tantorum seminum cumulo, ipsa cenae nuptiali concessit. Nec Psyche manus admolitur inconditae illi et inextricabili

---

acervatim (*adv.*): without order
admolior, (4), **admolitus sum**: to exert oneself (to)
ante: before (+ *acc.*)
approbo, (1): to approve
assigno, (1): to assign
cena, **-ae** *f.*: dinner
commisceo, (2), **commiscui**, **commixtus**: to combine
concedo, (3), **concessi**: depart
confundo, (3), **confudi**, **confusus**: to jumble
congeries, **-ei** *f.*: a heap
cumulus, **-i** *m*: a heap
deformis, **-e**: ugly
discerno, (3): to distinguish, sort out
dispono, (3), **disposui**, **dispositus**: to distribute
expedio, (4), **expedivi**, **expeditus**: to be complete, make ready
frux, **-ugis** *f.*: produce, virtue
granum, **-i** *n*: grain
grumulus, **-i** *m*: a little heap
inconditus, **-a**, **-um**: disordered
inextricabilis, **-e**: impossible to disentangle or sort out
ministerium, **-i** *n*: service
opus, **-eris** *n*: work
passivus, **-a**, **-um**: random
periclitor, (1), **periclitatus sum**: to test
promereor, (2), **promeritus sum**: to gain
rite: (*adv.*) duly
sedulus, **-a**, **-um**: attentive
sejugatus, **-a**, **-um**: separated
semen, **-inis** *n*: a seed
singulus, **-a**, **-um**: individual
vespera, **-ae** *f.*: evening

---

nullo alio: abl. means, "deserve *by no other way*"
sed tantum: "*but only* by service"
sedulo ministerio: abl. means, "by attentive service"
promereri: pr. inf. deponent complementing *videris*, "you seem *to deserve*"
Discerne: imper., "sort out!"
singulis granis...dispositis atque sejugatis: abl. abs., "with the individual grains having been distributed and separated"
approbato: fut. act. imper., "let the work be approved!"
mihi: dat. agent, "approved *by me*"
assignato...cumulo: abl. abs., "the heap having been assigned"
cenae nuptiali: dat. purp., "departed *for a wedding dinner*"
inconditae...moli: dat. after compound verb, "put her hands *to that mass*"

moli, sed immanitate praecepti consternata silens obstupescit. Tunc formicula illa parvula atque ruricola certa difficultatis tantae laborisque miserta contubernalis magni dei socrusque saevitiam exsecrata, discurrens naviter convocat corrogatque cunctam formicarum accolarum classem: "Miseremini, terrae omniparentis agiles alumnae, miseremini et Amoris uxori, puellae lepidae, periclitanti prompta velocitate succurrite." Ruunt aliae superque aliae sepedum populorum undae summoque studio singulae granatim totum

---

accola, **-ae** *f*: a neighbor
agilis, **-e**: nimble
alumna, **-ae** *f*: a nursling
Amor, **-oris** *m*: Amor, Cupid
certus, **-a**, **-um**: certain of, knowledgeable of (+ *gen.*)
classis, **-is** *f*: a class
consterno, (1): to confound
contubernalis, **-is** *m*: a bedmate
convoco, (1): to assemble
corrogo, (1): to summon to a gathering
cunctus, **-a**, **-um**: entire
difficultas, **-atis** *f*: hardship
discurro, (3): to dash about
exsecror, (1), **exsecratus sum**: to detest
formica, **-ae** *f*: an ant
formicula, **-ae** *f*: a little ant
granatim: grain by grain
immanitas, **-atis** *f*: frightfulness, vast size
lepidus, **-a**, **-um**: charming
misereor, (2), **misertus sum**: to pity
moles, **-is** *f*: a mass
naviter: (*adv.*) diligently
obstupesco, (3): to be stupefied
omniparens, **-entis** (*gen.*): parent or creator of all things
parvulus, **-a**, **-um**: very small
periclitor, (1), **periclitatus sum**: to put to the test, be in danger
populus, **-i** *m*: a host, group of people
praeceptum, **-i** *n*: order
promptus, **-a**, **-um**: eager
ruo, (3): to rush on
ruricola, **-e** *f*: a country-dweller
saevitia, **-ae** *f*: cruelty
sepes, **sepedis**: six-footed
sileo, (2): to be silent, be still
singulus, **-a**, **-um**: each, apiece (*pl.*)
socrus, **-us** *f*: a mother-in-law
studium, **-i** *n*: zeal
succurro, (3): to help
unda, **-ae** *f*: a wave
velocitas, **-atis** *f*: speed

---

immanitate: abl. means, "confounded *by the vast size*"
certa: "having certain knowledge of," by virtue of the work of ants
miserta: part. deponent, "having pitied" + gen.
Miseremini: imper., "take pity on!" + dat.
alumnae: vocative, "Oh Nurslings"
periclitanti: dat. agreeing with *uxori*, "come to the aid of the wife *being in danger*"
prompta velocitate: abl. manner, "with eager speed"
succurrite: imper., "come to the aid of!" + dat.
aliae superque aliae…undae: nom., "another and another wave in addition"
summo studio: abl. manner, "organized *with the highest zeal*"

digerunt acervum separatimque distributis dissitisque generibus e conspectu perniciter abeunt.

Venus, displeased, assigns another task: that Psyche must retrieve some golden wool from sheep near the river.

[11] Sed initio noctis e convivio nuptiali vino madens et fragrans balsama Venus remeat totumque revincta corpus rosis micantibus, visaque diligentia miri laboris: "non tuum," inquit, "nequissima, nec tuarum manuum istud opus, sed illius cui tuo, immo et ipsius, malo placuisti," et frusto cibarii panis ei projecto cubitum facessit.

abeo, **-ire**, **-ivi**, **-itus**: to disappear
acervus, **-i** *m*: a heap
balsamum, **-i** *n*: balsam
cibarius, **-a**, **-um**: plain
conspectus, **-us** *m*: a sight
convivium, **-i** *n*: a banquet
cubitus, **-us** *m*: a bed
digero, (3): to organize
diligentia, **-ae** *f*: diligence
dissero, (3), **dissevi**, **dissitus**: to plant at intervals, distribute
distribuo, (3), **distribui**, **distributus**: to divide
facesso, (3), **facessi**: to go away
fragrans, **-antis** (*gen.*): smelling, fragrant
frustum, **-i** *n*: a morsel, crumb
genus, **-eris** *n*: a variety
immo: more correctly
initium, **-i** *n*: a beginning
madeo, (2): to be dripping
mico (1): to gleam
mirus, **-a**, **-um**: extraordinary
nequissimus, **-a**, **-um**: most vile
nuptialis, **-e**: of a wedding
opus, **-eris** *n*: work
panis, **-is** *m*: bread
perniciter: (*adv.*) briskly
placeo, (2), **placui**: to please (+ *dat.*)
projicio, (3), **projeci**, **projectus**: to throw down
remeo, (1): to return
revincio, (4), **revinxi**, **revinctus**: to bind fast
rosa, **-ae** *f*: a rose
separatim (*adv.*): apart
totus, **-a**, **-um**: entire
vinum, **-i** *n*: wine

distributis dissitisque generibus: abl. abs., "once the varieties had been divided apart and distributed"
initio: abl. time, "*in the beginning* of night"
vino: abl. specification, "dripping *with wine*"
balsama: acc. respect with *fragrans*, "fragrant *with balsam*"
rosis micantibus: abl. means, "head bound *with gleaming roses*"
visa diligentia: abl. abs., "the diligence having been seen"
Non tuum: nom. pred., "this work is *not yours*"
cui...placuisti: perf. in relative clause "of that one *to whom you were pleasing*"
tuo...malo: abl. of result, "to your harm"
immo et ipsius (sc. malo): "*more correctly* to the harm *himself*"
frusto...projecto: abl. abs., "a morsel having been thrown down"

Interim Cupido solus interioris domus unici cubiculi custodia clausus coercebatur acriter, partim ne petulanti luxurie vulnus gravaret, partim ne cum sua cupita conveniret. Sic ergo distentis et sub uno tecto separatis amatoribus tetra nox exanclata.

Sed Aurora commodum inequitante vocatae Psychae Venus infit talia: "videsne illud nemus, quod fluvio praeterluenti ripisque longis attenditur, cuius imi frutices vicinum fontem despiciunt?

acriter: (*adv.*) steadfastly
attendo, (3): to stretch toward, extend
Aurora, **-ae** *f.* Dawn
claudo, (3), **clausi**, **clausus**: to confine
coerceo, (2): to restrain
commodum (*adv.*): even now
convenio, (4): to come together
cubiculum, **-i** *n*: a bedroom
Cupido, **-inis** *m*: Cupid, son of Venus
cupita, **-ae** *f.* beloved
custodia, **-ae** *f.* prison
despicio, (3): to look down on
distineo, (2), **distinui**, **distentus**: to keep apart
domus, **-us** *f.* a house
exanclo, (1): to suffer, go through
fluvius, **-i** *m*: a river
fons, **fontis** *m*: a spring
frutex, **-icis** *m*: a shrub
gravo, (1): to aggravate
imus, **-a**, **-um**: lowest
inequito, (1): to ride over
infit: she begins
interim: meanwhile
interior, **-ius**: interior
luxuries, **-ei** *f.* extravagance
nemus, **-oris** *n*: wood
partim: (*adv.*) partly
petulans, **-antis** (*gen.*): wanton
praeterluo, (3): to wash by/past
ripa, **-ae** *f.* a bank
separo, (1): to separate
tectum, **-i** *n*: a roof
teter, **-tra**, **-trum**: horrible
unicus, **-a**, **-um**: single
vicinus, **-a**, **-um**: neighboring
voco, (1): to summon
vulnus, **-eris** *n*: a wound

custodia: abl. place where, "in the prison"
ne...gravaret: impf. subj. in purp. clause, "lest he aggravate"
petulanti luxurie: abl. means, "aggravate *with wanton extravagance*"
ne...conveniret: impf. subj. purp. clause, "lest he come together with"
distentis...separatis amatoribus: abl. abs., "the lovers having been kept apart and separated"
exanclata (sc. est): "the night *was spent*"
Aurora...inequitante: abl. abs., "with Dawn riding over"
vocatae: dat., "to Psyche *having been summoned*"
fluvio praeterluenti ripis longis: dat. after *attenditur*, "extends *along the river washing past and its long banks*"

Oves ibi nitentes aurique colore florentes mihi incustodito pastu vagantur. Inde de coma pretiosi velleris floccum mihi confestim quoquo modo quaesitum afferas censeo."

Psyche despairs and intends to drown herself, but a reed offers help.

[12] Perrexit Psyche volenter non obsequium quidem illa functura sed requiem malorum praecipiti fluvialis rupis habitura. Sed inde de fluvio musicae suavis nutricula leni crepitu dulcis aurae divinitus inspirata sic vaticinatur harundo viridis: "Psyche tantis

---

affero, affere, attuli, allatus: to convey
aura, -ae *f.* breeze
aurum, -i *n*: gold
censeo, (3): to decree
color, -is *m*: color
coma, -ae *f.* wool
confestim: (*adv.*) without delay
crepitus, -us *m*: rustling
divinitus: (*adv.*) divinely
floccus, -i *m*: a tuft
floreo, (2): to flourish, be bright
fluvialis, -e: of a river
fungor, (3), **functus sum**: to perform
harundo, -inis *f.* a reed
incustoditus, -a, -um: unsupervised
inde: from that place
inspiro, (1): to inspire
lenis, -e: light
modus, -i *m*: a means, way
musica, -ae *f.* music
niteo, (2): to shine
nutricula, -ae *f.* a nurse
obsequium, -i *n*: subservience
ovis, -is *f.* a sheep
pastus, -us *m*: a pasture
pergo, (3), **perrexi**: to proceed
praecipitium, -i *n*: a precipice, a falling headlong
pretiosus, -a, -um: precious
quaero, (3), **quaesivi, quaesitus**: to obtain
requies, -ei *f.* respite
rupes, -is *f.* a cliff
suavis, -e: pleasant
vagor, (1), **vagatus sum**: to roam
vaticinor, (1), **vaticinatus sum**: to prophesy
vellus, -eris *n*: fleece
viridis, -e: green
volenter: (*adv.*) willingly

---

colore: abl. desc., "shining *with the color* of gold"
incustodito pastu: abl. circumstance, "in unsupervised pasture"
floccum...quaesitum: "convey *a tuft...having been obtained*"
quoque modo: abl. means, "by whatever means"
afferas: pr. subj. in ind. command, "I decree *that you convey*"
functura: fut. act. part. expressing purpose, "not *in order to perform*"
malorum: gen. separation, "respite *from her evils*"
praecipitio: abl. means, "have respite *by a headlong fall*"
habitura: fut. act. part. expressing purpose, "but *in order to have* respite"
nutricula: nom. appositive to the subject below, *harundo viridis*, "a green reed, *a nurse* of sweet music"
leni crepitu: abl. means, "prophesied *with the light rustling* of a sweet breeze"

aerumnis exercita, neque tua miserrima morte meas sanctas aquas polluas nec vero istud horae contra formidabiles oves feras aditum, quoad de solis fraglantia mutuatae calorem truci rabie solent efferri cornuque acuto et fronte saxea et non nunquam venenatis morsibus in exitium saevire mortalium; se dum meridies solis sedaverit vaporem et pecua spiritus fluvialis serenitate conquieverint, poteris

---

acutus, **-a**, **-um**: sharp
aditus, **-us** *m*: an attack
aerumna, **-ae** *f.* a task
aqua, **-ae** *f.* water
calor, **-oris** *m*: heat
conquiesco, (3), **conquievi**: take repose
contra: against (+ *acc.*)
cornu, **-us** *n*: a horn
effero, **efferre**, **extuli**, **elatus**: to raise, (pass.) to be carrried away
exercito, (1): to harrass
exitium, **-i** *n*: destruction
fluvialis, **-e**: river
formidabilis, **-e**: terrifying
fraglantia, **-ae** *f.* burning
frons, frontis *m*: a brow
hora, **-ae** *f.* time
meridies, **-ei** *m*: midday
morsus, **-us** *m*: teeth
mortalis, -e: mortal
mutuor, (1), **mutuatus sum**: to borrow
nunquam: never
ovis, **-is** *f.* a sheep
pecu, **-us** *n*: a flock
polluo, (3): to stain, dishonor
quoad: as long as
rabies, **-ei** *f.* madness
saevio, (4): to rage
sanctus, **-a**, **-um**: venerable, sacred
saxeus, **-a**, **-um**: stony
sedo, (1): to allay, diminish
serenitas, **-atis** *f.* fine weather
sol, solis *m*: sun
soleo, (2), **solitus sum**: to become accustomed to
spiritus, **-us** *m*: air
trux, **-ucis**: savage
vapor, **-oris** *m*: a fever
veneno, (1): to imbue or infect with poison

---

tantis aerumnis: abl. means, "harrassed *by so great tasks*"
tua miserrima morte: abl. means, "pollute *with your most wretched death*"
neque...polluas nec...feras: pr. subj. jussive, "*may you neither stain...nor bring* an attack"
istud horae: "at the very point of the hour," i.e. at this moment
mutuatae: nom., "*having borrowed* heat from the sun"
efferri: pr. inf. pass. complementing *solent*, "they are accustomed *to be carried away*"
truci rabie: abl. means, "carried away *by a savage madness*"
cornu acuto et fronte saxea et non nunquam venenatis morsibus: abl. means, "rage *with a sharp horn and a stony brow and teeth sometimes having been imbued with poison*"
in exitium: expressing purp., "for the destruction"
saevire: also complementing *solent*, "accustomed *to rage*"
dum...sedaverit...conquieverint: fut. perf., "*until* the day *will have allayed* and the flocks *will have taken repose*"
serenitate: abl. circumstance, "in the fine weather"

sub illa procerissima platano, quae mecum simul unum fluentum bibit, latenter abscondere. Et cum primum mitigata furia laxaverint oves animum, percussis frondibus attigui nemoris lanosum aurum reperies, quod passim stirpibus convexis obhaerescit."

Psyche succeeds with the advice of the reed, but Venus is irritated again and sets another task.

[13] Sic harundo simplex et humana Psychen aegerrimam salutem suam docebat. Nec auscultatu impaenitendo, diligenter instructa, illa cessavit, sed observatis omnibus furatrina facili

---

abscondeo, (2): to hide
aeger, **-gra**, **-grum**: sorrowful
attiguus, **-a**, **-um**: adjoining, neighboring
auscultatus, **-us**, *m*: a listening, obedience
bibo, (3): to drink
cesso, (1): to be inactive
convexus, **-a**, **um**: vaulted, curved
diligenter: (*adv.*) carefully
doceo, (2): to teach, show
facilis, **-e**: easy
fluentum, **-i** *n*: river
frons, **-ondis** *f*: foliage
furatrina, **-ae** *f*: theft
furia, **-ae** *f*: frenzy
harundo, **-inis** *f*: a reed
humanus, **-a**, **-um**: kind
impaeniteo, (2): to not repent
instruo, (3), **instruxi**, **instructus**: to instruct
lanosus, **-a**, **-um**: woolly
latenter: (*adv.*) without being perceived
laxo, (1): to relax
mitigo, (1): to soothe
nemus, **-oris** *n*: wood
obhaeresco, (3): to adhere to (+ *dat.*)
observo, (1): to heed
passim: everywhere
percutio, (3), **percussi**, **percussus**: to strike
platanus, **-i** *f*: a plane-tree
procerus, **-a**, **-um**: tall
reperio, (4): to obtain
salus, **-utis** *f*: salvation
simplex, **-icis** (*gen.*): simple
simul: (*adv.*) simultaneously
stirps, **-irpis** *f*: a trunk (of a plant)

---

cum primum...laxaverint oves: fut. perf. in cum temporal clause, "as soon as the sheep will have relaxed"
mitigata furia: abl. abs., "with the frenzy having been soothed"
percussis frondibus: abl. abs., "*with the foliage* of the nearby woods *having been struck*"
stirpibus convexis: dat. after compound verb, "cling *to the curved trunks*"
auscultatu paenitendo: abl. abs. expressing manner "with an obedience that would be repented," i.e. this is the manner in which she did not (*nec*) cease
instructa: nom. agreeing with *illa*, "*having been instructed* carefully"
observatis omnibus: abl. abs., "all things having been heeded"
furatrina facili: abl. means, "gather *with an easy theft*"

flaventis auri mollitie congestum gremium Veneri reportat. Nec tamen apud dominam saltem secundi laboris periculum secundum testimonium meruit, sed contortis superciliis subridens amarum sic inquit: "nec me praeterit huius quoque facti auctor adulterinus. Sed jam nunc ego sedulo periclitabor an oppido forti animo singularique prudentia sis praedita. Videsne insistentem celsissimae illi rupi montis ardui verticem, de quo fontis atri fuscae defluunt undae proxumaeque conceptaculo vallis inclusae Stygias inrigant

---

adulterinus, **-a**, **-um**: false
amarum: (*adv.*) bitterly
apud: in the view of (+ *acc.*)
arduus, **-a**, **-um**: steep
ater, **-tra**, **-trum**: black
auctor, **-oris** *m*: an originator
celsus, **-a**, **-um**: high
conceptaculum, **-i** *n*: a receptacle
congero, (3), **congessi**, **congestus**: to pile on, gather
contorqueo, (2), **contorsi**, **contortus**: to twist
defluo, (3): to fall
factum, **-i** *n*: an achievement
flaveo, (2): to be yellow colored
fons, **fontis** *m*: a spring, source
fortis, **-e**: strong
fuscus, **-a**, **-um**: dark
gremium, **-i** *n*: a lap
includo, (3), **inclusi**, **inclusus**: to enclose
inrigo, (1): to irrigate
insisto, (3): to stand upon
mereo, (2), **merui**: merit
mollities, **-ei** *f*: softness
mons, **montis** *m*: a mountain
oppido: (*adv.*) exceedingly
periclitor, (1), **periclitatus sum**: to test
periculum, **-i** *n*: peril
praeditus, **-a**, **-um**: gifted
praetereo, **-ire**, **-ivi**, **-itus**: to pass by, escape
proxumus, **-a**, **-um**: nearest
prudentia, **-ae** *f*: good sense
reporto, (1): to carry back
rupes, **-is** *f*: a cliff
saltem: even, at least
secundus, **-a**, **-um**: second, favorable
sedulo: (*adv.*) carefully
singularis, **-e**: remarkable
Stygius, **-a**, **-um**: Stygian, of the underworld
subrideo, (2): to smile
supercilium, **-i** *n*: a brow
testimonium, **-i** *n*: testimony
unda, **-ae** *f*: a wave
vallis, **-is** *f*: a valley
vertex, **-icis** *m*: a peak

---

mollitie: abl. specification, "gathered *with softness*"
contortis superciliis: abl. desc., "with a twisted brow," a sign of annoyance
secundi laboris periculum secundum testimonium: "nor even *the danger of the second labor* merit *a favorable testimony*;" note the pun on *secundus*, meaning "following" in order (i.e. second) and as in a favorable wind, one that *follows* a ship
an...sis: pr. subj. in ind. quest., "test *whether you may be*"
forti animo singularique prudentia: abl. specification, "gifted *with a strong mind and remarkable good sense*"
celsissimae illi rupi: dat. after compound verb, "standing over *that very high cliff*"
proxumae...vallis: gen., "receptacle *of a nearby valley*"
conceptaculo: abl. place where, "enclosed *in the receptacle*"
inclusae: agreeing with *undae*, "waves *having been enclosed*"

paludes et rauca Cocyti fluenta nutriunt? Indidem mihi de summi fontis penita scaturrigine rorem rigentem hauritum ista confestim defer urnula." Sic aiens crustallo dedolatum vasculum insuper ei graviora comminata tradidit.

Psyche is again on the verge of suicide.

[14] At illa studiose gradum celerans montis extremum petit cumulum, certe vel illic inventura vitae pessimae finem. Sed cum primum praedicti jugi conterminos locos appulit, videt rei vastae letalem difficultatem. Namque saxum, immani magnitudine

---

appello, (3), **appuli**: to land, arrive
celero, (1): to quicken
Cocytus, **-i** *m*: Cocytus, the river of wailing
comminor, (1), **comminatus sum**: to threaten
confestim (*adv.*): immediately
conterminus, **-a**, **-um**: adjacent to (+ *gen.*)
crustallum, **-i** *n*: crystal
cumulus, **-i** *m*: a peak
dedolo, (1): to hew smooth
defero, **-ferre**, **-tuli**, **-latus**: to bring
difficultas, **-atis** *f.* difficulty
extremus, **-a**, **-um**: farthest
finis, **-is** *m*: an end
fluentum, **-i** *n*: a stream
gradus, **-us** *m*: a step
gravis, **-e**: serious
haurio, (4), **hausi**, **hauritus**, **-a**, **-um**: draw out
illic: in that place
immanis, **-e**: immense
indidem: from the same place
insuper: (*adv.*) in addition
invenio, (4), **inveni**, **inventus**: to contrive
jugum, **-i** *n*: a ridge, summit
letalis, **-e**: lethal
magnitudo, **-inis** *f.* size
nutrio, (4): to feed
palus, **-udis** *f.* a swamp
penitus, **-a**, **-um**: inner
pessimus, **-a**, **-um**: worst
peto, (3): to make for
praedictus, **-a**, **-um**: previously named
raucus, **-a**, **-um**: raucous
rigens, **-entis** (*gen.*): freezing cold
ros, **roris** *m*: spray of water
saxum, **-i** *n*: a stone
scaturrigo, **-inis** *f.* bubbling
studiose: (*adv.*) eagerly
summus, **-a**, **-um**: the top of
trado, (3), **tradidi**: to hand over
urnula, **-ae** *f.* a little jar
vasculum, **-i** *n*: a small vessel
vastus, **-a**, **-um**: monstrous
vita, **-ae** *f.* life

---

hauritum: perf. part. of *haurio*, (=*haustum*), "water having been drawn out"
ista...urnula: abl. means, "drawn *with that little jar of yours*"
aiens: a rare pr. part. of *aio*, "saying"
crustallo: abl. source, "hewn *from crystal*"
inventura: fut. act. part. expressing purp., "went there *in order to contrive*"
cum primum...appulit: cum temporal clause, "as soon as she has landed"
praedicti jugi: gen. after *conterminos*, "next to *the previosuly mentioned ridge*"
immani magnitudine: abl. specification, "lofty *with immense size*"

procerum et inaccessa salebritate lubricum, mediis e faucibus lapidis fontes horridos evomebat, qui statim proni foraminis lacunis editi perque proclive delapsi et angusti canalis exarato contecti tramite proxumam convallem latenter incidebant. Dextra laevaque cautibus cavatis proserpunt, ecce, longa colla porrecti, saevi dracones inconivae vigiliae luminibus addictis et in perpetuam lucem pupulis excubantibus. Jamque et ipsae semet muniebant vocales aquae. Nam et, "Discede," et, "quid facis? Vide," et, "quid agis?

---

addico, (3), **addixi**, **addictus**: to devote, dedicate (+ *dat.*)
angustus, **-a**, **-um**: steep
aqua, **-ae** *f.* water
canalis, **-is** *n*: a channel
cautes, **-is** *f.* a crag
cavatus, **-a**, **-um**: hollow
collum, **-i** *n*: a neck
contego, (3), **contexi**, **contectus**: to conceal
convallis, **-is** *f.* a valley, ravine
delabor, (3), **delapsus sum**: to flow down
dexter, **-tra**, **trum**: on the right side
discedo, (3): to withdraw
draco, **-onis** *m*: a dragon, snake
ecce: behold!
edo, (3), **edidi**, **editus**: to eject
evomo, (3): to vomit out
exaro, (1): to plow
excubo, (1): to be attentive, stay awake
faux, **faucis** *f.* a chasm
foramen, **-inis** *n*: a fissure
horridus, **-a**, **-um**: wild
inaccessus, **-a**, **-um**: inaccessible
incido, (3): to fall upon
inconivus, **-a**, **um**: unsleeping
lacuna, **-ae** *f.* a hollow, cleft
laevus, **-a**, **-um**: on the left side
lapis, **-idis** *m*: a stone, milestone, jewel
latenter: (*adv.*) secretly
lubricus, **-a**, **-um**: slippery
lumen, **-inis** *n*: an eye
lux, **lucis** *f.* daylight, vision
medius, **-a**, **-um**: middle
munio, (4): to protect
perpetuus, **-a**, **-um**: perpetual
porrigo, (3), **porrexi**, **porrectus**: to stretch out
procerus, **-a**, **-um**: lofty
proclivis, **-is** *n*: a downward slope
pronus, **-a**, **-um**: prone
proserpo, (3): to creep forward
proxumus, **-a**, **-um**: nearest
pupula, **-ae** *f.* pupil of the eye
saevus, **-a**, **-um**: fierce
salebritas, **-ates** *f.* ruggedness
trames, **-itis** *m*: a track
vigilia, **-ae** *f.* a watch, wakefulness
vocalis, **-e**: causing speech

---

inaccessa salebritate: abl. specification, "slippery *with inaccessible ruggedness*"
qui...editi...delapsi...contecti: perf. part. "the waters *which, having been ejected... having fallen down... having been hidden*"
lacunis: abl. sep., "ejected *from the hollows*"
exarato...tramite: abl. means, "hidden *by the plowed track* of a narrow channel"
Dextra laevaque: abl. place, "on the right side and on the left side"
cautibus cavatis: abl. place from which, "from the hollow crags"
luminibus addictis: abl. abs., "*with eyes devoted to* wakefulness"
pupulis excubantibus: abl. abs., "with pupils staying awake"
semet: strengthened form of **se**: "the waters tried to protect *themselves*"

Cave," et, "Fuge," et, "Peribis," subinde clamant. Sic impossibilitate ipsa mutata in lapidem Psyche, quamvis praesenti corpore, sensibus tamen aberat et inextricabilis periculi mole prorsus obruta lacrumarum etiam extremo solacio carebat.

The eagle of Jupiter, in honor of Cupid, performs Psyche's task.

[15] Nec Providentiae bonae graves oculos innocentis animae latuit aerumna. Nam supremi Iovis regalis ales illa repente propansis utrimque pinnis affuit, rapax aquila, memorque veteris obsequii, quo ductu Cupidinis Iovi pocillatorem Phrygium sustulerat,

---

absum, **abesse**, **afui**, **afuturus**: to be absent
adsum, **adesse**, **affui**, **affuturus**: to arrive, be present
aerumna, **-ae** *f.* distress
ales, **-itis** *f.* a bird
anima, **-ae** *f.* soul
aquila, **-ae** *f.* an eagle
bonus, **-a**, **-um**: good
careo, (2): to be without, lack
caveo, (2): to beware
clamo, (1): to shout out
ductus, **-us** *m*: a leading, conducting
fugio, (3): to flee
gravis, **-e**: grave, earnest
impossibilitas, **-atis** *f.* impossibility
inextricabilis, **-e**: impossible to disentangle
innocens, **-entis** (*gen.*): innocent
lacruma, **-ae** *f.* a tear
lapis, **-idis** *m*: a stone
lateo, (2), **latui**: to lie hidden from
memor, **-oris** (*gen.*): mindful
moles, **-is** *f.* burden
muto, (1): to change
obruo, (3), **obrui**, **obrutus**: to overwhelm
obsequium, **-i** *n*: deference
pereo, **-ire**, **-ivi**, **-itus**: to die
periculum, **-i** *n*: danger
Phrygius, **-a**, **-um**: Phrygian (Trojan)
pocillator, **-oris** *m*: a cupbearer
praesens, **-entis** (*gen.*): present
propando, (3), **propansi**, **propansus**: to spread out
prorsus: (*adv.*) entirely
Providentia, **-ae** *f.* Providence
rapax, **-acis** (*gen.*): rapacious
regalis, **-e**: royal
repente: (*adv.*) suddenly
sensus, **-us** *m*: sense
solacium, **-i** *n*: solace
subinde: (*adv.*) repeatedly
suffero, **sufferre**, **sustuli**, **sublatus**: to bear
supremus, **-a**, **-um**: greatest
utrimque: on each side
vetus, **veteris** (*gen.*): long established

---

impossibilitate: abl. cause, "having been turned *because of the impossibility*"
praesenti corpore: abl. abs. concessive, "although her body being present"
sensibus: abl. specification, "absent *in the senses*"
mole: abl. means, "overwhelmed *by the burden*"
extremo solacio: abl. sep. with *carebat*, "she was without *the last solace*"
graves oculos: acc. obj. of *latuit*, "lie hidden from *earnest eyes*"
propansis utrimque pinnis: abl. abs., "with wings spread out on each side"
quo: abl. time, "at which time"
ductu: abl. means, "*by the leading* of Cupid"
pocillatorem: "the cup-bearer," i.e. Ganymede
sustulerat: plupf., "he had borne aloft"

opportunam ferens opem deique numen in uxoris laboribus percolens alti culminis diales vias deserit et ob os puellae praevolans incipit: "at tu, simplex alioquin et expers rerum talium, sperasne te sanctissimi nec minus truculenti fontis vel unam stillam posse furari vel omnino contingere? Diis etiam ipsique Jovi formidabiles aquas istas Stygias vel fando comperisti, quodque vos dejeratis per numina deorum deos per Stygis majestatem solere. Sed cedo istam urnulam."

---

alioquin (*adv.*): in general
altus, **-a**, **-um**: profound
aqua, **-ae** *f.* water
cedo, (3): to grant
comperio, (4), **comperi**, **compertus**: to hear, discover
contingo, (3): touch
culmen, **-inis** *n*: height
dejero, (1): to swear
desero, (3): to depart
Dialis, **-e**: of Jupiter
expers, **-ertis** (*gen.*): lacking experience of + gen.
fero, **ferre**, **tuli**, **latus**: to bring
for, (1), **fatus sum**: to speak, talk, say
formidabilis, **-e**: terrifying
furor, (1), **furatus sum**: to steal
incipio, (3): to begin
majestas, **-atis** *f.* majesty
opportunus, **-a**, **-um**: advantageous
ops, **opis** *f.* help
percolens, **-entis** (*gen.*): honoring completely
praevolo, (1): to fly before
sanctus, **-a**, **-um**: sacred
simplex, **-icis**: simple
soleo, (2), **solitus sum**: to be in the habit of
spero, (1): to hope
stilla, **-ae** *f.* a drop
Stygius, **-a**, **-um**: Stygian of the underworld
Styx, **Stygis** *f.* the Styx River
truculentus, **-a**, **-um**: ferocious
urnula, **-ae** *f.* a little pot
via, **-ae** *f.* a way

---

dei numen: "the power of the god," i.e. Cupid
uxoris: "in the labors *of the wife*," i.e. Psyche
te...posse: ind. st. after *speras*, "do you hope *that you are able?*" + inf.
Diis...ipsique Jovi: dat. of reference, "terrifying *to the gods and to Jupiter himself*"
vel fando: supine abl. source, "you have learned *at least from speaking*," i.e. from hearsay
quodque (=quodaque)...dejeratis: "and just as you (i.e. humans) swear"
deos...solere: ind. st. after *comperisti*, "learned *that the gods are accustomed*," (sc. "to swear")
cedo: irregular imper. of *cedo*, "grant!"

Et protinus adreptam completum festinat, libratisque pinnarum nutantium molibus inter genas saevientium dentium et trisulca vibramina draconum remigium dextra laevaque porrigens nolentes aquas, et ut abiret innoxius, praeminantes excipit, commentus ob jussum Veneris petere eique se praeministrare, quare paulo facilior adeundi fuit copia.

---

abeo, **-ire**, **-ivi**, **-itus**: to depart
adeo, **-ire**, **-ivi**, **-itus**: to approach
adripio, (3), **adripui**, **adreptus**: to snatch
comminiscor, (1), **commentus sum**: to pretend
compleo, (2), **-evi**, **-etum**: to fill up
copia, **-ae** *f.* supply, means
dens, **-entis** *m*: a tooth
draco, **-onis** *m*: a dragon
excipio, (3): to receive, collect
facilis, **-e**: easy
gena, **-ae** *f.* a cheek, jaw
innoxius, **-a**, **-um**: unharmed
jussus, **-us** *m*: an order
laevus, **-a**, **um**: to left side
libro, (1): to balance
moles, **-is** *f.* a mass
nolo, **nolle**, **nolui**: to be unwilling
nuto, (1): to nod, flutter
peto, (3): to attack
porrigo, (3): to extend
praeministro, (1): to attend to
praemino, (1): to threaten thoroughly
protinus: (*adv.*) without pause
quare: whereby
remigium, **-i** *n*: rowing, oarage
saevio, (4): to rage
trisulcus, **-a**, **-um**: triple-forked
vibramen, **-inis** *n*: a quivering

---

adreptam (sc. urnulam): "to fill (the pot) *having been snatched up*"
completum: supine acc. indicating purp., "in order to fill (the pot)."
libratis...molibus: abl. abs., "with the weight having been balanced"
inter genas...et vibramina: "extending his oarage *between the jaws and the fangs* of the snakes"
remigium: "oarage" of feathers, i.e. wings
nolentes...praeminantes: pr. part. concess., "waters, *although unwilling ... warning*"
ut abiret: impf. subj. in noun clause after *praeminantes*, "waters warning *him to depart* [while] unharmed"
petere eique se praeministrare: ind. st. after *commentus*, "pretending *that he was seeking and attending to her*"
paulo: abl. degree of difference after *facilior*, "easier *by a little*"
adeundi: gerund gen. after *copia*, "means *of approaching*"

Venus sets one more task for Psyche: she must enter the underworld and retrieve some of Proserpina's beauty for Venus.

[16] Sic acceptam cum gaudio plenam urnulam Psyche Veneri citata rettulit. Nec tamen nutum deae saevientis vel tunc expiare potuit. Nam sic eam majora atque pejora flagitia comminans appellat renidens exitiabile: "Jam tu quidem magna videris quaedam mihi et alta prorsus malefica, quae talibus praeceptis meis obtemperasti naviter. Sed adhuc istud, mea pupula, ministrare debebis. Sume istam pyxidem," et dedit; "protinus usque ad inferos et ipsius Orci ferales penates te derige. Tunc conferens pyxidem Proserpinae:

---

accipio, (3), **accepi**, **acceptus**: to receive
adhuc: still
altus, **-a**, **-um**: noble, profound
appello, (1): to address
citatus, **-a**, **-um**: quick
comminor, (1), **comminatus sum**: to threaten
confero, **-ferre**, **-tuli**, **collatus**: to bestow
debeo, (2): to be obliged to + inf.
derigo, (3): to direct
do, (1), **dedi**: to give
exitiabilis, **-e**: deadly
expio, (1): to expiate, appease
feralis, **-e**: funereal
flagitium, **-i** *n*: outrage
gaudium, **-i** *n*: joy
inferus, **-i** *m*: the dead
major, **-us**: larger
malefica, **-ae** *f.* a witch
ministro, (1): to attend (to)
naviter (*adv.*): diligently
nutus, **-us** *m*: will
obtempero, (1): to comply
Orcus, **-i** *m*: Dis, god of the underworld
pejor, **-us**: worse
Penas, **-atis** *m*: Penates, gods of home; dwelling
plenus, **-a**, **-um**: full
prorsus (*adv.*): absolutely
pupula, **-ae** *f.* a little girl, pupil
pyxis, **-idis** *f.* a small box
refero, **referre**, **rettuli**, **relatus**: to carry back
renideo, (2): to gleam, smile
saevio, (4): to be ferocious
sumo, (3): to take up
urnula, **-ae** *f.* a little pot
video, (2): to seem (pass.)

---

cum gaudio: abl. manner, "received *with joy*"
vel tunc: "not *even then*"
majora atque pejora flagitia: acc. dir. obj. of *comminans*, "threatening *larger and worse outrages*"
exitiabile: neut. adverbial, "smiling *in a deadly manner*"
magna...quaedam...et alta...malefica: nom. s. pred., "seem to be *a certain great and profound witch*"
talibus praeceptis meis: dat. with compound verb, "complied with *my such demands*"
obtemperasti (=obtemperavasti): *perf.* "you who have complied"
debebis: fut., "you will need to" + inf.

'petit de te Venus," dicito, "modicum de tua mittas ei formonsitate, vel ad unam saltem dieculam sufficiens. Nam quod habuit, dum filium curat aegrotum, consumpsit atque contrivit omne.' sed haud immaturius redito, quia me necesse est indidem delitam theatrum deorum frequentare."

Again planning to commit suicide, Psyche climbs to the top of a tower that stops her by offering advice.

[17] Tunc Psyche vel maxime sensit ultimas fortunas suas et velamento rejecto ad promptum exitium sese compelli manifeste

---

aegrotus, **-a**, **-um**: love-sick
compello, (3): to force
consumo, (3), **consumpsi**: to consume
contero, (3), **contrivi**: to use up
curo, (1): to take care of
delino, (3), **delivi**, **delitus**: to anoint
diecula, **-ae** *f.* little day
exitium, **-i** *n*: death
formonsitas, **-atis** *f.* beauty
fortuna, **-ae** *f.* fortune
frequento, (1): to visit
habeo, (2), **habui**: to have
haud: by no means
immaturius: (*adv.*) more untimely, later
indidem (*adv.*): from the same place
manifeste: (*adv.*) undoubtedly
mitto, (3): to send
modicum, **-i**, *n*: a small amount
peto, (3): to desire
promptus, **-a**, **-um**: manifest
redeo, **-ire**, **-ivi**, **-itus**: to return
rejicio, (3), **rejeci**, **rejectus**: to throw back, remove
saltem (*adv.*): at least
sentio, (4), **sensi**: feel
sufficio, (3): to suffice
theatrum, **-i** *n*: a theater
ultimus, **-a**, **-um**: last, worst
velamentum, **-i** *n*: a cover, veil

---

dicito: fut. imper., "you must say!"
mittas: pr. subj. in ind. command, "seeks *that you send*"
ad unam...dieculam: after *sufficiens* expressing purp., "sufficient *for one little day*"
quod habuit: perf., "*what she has had* she consumed"
redito: fut. imper., "you must return!"
delitam: perf. part., "me *having been anointed*"
me...frequentare: acc. + inf. after *necesse est*, "necessary *that I visit*"
ultimas: acc. pred., "sensed her fortune to be *worst*"
velamento rejecto: abl. abs., "with the veil having been removed," i.e. pretense having been dropped
sese compelli: pr. passive inf. in ind. st. after *comperit*, "realizes *that she is forced*"

comperit. Quidni? Quae suis pedibus ultro ad Tartarum manesque commeare cogeretur. Nec cunctata diutius pergit ad quampiam turrim praealtam, indidem sese datura praecipitem: sic enim rebatur ad inferos recte atque pulcherrime se posse descendere. Sed turris prorumpit in vocem subitam et: "quid te," inquit, "praecipitio, misella, quaeris extinguere? Quidque jam novissimo periculo laborique isto temere succumbis? Nam si spiritus corpore tuo semel fuerit sejugatus, ibis quidem profecto ad imum Tartarum, sed inde nullo pacto redire poteris. Mihi ausculta.

---

ausculto, (1): to listen to (+ *dat.*)
cogo, (3): to compel
commeo, (1): to go to
comperio, (4), **comperi**: discover
cunctor, (1), **cunctatus sum**: to delay
descendo, (3): to descend
diutius: longer
eo, ire, ivi, itus: to pass
extinguo, (3): to kill
imus, -a, -um: deepest
indidem (*adv.*): from the same place
inferus, -i *m*: the dead
manis, -is *m*: shades of dead (*pl.*)
misellus, -a, -um: wretched
pactum, -i *n*: manner
pes, pedis *m*: foot
praealtus, -a, -um: very high
praeceps, -ipitis (*gen.*): headlong
praecipitium, -i *n*: fall, throw down
profecto: (*adv.*) surely, certainly
prorumpo, (3): to break out
quaero, (3): to seek
quidni: why not?
quispiam, quaepiam, quodpiam: any
recte: (*adv.*) rightly
redeo, -ire, -ivi, -itus: to return
reor, (2), **ratus sum**: to suppose
sejugatus, -a, -um: separated
semel: one time
spiritus, -us *m*: life
subitus, -a, -um: unexpected
succumbo, (3): to break down
Tartarus, -i *m*: Tartarum
temere: (*adv.*) blindly
turris, -is *f*: a tower
ultro: (*adv.*) unaided, spontaneously

Quae...cogeretur: impf. subj. in causal relative clause of characteristic, "she *who would be compelled*" + inf., i.e. since she would be compelled
suis pedibus: abl. means, "to go *on her own feet*"
sese datura: fut. act. part. indicating purp., "she intending *to give herself headlong*"
se posse: ind. st. after *rebatur*, "was thinking *that she could*" + inf.
novissimo periculo laborique isto: dat. with compound verb, "succumb to *the newest danger and this task of yours*"
si...fuerit sejugatus: fut. perf. in fut. more vivid protasis, "if your spirit will have been separated"
corpore tuo: abl. sep., "separated *from your body*"
nullo pacto: abl. manner, "able *in no manner*"

The tower explains to Psyche how to enter the underworld and cross the river Styx.

[18] Lacedaemo Achaiae nobilis civitas non longe sita est: huius conterminam deviis abditam locis quaere Taenarum. Inibi spiraculum Ditis et per portas hiantes monstratur iter invium, cui te limine transmeato simul commiseris, jam canale directo perges ad ipsam Orci regiam. Sed non hactenus vacua debebis per illas tenebras incedere, sed offas polentae mulso concretas ambabus gestare manibus at in ipso ore duas ferre stipes. Jamque confecta

---

abdo, (3), **abdidi**, **abditus**: to hide
Achaia, **-ae** *f.* Achaia, region in the northwest Peloponnese in Greece
ambo, **-ae**, **-o**: both
canale, **-is** *m*: a channel
civitas, **-atis** *f.* a city
committo, (3), -misi, missus: to commit
concretus, **-a**, **-um**: dense, kneeded together
conficio, (3), **confeci**, **confectus**: to complete
conterminus, **-a**, **-um**: neighboring, adjacent to (+ *gen.*)
debeo, (2): to be obliged to
devius, **-a**, **-um**: remote
directo: (*adv.*) in straight line
Dis, **Ditis** *m*: Dis, the underworld
fero, **ferre**, **tuli**, **latus**: to bring
gesto, (1): to carry
hactenus (*adv.*): in this way
hio, (1): to be wide open, gape
incedo, (3): to walk
inibi (*adv.*): in that place
invius, **-a**, **-um**: impassable
iter, **itineris** *n*: a path, pass
Lacedaemo, **-onis** *m*: Lacedaemon, the region of Sparta
limen, **-inis** *n*: a threshold
longe: (*adv.*) far
monstro, (1): to reveal
mulsum, **-i** *n*: honeyed wine
nobilis, **-e**: noble
offa, **-ae** *f.* a lump of food, cake
Orcus, **-i** *m*: Dis, god of the underworld
polenta, **-ae** *f.* barley-meal
porta, **-ae** *f.* a gate
quaero, (3): to seek
regia, **-ae** *f.* a palace
simul (*adv.*): at same time
sino, (3), **sivi**, **situs**: to allow
spiraculum, **-i** *n*: vent, breathing-passage
stips, **-ipis** *f.* a small offering (coin)
Taenarus, **-i** *f.* Taenarum, well-known entrance to the underworld
tenebra, **-ae** *f.* darkness (*pl.*)
transmeo, (1): to cross
vacuus, **-a**, **-um**: empty

---

iter invium: an oxymoron, "an impassable pass"
cui...commiseris: fut. perf. "*to which* path *you will have committed* yourself"
limine transmeato: abl. abs., "with the threshold having been crossed"
simul...iam: "*once* you have...*then* you will"
canale directo: abl. means, "go *by a direct channel*"
vacua: nom. s., "you...*empty*," i.e. empty-handed
polentae: gen. of quality, "cakes *of barley*"
mulso: abl. specification, "kneeded *with honeyed wine*"
ambabus...manibus: abl. means, "in both hands"

bona parte mortiferae viae continaberis claudum asinum lignorum gerulum cum agasone simili, qui te rogabit decidentis sarcinae fusticulos aliquos porrigas ei, sed tu nulla voce deprompta tacita praeterito. Nec mora, cum ad flumen mortuum venies, cui praefectus Charon protenus expetens portorium sic ad ripam ulteriorem sutili cumba deducit commeantes. Ergo et inter mortuos avaritia vivit nec Charon, ille Ditis exactor tantus deus, quicquam gratuito facit:

---

agaso, **-onis** *m*: a driver
asinus, **-i** *m*: an ass, donkey
avaritia, **-ae** *f.* greed
Charon, -onis, *m*: Charon, ferryman of the dead
claudus, **-a**, **-um**: lame
commeo, (1): to travel
continor, (1), **continatus sum**: to encounter
cumba, **-ae** *f.* a small boat
decido, (3), **decidi**, **decisus**: to fall
deduco, (3): to escort
depromo, (3), **deprompsi**, **depromptus**: to utter
Dis, Ditis *m*: Dis, the underworld
exactor, **-oris** *m*: an exactor
expeto, (3): to ask for
flumen, **-inis** *n*: a river
fusticulus, **-i** *m*: a little stick
gerulus, **-i** *m*: a bearer
gratuitus, **-a**, **-um**: without pay
lignum, **-i** *n*: firewood
mora, **-ae** *f.* delay
mortifer, **-a**, **-um**: deadly
mortuus, **-i** *m*: the dead
pars, **partis** *f.* a part
porrigo, (3): to extend, hand X (*acc.*) to Y (*dat.*)
portorium, **-i** *n*: port duty, toll
praefectus, **-i** *m*: a commander
praetereo, **-ire**, **-ivi**, **-itus**: to pass by
protenus: (*adv.*) immediately
ripa, **-ae** *f.* a bank
rogo, (1): to ask
sarcina, **-ae** *f.* a burden
similis, **-e**: similar
sutilis, **-e**: patched, made by sewing
tacitus, **-a**, **-um**: silent
ulterior, **-ius**: last
via, **-ae** *f.* a road
vivo, (3): to live

---

gestare…ferre: also complementing *debebis*, "you will need *to carry…to bring*"
confecta bona parte: abl. abs., "with a good part having been completed"
decidentis…fusticulos: acc., "the sticks falling" + gen.
porrigas: pr. subj. in ind. command, "ask *that you hand* sticks to him"
nulla voce deprompta: abl. abs., "with no voice having been uttered"
praeterito: future imperative, "you must pass by!"
cui: dat. of possession, "the river, *whose* commander"
commeantes: acc. dir. obj., "transports *those traveling*"
et inter mortuos: "even among the dead"

set moriens pauper viaticum debet quaerere, et aes si forte prae manu non fuerit, nemo eum exspirare patietur. Huic squalido seni dabis nauli nomine de stipibus quas feres alteram, sic tamen ut ipse sua manu de tuo sumat ore. Nec setius tibi pigrum fluentum transmeanti quidam supernatans senex mortuus putris adtollens manus orabit ut eum intra navigium trahas, nec tu tamen inclita adflectare pietate.

---

adflecto, (1): to influence
adtollo, (3): to raise
aes, **aeris** *n*: money
alter, **-era**, **-erum**: one (of two)
debeo, (2): to be obliged to (+ *inf.*)
exspiro, (1): to die
fero, **ferre**, **tuli**, **latus**: to bring
fluentum, **-i** *n*: a stream
fors, **fortis** *f.* chance
inclitus, **-a**, **-um**: celebrated, renowned
morior, (3), **mortuus sum**: to die
naulum, **-i** *n*: a fare, passage money
navigium, **-i** *n*: a vessel
nemo, **-inis** *n*: no one
nomen, **-inis** *n*: an account
oro, (1): to beg
os, **oris** *n*: a mouth
patior, (3), **passus sum**: to allow (+ *inf.*)
pauper, **pauperis** *m*: a poor man
pietas, **-atis** *f.* loyalty
piger, **-a**, **-um**: slow
prae: (*adv.*) before
puter, **-tris**, **-tre**: decaying
quaero, (3): to obtain
senex, **-is** *m*: an old man
set: but
squalidus, **-a**, **-um**: filthy
stips, **-ipis** *f.* a small offering (coin)
sumo, (3): to obtain
supernato, (1): to float
traho, (3): to drag
transmeo, (1): to cross
viaticum, **-i** *n*: a traveling allowance

---

si...non fuerit: fut. perf. in fut. more vivid protasis, "unless there will be"
forte: abl. circumstance, "by chance"
Huic squalido seni: dat. ind. obj., "to this filthy old man"
nomine: abl. specification, "*for the payment* of fare," cf. 6.8
ut...sumat: pr. subj. in result clause, "in such a way *that he obtains*"
sua manu: abl. means, "with his own hand"
Nec setius: "no less," i.e. likewise
transmeanti: dat. ind. obj., "to you *crossing*"
putris...manus: acc. dir. obj. of *adtollens*, "raising *decaying hands*"
ut...trahas: pr. subj. in ind. command, "will beg *that you drag*"
nec...adflectare: pass. imper., "do not be influenced!"

The tower continues, explaining to Psyche how to treat those she encounters and return from the underworld. Above all, the tower warns not look into the box that Proserpina has filled for Venus.

[19] Transito fluvio modicum te progressam textrices orabunt anus telam struentes manus paulisper accommodes, nec id tamen tibi contingere fas est. Nam haec omnia tibi et multa alia de Veneris insidiis orientur, ut vel unam de manibus omittas offulam. Nec putes futile istud polentacium damnum leve; altera enim perdita lux haec tibi prorsus denegabitur. Canis namque praegrandis terjugo et satis amplo capite praeditus, immanis et formidabilis, tonantibus oblatrans faucibus mortuos, quibus jam nil mali potest

---

accommodo, (1): to apply
alter, **-era**, **-erum**: one (of two), either
amplus, **-a**, **-um**: ample
anus, **-a**, **-um**: aged
canis, **-is** *m*: a dog
contingo, (3): to touch
damnum, **-i** *n*: loss
denego, (1): to deny
fas: allowable, permitted (+ *inf.*)
faux, **faucis** *f.* a maw
fluvius, **-i** *m*: a river
formidabilis, **-e**: terrifying
futilis, **-e**: worthless
immanis, **-e**: monstrous
insidia, **-ae** *f.* a trap
levis, **-e**: trifling
lux, **lucis** *f.* light, life
modicum, **-i**, *n*: a short distance
oblatro, (1): to bark at
offula, **-ae** *f.* a little lump of food, cake
omitto, (3): to let go
orior, (3), **oritus sum**: to emerge
oro, (1): to ask
paulisper: (*adv.*) for only a short time
perdo, (3), **perdidi**, **perditus**: to lose
polentacius, **-a**, **-um**: of barley-meal
praeditus, **-a**, **-um**: endowed with
praegrandis, **-e**: very large
progredior, (3), **progressus sum**: to advance
prorsus: (*adv.*) entirely
puto, (1): to suppose
struo, (3): to construct
tela, **-ae** *f.* warp
terjugus, **-a**, **-um**: threefold
textrix, **-icis** *f.* female weaver, the Fates
tono, (1): to thunder
transeo, **-ire**, **-ivi**, **-itus**: to cross

Transito fluvio: abl. abs., "with the river having been crossed"
accomodes: pr. subj. in ind. command, "will beg *that you apply*"
ut...omittas: pr. subj. in purp. clause, "will emerge *so that you might let go*"
Nec putes: pr. subj. in prohibition, "do not suppose"
polentacium damnum (=polentae damnum): "loss of a barley cake"
leve: acc. pred., "this loss to be *trifling*"
altera...perdita: abl. abs., "with either having been lost"
terjugo et...amplo capite: abl. desc., "endowed with *a threefold and ample head*" (the dog is Cerberus)
tonantibus...faucibus: abl. specification, "barking *with a thundering maw*"
quibus: ind. obj., "the dead *to whom* he can do"

facere, frustra territando ante ipsum limen et atra atria Proserpinae semper excubans servat vacuam Ditis domum. Hunc offrenatum unius offulae praeda facile praeteribis ad ipsamque protinus Proserpinam introibis, quae te comiter excipiet ac benigne, ut et molliter assidere et prandium opipare suadeat sumere. Sed tu et humi reside et panem sordidum petitum esto. Deinde nuntiato quid adveneris susceptoque quod offeretur rursus remeans canis

---

advenio, (4): to arrive
assido, (3): to sit down
ater, **-tra**, **-trum**: gloomy
atrium, **-i** *n*: an atrium
benigne: (*adv.*) kindly
canis, **-is** *m*: a dog
comiter: (*adv.*) courteously
edo, **esse**: eat
excipio, (3): to receive
excubo, (1): to keep watch
frustra (*adv.*): in vain
humi (**loc.**): on the ground
introeo, **-ire**, **-ivi**, **-itus**: to enter
limen, **-inis** *n*: a threshold
molliter: (*adv.*) calmly
nuntio, (1): to announce
offero, **offerre**, **obtuli**, **oblatus**: to offer
offrenatus, **-a**, **-um**: tamed
opipare: (*adv.*) sumptuously
panis, **-is** *m*: bread
peto, (3), **petivi**, **petitus**: to ask (for)
praeda, **-ae** *f*: loot, prize
praetereo, **-ire**, **-ivi**, **-itus**: to pass by
prandium, **-i** *n*: lunch
remeo, (1): to return
resideo, (2): to sit down on
rursus (*adv.*): backward
servo, (1): to guard
sordidus, **-a**, **-um**: paltry
suadeo, (2): to persuade
sumo, (3): to accept
suscipio, (3), **suscepi**, **susceptus**: to accept
territo, (1): to intimidate
unus, **-a**, **-um** (*gen.* **–ius**): one
vacuus, **-a**, **-um**: empty

---

territando: gerund abl. means, "he guards *by terrifying*"
praeda: abl. means, "tamed *by the prize*"
ut...suadeat: pr. subj. in purp. clause, "in order to persuade" + inf.
prandium...sumere: "to take lunch"
reside: imper., "sit down on!"
petitum: perf. part., "bread, *having been sought*"
esto: fut. imper. of *edo*, "eat!"
nuntiato: perf. part. in abl. abs. with clause *quid adveneris* as subject, "why you have arrived *having been announced*"
quid adveneris: perf. subj. in ind. quest., "*why you have arrived*"
susecepto: perf. part. in abl. abs. with clause *quid offeretur* as subject, "what will be offered *having been received*"
quod...offeretur: fut. pass. in rel. clause, "*that which will be offered*"

saevitiam offula reliqua redime ac deinde avaro navitae data quam reservaveris stipe transitoque eius fluvio recalcans priora vestigia ad istum caelestium siderum redies chorum. Sed inter omnia hoc observandum praecipue tibi censeo: ne velis aperire vel inspicere illam quam feres pyxidem vel omnino divinae formonsitatis abditum curiosius temptare thensaurum."

---

abdo, (3), **abdidi**, **abditus**: to hide
aperio, (4): to open
avarus, **-a**, **-um**: greedy
caelestis, **-e**: heavenly
censeo, (3): to recommend
chorus, **-i** *m*: a chorus
curiosius (**comp. adv.**): more curiously
do, (1): to give
fero, **ferre**, **tuli**, **latus**: to bear
formonsitas, **-atis** *f*: beauty
inspicio, (3): to look into
navita, **-ae** *m*: a sailor
observo, (1): to heed
omnino (*adv.*): generally
praecipue: (*adv.*) especially
prior, **-us**: former
pyxis, **-idis** *f*: a small box
recalco, (1): to tread again
redeo, **-ire**, **-ivi**, **-itus**: to return
redimo, (3): to buy off
reliquus, **-a**, **-um**: remaining
reservo, (1): to reserve
saevitia, **-ae** *f*: rage
sidus, **-eris** *n*: a star
tempto, (1): to test
thensaurus, **-i** *m*: treasure
transeo, **-ire**, **-ivi**, **-itus**: to cross

---

offula reliqua: abl. means, "buy off *with the remaining little lump of food*"
redime: imper., "buy off!"
avaro navitae: dat., "given *to the greedy sailor,*" i.e. Charon
data…stipe: abl. abs. "the coin having been given"
quam reservaveris: fut. perf., "coin *which you will have saved*"
transito…fluvio: abl. abs., "with the river having been crossed"
redies (=redibis): "you will return"
hoc observandum (sc. esse): gerundive in ind. st., "recommend *that this be heeded* especially"
ne velis: pr. subj. in prohibition, "do not want" + inf.
quam feres: fut., "the box *which you will be carrying*"

Psyche follows the tower's instructions, but she succumbs to her curiosity.

[20] Sic turris illa prospicua vaticinationis munus explicuit. Nec morata Psyche pergit Taenarum sumptisque rite stipibus illis et offulis infernum decurrit meatum transitoque per silentium asinario debili et amnica stipe vectori data neglecto supernatantis mortui desiderio et spretis textricum subdolis precibus et offulae cibo sopita canis horrenda rabie domum Proserpinae penetrat. Nec

---

amnicus, **-a**, **-um**: of a river
asinarius, **-i** *m*: an ass-driver
canis, **-is** *m*: a dog
cibus, **-i** *m*: a morsel
debilis, **-e**: crippled
decurro, (3): to hurry down
desiderium, **-i** *n*: a desire, request
do, (1), **dedi**, **datus**: to pay
explico, (1), **explicui**: unfold, set forth
horrendus, **-a**, **-um**: horrible
infernus, **-a**, **-um**: infernal
meatus, **-us** *m*: a passage-way
moror, (1), **moratus sum**: to delay
mortuus, **-i** *m*: a corpse, the dead
munus, **-eris** *n*: service
neglego, (3), **neglexi**, **neglectus**: to ignore
penetro, (1): to enter
prospicuus, **-a**, **-um**: provident
rabies, **-ei** *f*: madness
rite: (*adv.*) duly
silentium, **-i** *n*: silence
sopio, (4), **sopivi**, **sopitus**: to render insensible
sperno, (3), **sprevi**, **spretus**: to spurn
subdolus, **-a**, **-um**: treacherous
sumo, (3), **sumpsi**, **sumptus**: to take up, obtain
supernato, (1): to float
Taenarus, **-i** *f*: Taenarus
textrix, **-icis** *f*: a female weaver, the Fates
transeo, **-ire**, **-ivi**, **transitus**: to go over, cross
turris, **-is** *f*: a tower
vaticinatio, **-onis** *f*: prophecy
vector, **-oris** *m*: a passenger

Nec morata: perf. part., "and Psyche *not having delayed*"
sumptis...stipibus illis et offulis: abl. abs., "with those coins and little lumps of food having been taken up"
transito...asinario debili: abl. abs., "with the crippled ass-driver having been passed by"
amnica stipe...data: abl. abs., "with the river fare having been paid"
neglecto...desiderio: abl. abs., "with the request having been ignored"
spretis...subdolis precibus: abl. abs., "with the treacherous requests having been spurned"
cibo: abl. means, "rendered insensible *by the morsel*"
sopita...horrenda rabie: abl. abs., "with the horrible madness having been rendered insensible"

offerentis hospitae sedile delicatum vel cibum beatum amplexa sed ante pedes eius residens humilis cibario pane contenta Veneriam pertulit legationem. Statimque secreto repletam conclusamque pyxidem suscipit et offulae sequentis fraude caninis latratibus obseratis residuaque navitae reddita stipe longe vegetior ab inferis recurrit. Et repetita atque adorata candida ista luce, quanquam festinans obsequium terminare, mentem capitur temeraria curiositate et: "Ecce," inquit, "inepta ego divinae formonsitatis gerula, quae

---

adoro, (1): to adore
amplector, (3), **amplexus sum**: to embrace
beatus, **-a**, **-um**: sumptuous
candidus, **-a**, **-um**: bright
caninus, **-a**, **-um**: of a dog
capio, (3): to seize
cibarius, **-a**, **-um**: common
cibus, **-i** *m*: food
concludo, (3), **conclusi**, **conclusus**: to shut up
contentus, **-a**, **-um**: content
curiositas, **-atis** *f*: curiosity
delicatus, **-a**, **-um**: luxurious
festino, (1): to hurry (+ *inf.*)
fraus, **fraudis** *f*: trickery
gerula, **-ae** *f*: a bearer
hospita, **-ae** *f*: a hostess
humilis, **-e**: humble
ineptus, **-a**, **-um**: foolish
inferus, **-i** *m*: region below
latratus, **-us** *m*: barking
legatio, **-onis** *f*: a mission
longe: (*adv.*) by far
lux, **lucis** *f*: light
mens, **mentis** *f*: mind
navita, **-ae** *m*: a sailor
obsequium, **-i** *n*: service
obsero, (1): to bolt, bar
offero, **offerre**, **obtuli**, **oblatus**: to offer
panis, **-is** *m*: bread
perfero, **-ferre**, **-tuli**, **-latus**: to carry through
pes, **pedis** *m*: a foot
quanquam: although
recurro, (3): to run back
reddo, (3), **reddidi**, **redditus**: to deliver, render
repeto, (3), **repetivi**, **repetitus**: to return to
repleo, (2), **replevi**, **repletus**: to fill again
resideo, (2): to settle
residuus, **-a**, **-um**: remaining
secretum, **-i** *n*: a secret
sedile, **-is** *n*: seat
sequens, **-entis** (*gen.*): next, second
stips, **-ipis** *f*: a small offering (coin)
suscipio, (3): to take up
temerarius, **-a**, **-um**: rash
termino, (1): to conclude
vegetus, **-a**, **-um**: vigorous

Nec...amplexa: perf. part., "not having embraced"
offerentis hospitae: gen., "the feet *of her host offering* them"
cibario pane: abl. specification, "content *with plain bread*"
secreto: abl. manner, "shut up *secretly*"
fraude: abl. means, "barred *by the trickery*"
caninis latratibus obseratis: abl. abs., "with the dog-barking having been barred"
residua...reddita stipe: abl. abs., "with the remaining coin having been rendered"
repetita atque adorata...luce: abl. abs., "light having been returned to and adored"
mentem: acc. respect, "she is seized *with respect to the mind*"

nec tantillum quidem indidem mihi delibo vel sic illi amatori meo formonso placitura," et cum dicto reserat pyxidem.

Psyche falls into a deep sleep, but Cupid appears to revive her.

[21] Nec quicquam ibi rerum nec formonsitas ulla, sed infernus somnus ac vere Stygius, qui statim coperculo relevatus invadit eam crassaque soporis nebula cunctis eius membris perfunditur et in ipso vestigio ipsaque semita conlapsam possidet. Et jacebat immobilis et nihil aliud quam dormiens cadaver.

Sed Cupido jam cicatrice solida revalescens nec diutinam suae Psyches absentiam tolerans per altissimam cubiculi quo cohibebatur

---

absentia, **-ae** *f.* absence
altus, **-a**, **-um**: high
amator, **-oris** *m*: a lover
cadaver, **-eris** *n*: a corpse
cicatrix, **-icis** *f.* a scar
cohibeo, (2): to contain
conlabor, (3), **conlapsus sum**: to collapse
coperculum, **-i** *n*: a cover
crassus, **-a**, **-um**: thick
cubiculum, **-i** *n*: a bedroom
cunctus, **-a**, **-um**: all
delibo, (1): to skim off
dictum, **-i** *n*: an utterance
diutinus, **-a**, **-um**: long lasting
dormio, (4): to sleep
formonsus, **-a**, **-um**: handsome
immobilis, **-e**: unmoving
indidem (*adv.*): from the same place
infernus, **-a**, **-um**: infernal
invado, (3): to attack
jaceo, (2): to lie
membrum, **-i** *n*: a limb
nebula, **-ae** *f.* a mist
nihil: nothing
perfundo, (3): to pour over
placeo, (2), **placui**, **placitus**: to please, give pleasure to (+ *dat.*)
possideo, (3): to seize
relevo, (1): to relieve
resero, (1): to open up
revalesco, (3): to grow well again
semita, **-ae** *f.* a path
solidus, -a, -um (1): whole
sopor, **-oris** *m*: a deep sleep
Stygius, **-a**, **-um**: Stygian, of the underworld
tantillus, **-a**, **-um**: so small a quantity
tolero, (1): tolerate
vere: (*adv.*) truly
vestigium, **-i** *n*: a spot, track

---

quae nec...delibo: "I *who do not skim off*"
placitura: fut. act. part. expressing purpose, "in order to be pleasing to"
cum dicto: abl. of circumstance, "*with the utterance* she unlocks"
coperculo: abl. separation, "relieved *from the cover*"
soporis: gen. characteristic, "a thick mist *of sleep*"
cunctis...membris: abl. with *perfunditur*, "pours over *all limbs*"
cicatrice solida: abl. abs., "with the scar being whole"
per altissimam...fenestram: "through the highest window"
quo: abl. place where, "the bedroom *in which*"

elapsus fenestram refectisque pinnis aliquanta quiete longe velocius provolans Psychen accurrit suam detersoque somno curiose et rursum in pristinam pyxidis sedem recondito Psychen innoxio punctulo sagittae suae suscitat et: "Ecce," inquit, "rursum perieras, misella, simili curiositate. Sed interim quidem tu provinciam quae tibi matris meae praecepto mandata est exsequere naviter; cetera egomet videro." His dictis amator levis in pinnas se dedit, Psyche vero confestim Veneri munus reportat Proserpinae.

---

accurro, (3), **accucurri**: to hasten (to)
aliquantus, **-a**, **-um**: a certaian amount of
confestim (*adv.*): at once
curiose: (*adv.*) carefully
curiositas, **-atis** *f.* meddlesomeness
detergeo, (2), **detersi**, **detersus**: to wipe away
egomet: I myself
elabor, (3), **elapsus sum**: to escape
exsequor, (3), **exsecutus sum**: to carry out
fenestra, **-ae** *f.* a window
innoxius, **-a**, **-um**: harmless
interim: meanwhile
levis, **-e**: nimble
mando, (1): to command
misellus, **-a**, **-um**: wretched
munus, **-eris** *n*: tribute
naviter: (*adv.*) diligently
pereo, **-ire**, **-ivi**, **-itus**: to be destroyed
praeceptum, **-i** *n*: an order
pristinus, **-a**, **-um**: former
provincia, **-ae** *f.* duty
provolo, (1): to fly forward
punctulum, **-i** *n*: a pin prick
quies, **-etis** *f.* rest
recondo, (3), **recondidi**, **reconditus**: to put away
reficio, (3), **refeci**, **refectus**: to restore
reporto, (1): to carry back
sagitta, **-ae** *f.* an arrow
sedes, **-is** *f.* home
similis, **-e**: similar
suscito, (1): to awaken
velocius: (*adv.*) swiftly

---

refectis pinnis: abl. abs., "with wings having been restored"
aliquanta quiete: abl. means, "restored *by a certain amount of rest*"
deterso somno...recondito: abl. abs., "with sleep having been wiped away...and put away into"
innoxio punctulo: abl. means, "he awakens *with a harmless pinprick*"
perieras: syncopated plupf. (=*periveras*) in vivid past contrafactual protasis "you would have been destroyed"
simili curiositate: abl. cause, "by a similar meddlesomeness"
quae...mandata est: "the duty *which was commanded*"
praecepto: abl. means, "commanded *by the order*"
exsequere: imper., "carry out!"
His dictis: abl. abs., "with these having been said"

Cupid entreats Jupiter regarding his marriage to Psyche, and Jupiter consents to the marriage.

[22] Interea Cupido amore nimio peresus et aegra facie matris suae repentinam sobrietatem pertimescens ad armillum redit alisque pernicibus caeli penetrato vertice magno Iovi supplicat suamque causam probat. Tunc Juppiter prehensa Cupidinis buccula manuque ad os suum relata consaviat atque sic ad illum: "licet tu," inquit, "domine fili, numquam mihi concessu deum decretum servaris honorem, sed istud pectus meum, quo leges elementorum

---

aeger, **-gra**, **-grum**: ill
ala, **-ae** *f.* a wing
armillum, **-i** *n*: wine jar
buccula, **-ae** *f.* a little cheek
caelum, **-i** *m*: heavens
causa, **-ae** *f.* a case
concessus, **-us** *m*: an agreement
consavio, (1): to kiss affectionately
decerno, (3), **decrevi**, **decretus**: to decree
dominus, **-i** *m*: a master
elementum, **-i** *n*: elements (*pl.*)
facies, **-ei** *f.* appearance
honor, **-oris** *m*: honor
lex, **legis** *f.* law
licet: it is permitted, although (+ subj.)
nimius, **-a**, **-um**: excessive
numquam: never
pectus, **-oris** *n*: a heart
penetro, (1): to enter
peredo, (3), **peredi**, **peresus**: to consume
pernix, **-icis** (*gen.*): swift
pertimesco, (3): to become very scared (of)
prehendo, (3), **prehendi**, **prehensus**: to take in hand
probo, (1): to recommend
refero, **referre**, **rettuli**, **relatus**: to return
repentinus, **-a**, **-um**: unexpected
servo, (1): to keep
sobrietas, **-atis** *f.* sobriety
supplico, (1): to supplicate
vertex, **-icis** *m*: a peak

---

amore nimio: abl. specification, "consumed *with excessive love*"
aegra facie: abl. description, "with an ill appearance"
ad armillum redit: "he returns to his wine-jar," a proverb meaning "to return to his old tricks"
alis pernicibus: abl. means, "entered *on swift wings*"
penetrato vertice: abl. abs., "with the peak having been entered"
prehensa…buccula: abl. abs., "with the little cheek having been taken in hand"
manu…relata: abl. abs., "with the hand having been placed"
licet: "it is permitted," introduces a series of concessive clauses with the perf. subj. "although you have…"
domine fili: vocative, "master and son"
concessu: abl. means, "decreed *by the agreement*"
servaris (=servaveris): perf. subj. after *licet*, "although you have never preserved"

et vices siderum disponuntur, convulneraris assiduis ictibus crebrisque terrenae libidinis foedaveris casibus contraque leges et ipsam Juliam disciplinamque publicam turpibus adulteriis existimationem famamque meam laeseris in serpentes in ignes in feras in aves et gregalia pecua serenos vultus meos sordide reformando, at tamen modestiae meae memor quodque inter istas meas manus creveris cuncta perficiam, dum tamen scias aemulos tuos cavere, ac si qua

---

adulterium, **-i** *n*: adultery
aemulus, **-i** *m*: a rival
assiduus, **-a**, **-um**: unremitting
avis, **-is** *f.* a bird
casus, **-us** *m*: calamity
caveo, (2): to beware
convulnero, (1): to inflict severe wounds
creber, **-bra**, **-brum**: frequent
cresco, (3), **crevi**: to grow up
disciplina, **-ae** *f.* instruction
dispono, (3): to ordain, arrange
existimatio, **-onis** *f.* an opinion, reputation
fama, **-ae** *f.* reputation
fera, **-ae** *f.* a wild beast
foedo, (1): to defile
gregalis, **-e**: of the flock
ictus, **-us** *m*: a blow
ignis, **-is** *m*: fire
Julius, **-a**, **-um**: Julian, of Julius
laedo, (3), **laesi**: to injure
libido, **-inis** *f.* lust
manus, **-us** *f.* a hand
memor, **-oris** (*gen.*): mindful of (+ *gen.*)
modestia, **-ae** *f.* restraint
pecu, **-us** *n*: a sheep
perficio, (3): to bring about
publicus, **-a**, **-um**: public
reformo, (1): to transform
serenus, **-a**, **-um**: fair, serene
serpens, **-entis** *m*: a serpent, snake
sidus, **-eris** *n*: a star
sordide: (*adv.*) unbecomingly
terrenus, **-a**, **-um**: earthly
turpis, **-e**: indecent
vicis, **-is** *f.* a turn

---

quo...disponuntur: "heart *by which are disposed*"
convulneraris (=convulneraveris): perf. subj. after *licet*, "although you have inflicted sever wounds upon"
assiduis ictibus: abl. means, "inflicted *with unremitting blows*"
crebris...casibus: abl. means, "violated *with frequent calamities*"
foedaveris: perf. subj. after *licet*, "although you have violated"
ipsam Juliam (sc. legem): "against *even the Julian law*," i.e. the Julian laws enacted by Augustus in 18-17 BCE that made adultery a public crime
turpibus adulteriis: abl. means, "violated *with indecent adulteries*"
laeseris: perf. subj. after licet, "although you have injured"
reformando: gerund abl. means, "injured *by transforming*"
quod...creveris: perf. subj. in causal clause, "and *because you grew up*"
dum...scias: subj. in proviso clause, "so long as you know"

nunc in terris puella praepollet pulcritudine, praesentis beneficii vicem per eam mihi repensare te debere."

Psyche is made immortal and the gods celebrate. After a time, Psyche gives birth to her daughter, called Pleasure.

[23] Sic fatus jubet Mercurium deos omnes ad contionem protinus convocare, ac si qui coetu caelestium defuisset, in poenam decem milium nummum conventum iri pronuntiare. Quo metu statim completo caelesti theatro pro sede sublimi sedens procerus Iuppiter sic enuntiat:

---

beneficium, **-i** *n*: a favor
caeleste, **-is** *n*: heavenly matters
caelestis, **-e**: heavenly
coetus, **-us** *m*: a meeting
compleo, (2), **complevi**, **completus**: to fill, occupy
contio, **-onis** *f.* an assembly
convenio, (4), **conveni**, **conventus**: to be appropriate to, use
convoco, (1): to convene
debeo, (2): to owe, ought
decem: ten
desum, **desse**, **defui**, **defuturus**: to be absent
enuntio, (1): to speak out
for, (1), **fatus sum**: to speak
jubeo, (2): to order
metus, **-us** *m*: fear
mille, **-is** *n*: thousand
nummus, **-i** *m*: a coin, sesterce
poena, **-ae** *f.* penalty
praepolleo, (2): to be very strong, to be preeminent
praesens, **-entis** (*gen.*): present
procerus, **-a**, **-um**: tall
pronuntio, (1): to relate
pulcritudo, **-inis** *f.* beauty
repenso, (1): to recompense, repay
sedeo, (2): to remain
sedes, **-is** *n*: a seat
sublimis, **-e**: lofty
theatrum, **-i** *n*: a theater
vicis, **-is** *f.* repayment

---

te debere: ind. st. after *scias*, "know *that you ought to*" + inf.
pulchritudine: abl. specification, "is preeminent *in beauty*"
Mercurium...convocare: ind. command, "orders *Mercury to convoke*"
si qui...defuisset: plupf. subj. in ind. st. after *pronuntiare*, representing a fut. more vivid protasis, "to announce *that if anyone were absent*," the direct statement would have been *si qui defuerit*
coetu: abl. sep., "absent *from the meeting*"
conventum iri: fut. pass. inf. in ind. st., "announce *that he will be sued*"
Quo metu: abl. cause, "because of which fear"
completo...theatro: abl. abs., "with the theater having been filled"

"Dei conscripti Musarum albo, adolescentem istum quod manibus meis alumnatus sim profecto scitis omnes. Cuius primae juventutis caloratos impetus freno quodam coercendos existimavi; sat est cotidianis eum fabulis ob adulteria cunctasque corruptelas infamatum. Tollenda est omnis occasio et luxuria puerilis nuptialibus pedicis alliganda. Puellam elegit et virginitate privavit: teneat, possideat, amplexus Psychen semper suis amoribus perfruatur."

---

adolescens, **-entis** *m*: a youth
adulterium, **-i** *n*: adultery
album, **-i** *n*: an official list, register
alligo, (1): to hinder, bind
alumnor, (1), **alumnatus sum**: to nurture
amplector, (3), **amplexus sum**: to embrace
caloratus, **-a**, **-um**: heated
coerceo, (2), **coercui**, **coercitus**: to curb
conscribo, (3), **conscripsi**, **conscriptus**: to enroll
corruptela, **-ae** *f*: corruption, seduction
cotidianus, **-a**, **-um**: daily
eligo, (3), **elegi**: to choose
existimo, (1): to judge
fabula, **-ae** *f*: a drama
frenus, **-i** *m*: a check
impetus, **-us** *m*: impetus, impulse
infamo, (1): to defame
juventus, **-utis** *f*: a youth
luxuria, **-ae** *f*: extravagance
Musa, **-ae** *f*: a Muse
occasio, **-onis** *f*: an opportunity
pedica, **-ae** *f*: a fetter
perfruor, (3), **perfructus sum**: to enjoy (+ *abl.*)
possideo, (2): to possess
privo, (1): to rob
profecto: (*adv.*) certainly
puerilis, **-e**: boyish
sat: enough
scio, (4): to know
teneo, (2): to hold
tollo, (3): to destroy, remove
virginitas, **-atis** *f*: maidenhood, virginity

Dei conscripti: vocative, "Gods having been enrolled," a parody of *patres conscripti*, the term used to address Roman senators
albo: abl. specification, "enrolled *on the register*"
quod...alumnatus sim: perf. subj. in ind. st. after *scitis*, "you know that I have nurtured"
impetus...coercendos (sc. esse): ind. st. after *existimavi*, "whose *impulses* I thought *ought to be curbed*"
freno quodam: abl. means, "curbed *by some check*"
eum...infamatum (sc. esse): perf. pass. inf. after *sat* (sc. *est*), "it is enough *that he has been defamed*"
Tollenda est...alliganda: pass. periph., "it must be removed...it must be hindered"
nuptialibus pedicis: abl. means, "bound *by marriage fetters*"
virginitate: abl. sep., "deprived her *of her virginity*"
teneat, possideat...perfruatur: subj. jussive, "let him hold, let him possess, let him enjoy"
suis amoribus: abl. after *perfruatur*, "enjoy *his own loves*"

Et ad Venerem conlata facie: "nec tu," inquit, "filia, quicquam contristere nec prosapiae tantae tuae statuque de matrimonio mortali metuas. Jam faxo nuptias non impares sed legitimas et jure civili congruas," et ilico per Mercurium arripi Psychen et in caelum perduci jubet. Porrecto ambrosiae poculo: "Sume," inquit, "Psyche, et immortalis esto, nec umquam digredietur a tuo nexu Cupido sed istae vobis erunt perpetuae nuptiae." [24] Nec mora, cum cena nuptialis affluens exhibetur. Accumbebat summum torum maritus Psychen gremio suo complexus. Sic et cum sua Junone Juppiter ac

---

accumbo, (3): to recline on (+ *acc.*)
affluens, **-entis** (*gen.*): sumptuous, overflowing
ambrosia, **-ae** *f.* food of the gods, ambrosia
arripio, (3): to seize
caelum, **-i** *n*: heavens
cena, **-ae** *f.* dinner
civilis, **-e**: civil
complector, (3), **complexus sum**: to embrace
confero, **-ferre**, **-tuli**, **conlatus**: to direct
congruus, **-a**, **-um**: agreeing with (+ *abl.*)
contristo, (1): to make gloomy
digredior, (3), **digressus sum**: to depart
exhibeo, (2), **exhibui**, **exhibitus**: to present
facies, **-ei** *f.* a face
gremium, **-i** *n*: a lap
ilico (*adv.*): immediately
immortalis, **-e**: immortal
impar, **-aris** (*gen.*): unequal
jus, **juris** *n*: law
legitimus, **-a**, **-um**: legitimate
matrimonium, **-i** *n*: marriage
metuo, (3): to fear
mora, **ae** *f.* delay
nexus, **-us** *m*: obligation, bind
nuptialis, **-e**: of a wedding
perduco, (3): to lead
perpetuus, **-a**, **-um**: everlasting
poculum, **-i** *n*: a cup
porrigo, (3), **porrexi**, **porrectus**: to extend
prosapia, **-ae** *f.* a family
status, **-us** *m*: status
summus, **-a**, **-um**: top of
sumo, (3): to take up
torus, **-i** *m*: a couch

---

conlata facie: abl. abs., "with the face having been directed"
nec contristere...metuas: pr. subj. in prohibition, "don't be made gloomy...don't fear"
prosapiae tantae tuae statuque: dat. of reference after *metuas*, "fear *for your great family and status*"
faxo: archaic fut. of *facio*, "I shall make"
jure civili: abl. specification, "agreeing *with civil law*"
arripi...perduci: pr. inf. pass. after *jubet*, "orders *to be snatched up...to be led*"
Porrecto...poculo: abl. abs., "with a cup having been extended"
Sume: imper., "take it up!"
esto: fut. imper., "*become* immortal!"
cum...exhibetur: cum temporal clause, "when it is presented," i.e. no delay *before*
summum torum: acc. with *accumbebat*, "was reclining *on top of the couch*"
gremio suo: abl. place where, "in his own lap"

deinde per ordinem toti dei. Tunc poculum nectaris, quod vinum deorum est, Jovi quidem suus pocillator ille rusticus puer, ceteris vero Liber, ministrabat, Vulcanus cenam coquebat; Horae rosis et ceteris floribus purpurabant omnia, Gratiae spargebant balsama, Musae quoque canora personabant. Tunc Apollo cantavit ad citharam, Venus suavi musicae superingressa formonsa saltavit, scaena sibi sic concinnata, ut Musae quidem chorum canerent, tibias

---

Apollo, **-inis** *m*: Apollo
balsamum, **-i** *n*: balsam
cano, (3): to sing
canorum, **-i** *n*: a melody
canto, (1): to sing, play
cena, **-ae** *f*: dinner
chorus, **-i** *m*: a chorus
cithara, **-ae** *f*: a cithara, lyre
concinno, (1): to arrange suitably
coquo, (3): to cook
flos, **-oris** *m*: a flower
formonsus, **-a**, **-um**: beautiful
Gratia, **-ae** *f*: the Graces
Hora, **-ae** *f*: Horae, the seasons
Liber, **-i** *m*: Liber, god of wine, associated with Dionysus
ministro, (1): to serve
Musa, **-ae** *f*: a Muse
musica, **-ae** *f*: music
nectar, **-aris** *n*: nectar
ordo, **-inis** *m*: rank, succession
persono, (1): to chant
pocillator, **-oris** *m*: a cupbearer
poculum, **-i** *n*: a cup
purpuro, (1): to make crimson
rosa, **-ae** *f*: a rose
rusticus, **-a**, **-um**: country
salto, (1): to dance
scaena, **-ae** *f*: a scene
spargo, (3): to scatter
suavis, **-e**: sweet
superingredior, (3), **-ingressus sum**: to advance over (+ *dat.*)
tibia, **-ae** *f*: a flute
totus, **-a**, **-um**: all
vinum, **-i** *n*: wine
Vulcanus, **-i** *m*: Vulcan, god of fire and the forge

---

pocillator ille: "that cupbearer," i.e. Ganymede
Vulcanus: Vulcan, the god of the forge, is humorously presented as cooking
rosis et ceteris floribus: abl. means, "were making everything crimson *with roses and other flowers*"
ad citharam...ad fistulam: "to the accompaniment of the cithara...of the pipe"
scaena...concinnatu: abl. abs., "with the scene having been arranged suitably"
ut...canerent...inflaret...diceret: impf. subj. in result clause, "in such a way *so that they would sing...so that he would play...so that he would sing*"

inflaret Saturus, et Paniscus ad fistulam diceret. Sic rite Psyche convenit in manum Cupidinis et nascitur illis maturo partu filia, quam Voluptatem nominamus.

---

convenio, (4), **conveni**: fit together, come together
dico, (3): to articulate, sing
fistula, **-ae** *f*: a shepherd's pipe
inflo, (1): to blow into, play a flute
maturus, **-a**, **-um**: timely
nascor, (3), **natus sum**: to be born
nomino, (1): to call
Paniscus, **-i** *m*: a little Pan
partus, **-us** *m*: birth
rite: (*adv.*) duly
Saturus, **-i**, *m*: Satyr, a half-man, half-goat creature
Voluptas, **-atis** *f*: Delight, Pleasure

---

illis: dat. of reference, "born *to these*"
maturo partu: abl. manner, "with a timely birth"

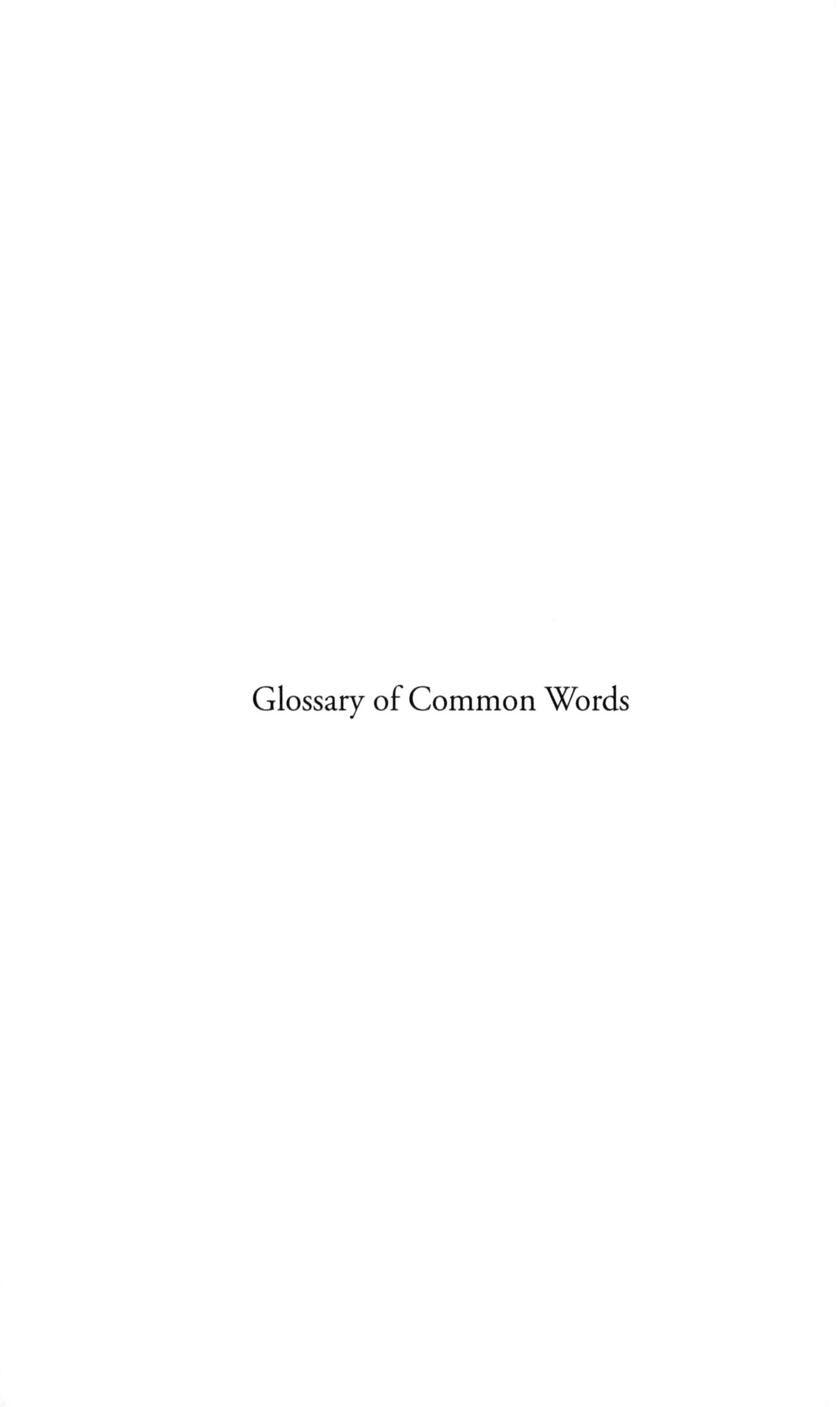

Glossary of Common Words

A a

a, **ab**, **abs**: from, by (+ *abl.*)

ac: and in addition, and also, and; (+ *comparative*) than

accipio, (3), **accepi**, **acceptus**: to accept, hear

ad: to, up to, towards (+ *acc.*)

adsum, **adesse**, **affui**: to be present, be near

aetas, **-atis** *f.*: age

ago, **agere**, **egi**, **actum**: to drive, do, act

alius, **-a**, **-ud**: other, another

amator, **-oris** *m*: a lover

amor, **-oris** *m*: love; Amor, -oris *m*: Amor, Cupid

amplexus, **-us** *m*: embrace, coil (snake)

an: or (in questions); utrum ... an: whether ... or

ancilla, **-ae** *f.*: a handmaid

animus, **-i** *m*: a heart, spirit, mind

ante: before, in front of (*adv.* and *prep.* + *acc.*)

at: but, but yet

atque: and in addition, and also, and; (after comparatives) than; simul atque: as soon as

audio, **-ire**, **-ivi**/**-ii**, **-itum**: to hear, listen to, obey

aureus, **-a**, **-um**: golden, gleaming

aurum, **-i** *n*: gold

autem: moreover, but, however

B b

beatus, **-a**, **-um**: blessed, happy, fortunate

bestia, **-ae** *f.*: a wild beast, creature

bonum, **-i** *n*: a good (thing), (*pl.*) wealth

bonus, **-a**, **-um**: good, noble

C c

caelum, **-i** *n*: sky, heavens

casus, **-us** *m*: a fall; chance, accident

censeo, **censere**, **censui**, **censum**: assess, rate; think, decide

certe: certainly, surely

confero, **-ferre**, **-tuli**, **collatus**: to confer, direct (a conversation)

confestim: (*adv.*) at once

consilium, **-i** *n*: a plan

contra: against, opposite (*adv. and prep.* + *acc.*)

cum: with (*prep.* + *abl.*); when, since, although (*conj.* + *subj.*)

cunctus, **-a**, **-um**: all

cupido, -inis *m*: desire

D d

de: down from, about, concerning (+ *abl.*)

debeo, (2), **debui**, **debitus**: ought to, must (+ *inf.*)

deinde: next

denique: finally

deus, **-i m; dea**, **-ae** *f.*: god; goddess

dico, **dicere**, **dixi**, **dictum**: to say, speak

do, **dare**, **dedi**, **datum**: to give

dominus, **-i m** / **domina**, **-ae** *f.*: master, lord; mistress

domus, **-i**/**-us** *f.*: a house, home

dum: while (+ *indic.*); until (+ *subj.*); provided that (+ *subj.*)

E e

ecce: behold!

ego, **mei**, **mihi**, **me**: I, me

enim: for, indeed

eo, **ire**, **ivi/ii**, **itus**: to go, walk

ergo: therefore

et: and

etiam: also, even

ex, **e**: out of, from (+ *abl.*)

extremus, **-a**, **-um**: extreme

F f

facio, **facere**, **feci**, **factum**: to do, make

fero, **ferre**, **tuli**, **latus**: to bear, carry

filia, **-ae f.**; **filius**, **-i** *m*: daughter; son

formonsitas, **-atis** *f*: beauty

fortuna, **-ae** *f*: fate, fortune

G g

gero, (3), **gessi**, **gestus**: to carry on

gravis, **-e**: heavy, serious

gremium, **-i** *n*: a lap, bosom

H h

hic, **haec**, **hoc**: this, these

homo, **hominis** *m*: a man, human being

I i

ibi: there

idem, **eadem**, **idem**: the same

ilico: (*adv.*) immediately

ille, **illa**, **illud**: that

immo: indeed, rather

in: in, on (+ *abl.*); into, onto (+ *acc.*)

inde: from there, from then

inquam, **inquis**, **inquit**, **inquiunt**: to say (used with direct speech)

inter: between, among; during (+ *acc.*)

interea: meanwhile

interim: meanwhile

is, **ea**, **id**: he, she, it

iste, **ista**, **istud**: that, that of yours

J j

jam, **jamque**: now; already

jubeo, **jubere**, **jussi**, **jussum**: to order, bid

L l

lacrima, **-ae** *f*: tear

laetus, **-a**, **-um**: glad, happy, joyful

latenter: (*adv.*) secretly

licet: even though

longe: far, far off

lucerna, **-ae** *f*: oil lamp

lumen, **luminis** *n*: light

M m

magnus, **-a**, **-um**: large, great

malus, **-a**, **-um**: bad, evil

manus, **-us** *f*: a hand, band of men

maritus, **-i** *m*: a husband

medius, **-a**, **-um**: middle, in the middle, central

metuo, **metuere**, **metui**: to fear, be afraid

meus, **-a**, **-um**: my, mine

modo: just, just now; **modo** ... **modo**: now ... now, at one moment ... at another, sometimes ... sometimes

modus, **-i** *m*: means, way

mons, **montis** *m*: a mountain

mox: soon

N n

nam, **namque**: for, indeed, really

ne: lest, that not (+ *subj.*)

nec: and not, nor; **nec** ... **nec**: neither ... nor

nemo, neminis, n: no one

nisi, **ni**: if not, unless

nomen, **-inis** *n*: a name

non: not

nos, **nostrum/nostri**, **nobis**, **nos**: we

nox, **noctis** *f*: night

nullus, **-a**, **-um**: not any, no one

nunc: now

O o

ob: against, on account of (+ *acc.*)

obsequium, **-i** *n*: compliance

oculus, **-i** *m*: an eye

offero, **offerre**, **obtuli**, **oblatum**: to present, offer, expose

omnino: (*adv.*) entirely

omnis, **-e**: all, every, as a whole

ops, **opis** *f*: power, assistance, resources, wealth

oro, **-are**: to ask, beg, pray

os, **oris** *n*: a mouth, face

P p

passim: everywhere, here and there

pectus, **-oris** *n*: a heart

per: through (+ *acc.*)

peto, **petere**, **petivi**, **petitum**: to seek, aim at

porrigo, (3) **porrexi**, **porrectus**: to extend

possum, **posse**, **potui**, -: to be able, be possible

praeceptum, **-i** *n*: an order

praeterea: besides, moreover

pretiosus, **-a**, **-um**: costly

prex, **precis** *f*: prayers, entreaties

primum: at first, firstly

pro: for, on behalf of, in proportion to (+ *abl.*)

propter: because of (+ *acc.*)

prorsus: (*adv.*) entirely, by all means

protinus: (*adv.*) at once, immeditaly

puella, **-ae** *f*: a girl

Q q

quam: how?; (after comparative) than

quamvis: however you like; although

quantum: (*adv.*) how much? how greatly? how much! how greatly! as much as

quasi: as if

-que: (*enclitic*) and

qui, **quae**, **quod**: who, which, what

quidem: certainly, at least; **ne...quidem**: not even

quis, **quid**: who? what? which?

quisquam, **quicquam/quidquam**: any (single) person, anyone at all

quo: for which reason; to or in what place; to what end, for what purpose?

quoad: so long as

quoque: also, too

R r

reddo, (3), **reddidi**, **redditus**: to deliver, render

rursus: back, again

S s

saevio, (4), **saevivi**, **saevitus**: to rage

saltem: (*adv.*) at least

scilicet: certainly, of course

scio, (4), **scivi**, **scitus**: to know

sed, set: but

semper: always, ever

si: if

sic: in this manner, thus; **sic** ... **ut**: in the same way as

similis, **-e**: like, similar

simul: at the same time

sive: whether; **sive** ... **sive**: whether ... or

sonus, **-i** *m*: a noise, sound

soror, **-oris** *f*: a sister

spes, **-ei** *f*: hope

spiritus, **-us** *m*: breath, life, spirit

statim: immediately

stips, **-ipis** *f*: a small offering (coin)

sub: under, close to (+ *acc.* or *abl.*)

sui, **sibi**, **se/sese**: him/her/itself, themselves

sum, **esse**, **fui**, **futurus**: to be, exist

super: over (*adv.* and *prep.* + *acc.*)

suscipio, **-cipere**, **-cepi**, **-ceptum**: to take up, accept, undertake

suus, **sua**, **suum**: his/her/its (own), (*pl.*) their (own)

T t

tam: so, so much

tamen: nevertheless, still

tandem: finally

totus, **-a**, **-um**: whole, entire

tu, **tui**, **tibi**, **te**: you (*sing.*)

tunc: then

U u

ubi: where, when

unus, **-a**, **-um**: one

ut, **uti**: as (+ *indic.*); so that, with the result that (+ *subj.*)

V v

vel: or else, or; even; **vel** ... **vel**: either ... or

venio, **venire**, **veni**, **ventus**: to come

vero: in fact, certainly, without doubt

verus, **-a**, **-um**: true, real, actual

via, **-ae** *f*: a way, road, journey

video, **videre**, **vidi**, **visum**: to see, (*pass.*) to seem

voco, **-are**, **-avi**, **-atum**: to call, summon

voluptas, **-atis** *f*: delight

vos, **vestrum**, **vobis**, **vos**: you (*pl.*)

vultus, **-us** *m*: a look, expression, face

NOTES

NOTES

NOTES

NOTES

CPSIA information can be obtained
at www.ICGtesting.com
Printed in the USA
LVHW081711100320
649602LV00010B/908

9 781940 997094